Much attention is given to the Holy Spirit today, but misconceptions, prejudices, and limited views concerning the Spirit tip this interest in His work off balance. In **Keep in Step With the Spirit**, J.I. Packer says that in order to live in the Spirit, we must both clearly understand Him and His work and unreservedly open up our lives to Him. Dr. Packer examines various popular doctrines of the Holy Spirit and shows that by overemphasizing particular dimensions of the Spirit's work, they overlook or minimize other attributes. Through a sound theological perspective, he brings the ministry of the Holy Spirit into sharp focus. By displaying how the Spirit operates in the church body and in your life as a believer, Dr. Packer helps you to pursue these and other goals:

- Faith
- Worship
- Discipline
- Prayer
- Obedience
- Evangelical enrichment

Keep In Step With The Spirit

J. I. Packer

Power Books

Fleming H. Revell Company
Old Tappan, New Jersey

Italics in Scripture quotations have been added by the author for emphasis.

Unless otherwise identified, Scripture quotations are from the Revised Standard Version of the Bible, copyrighted 1946, 1952, © 1971 and 1973.

Scripture quotations identified ASV are from the American Standard Version of the Revised Bible, copyrighted 1946 by the International Council of Religious Education, and are used by permission.

Scripture quotations identified NEB are from The New English Bible. Copyright © The Delegates of the Oxford University Press and the Syndics of the Cambridge University Press 1961, 1970. Reprinted by permission.

Scripture texts identified NIV are from Holy Bible, New International Version, copyright © 1978, New York International Bible Society. Used by permission.

Scripture quotations identified JERUSALEM are excerpts from *The Jerusalem Bible*, copyright © 1966 by Darton, Longman & Todd, Ltd. and Doubleday and Company, Inc. Used by permission of the publisher.

ALL THE THINGS YOU ARE written by Oscar Hammerstein II and Jerome Kern. Copyright © 1939 T. B. Harms Company. Copyright Renewed (c/o The Welk Music Group, Santa Monica, CA 90401). International Copyright Secured. All Rights Reserved. Made in U.S.A.

Material from preface to J. C. Ryle, *Holiness*, Evangelical Press 1979.

Material in chapter six based upon 'Theological Reflections on the Charismatic Movement', *Churchman*, 94 (Church Society, London 1980), pp. 7-25, 103-125.

Letter quoted from 'Interview with a Christian counselor,' *The Good Newspaper*, Box 219214, Houston, Texas 77218.

Library of Congress Cataloging in Publication Data

Packer, J. I. (James Innell)
  Keep in step with the spirit.

  1. Holy Spirit. 2. Spiritual life. 3. Gifts,
Spiritual. 4. Holiness. 5. Sanctification. I. Title.
BT121.2.P32   1984   231'.3   84-1304
ISBN 0-8007-5235-X

TO some friends in Texas:
Howard and Barbara Dan Butt,
Bill and Betty Ann Cody,
John and Telle DeFoore,
Woody and Lois Eagan,
Forest and Richie Bryant,
with love
and in gratitude

Contents

Preface

THE HOLY Spirit of God, the Lord, the life giver, who hovered over the waters at creation and spoke in history by the prophets, was poured out on Jesus Christ's disciples at Pentecost to fulfill the new Paraclete role that Jesus had defined for him. In his character as the second Paraclete, Jesus' deputy and representative agent in men's minds and hearts, the Spirit ministers today. *Paraclete (paraklētos* in Greek) means "Comforter, Counselor, Helper, Advocate, Strengthener, Supporter." Jesus, the original Paraclete, continues his ministry to mankind through the work of the second Paraclete. As Jesus Christ is the same yesterday, today, and forever, so is his Spirit; and in every age since Pentecost, wherever the gospel has gone, the Spirit has continued to do on a larger or smaller scale the things that Jesus promised he would do when sent in this new capacity.

It is well that he has! Had he ceased to do these things, the church would long ago have perished, for there would have been no Christians to compose it. The Christian's life in all its aspects—intellectual and ethical, devotional and relational, upsurging in worship and outgoing in witness—is supernatural; only the Spirit can initiate and sustain it. So apart from him, not only will there be no lively believers and no lively congregations, there will be no believers and no congregations at all. But in fact the church continues to live and grow, for the Spirit's ministry has not failed, nor ever will, with the passage of time.

Yet the Spirit's work in this world is observably more extensive and apparently more deep in some periods than in others. Nowadays, for instance, it seems to be more extensive in Africa, in Indonesia, in Latin America, in the United States, and in the Roman Catholic Church than it seemed to be fifty years ago. I say *seems* and *seemed* advisedly, for only God knows the reality here, and Bible warnings against judging by appearance in spiritual matters are many and strong. When it seemed to Elijah that he was the only loyal Israelite left, God told him that there were still 7,000 others, which should give us pause when we try to estimate what God was doing before we ourselves arrived or is now doing all around us. However, for what the impression is worth, it looks to me (and not only to me) as if, while compromise Christianities are falling apart, there is today a fresh breath of life from the Spirit in many parts of the world. Its depth is another question: A widely traveled leader has said that Christianity in North America is 3,000 miles wide and half an inch deep, and suspicions of shallowness have been voiced elsewhere, too. But however that may be, it is out of the sense that the Spirit is stirring us that this book has emerged.

It should be read as a set of pointers toward what Richard Lovelace calls a "unified field" theory of the Holy Spirit's work in the church yesterday, today, and tomorrow. Its contents have emerged rather like a menu for a four-course meal, thus:

Chapter 1 moves to the conclusion that the key thought unlocking understanding of the Spirit's new covenant ministry is that he mediates the personal presence and ministry of the Lord Jesus. This argument is meant to have the status of an appetizer.

Chapter 2 looks at biblical teaching about the Spirit from this point of view. It is, so to speak, the soup—thick, maybe, but (so I hope) nourishing. Perhaps, unlike other sorts of soup, it will manage to be both thick and clear at the same time; as the one who cooks it up, I certainly want it to be so.

Chapters 3, 4, 5, and 6 are the meat of the book—encounters with Wesley's perfectionism, classic Keswick teaching, and contemporary charismatic spirituality, and alongside them a restatement of an older view of life in the Spirit, which seems to me to be more deeply biblical than either.

Last, for dessert (the part of the meal in which sweetness should predominate), I offer some thoughts about the work of the Paraclete reviving the body of Christ. You may find it bittersweet; that, I think, will depend on you more than on me.

The title, *Keep in Step With the Spirit*, focuses the book's practical thrust throughout. The idea of "keeping in step" reflects Paul's thought in Galatians 5:25: "If we live by the Spirit, let us also walk by the Spirit." *Walk* there is not *peripateō*, as in verse 16, signifying literally the walker's moving of his limbs and metaphorically the activity of living, but *stoicheō*, which carries the thought of walking in line, holding to a rule, and thus proceeding under another's control.

Faith, worship, praise, prayer, openness and obedience to God, discipline, boldness, moral realism, and evangelical enrichment are the goals at which I aim. Says Paul again: ". . . Be filled with the Spirit; speaking one to another in psalms and hymns and spiritual songs, singing and making melody with your heart to the Lord; giving thanks always for all things in the name of our Lord Jesus Christ to God, even the Father; subjecting yourselves one to another in the fear of Christ" (Ephesians 5:18–21, ASV). My highest hope for this book is that it might help its readers to implement Paul's series of directives in that tremendous sentence. So I ask you now to check before God your willingness to learn this new supernatural life-style, at whatever cost to your present way of living; for there is nothing so Spirit quenching as to study the Spirit's work without being willing to be touched, humbled, convicted, and changed as you go along.

To study the Holy Spirit's work is an awesome venture for anyone who knows, even at secondhand, what the Spirit may do. In 1908 some missionaries in Manchuria wrote home as follows:

> A power has come into the church that we cannot control if we would. It is a miracle for stolid, self-righteous John

Chinaman to go out of his way to confess to sins that no torture of the Yamen could force from him; for a Chinaman to demean himself to crave, weeping, the prayers of his fellow-believers is beyond all human explanation.

Perhaps you will say it's a sort of religious hysteria. So did some of us . . . But here we are, about sixty Scottish and Irish Presbyterians who have seen it—all shades of temperament—and, much as many of us shrank from it at first, every one who has seen and heard what we have, every day last week, is certain there is only *one* explanation—that it is God's Holy Spirit manifesting himself. . . . One clause of the Creed that lives before us now in all its inevitable, awful solemnity is, *"I believe in the Holy Ghost."*[1]

"Inevitable, awful solemnity": Does that phrase fit our present perception of the Holy Spirit and his work? What happened in Manchuria in 1908, when the Spirit attacked and overthrew self-righteousness, got down to specifics in people's consciences, and robbed them of all inward rest and quietness till they confessed their sins and changed their ways, may be paralleled from the Acts of the Apostles. But where nothing of this kind happens, nor is even envisioned, claims that the Spirit is at work must be judged unreal. The Holy Spirit comes to make us holy, by making us know and feel the reality of God through his Son Jesus Christ—God's hatred of, recoil from, and wrath against our sins, and his loving insistence on changing and rebuilding our characters while he forgives us for Jesus' sake. Have we ever *felt* these things, that is, been stirred and shaken and altered by their impact? And are we inwardly ready now to embark on a study that may leave us feeling them?

"Reader," wrote John Owen the Puritan at the start of a treatise that had cost him seven years' hard labor, "if thou art, as many in this pretending age, a sign or title-gazer, and comest into books as Cato into the theatre, to go out again, thou hast had thy entertainment; farewell." At this moment I want to say that to anyone into whose hands this book has fallen. It asks for more than the casual glance that in this "pretending age" of ours is all that readers often give to the books whose pages they flip. Nor is it written to please those who are just curious to know what its author thinks these days about the Holy Spirit. It has been put together to help Christians who mean business with God and are prepared to be dealt with by him. It would be your wisdom, I think, quietly and prayerfully to read through Psalm 119 two or three times before going further. Stuffing our heads with idle thoughts, however true, puffs up, not builds up, and it is building up that we need. May the Lord have mercy on us all.

I would like to express my gratitude to the many over the years, on both sides of the Atlantic, who have helped me by their responses to earlier versions of this material and particularly to the faculty and students of Asbury Theological Seminary, to whom I ventured to present my encounter with John Wesley's teaching as the Ryan Lectures for 1982. Also I owe thanks to several gallant typists, most notably Mary Parkin, Nancy Morehouse, and Ann Norford and to Jim Fodor for the indexes.

Let me finally say that this is not a technical treatise, and therefore footnotes and references to other material have been kept to a minimum; nonetheless, it is a study book, and as in other study books I have written, biblical references in the text are meant to be looked up.

Getting the Spirit in Focus

Many books have already been written on the Holy Spirit: Why add to their number? Let me start my answer to this very proper question by telling you about my short sight.

Purblindness

If while looking at you I should take my glasses off, I should reduce you to a smudge. I should still know you were there; I might still be able to tell whether you were boy or girl; I could probably manage to avoid bumping into you. But you would have become so indistinct at the edges, and your features would be so blurred that adequate description of you (save from memory) would be quite beyond me. Should a stranger enter the room while my glasses were off, I could point to him, no doubt, but his face would be a blob, and I would never know the expression on it. You and he would be right out of focus, so far as I was concerned, until I was bespectacled again.

One of Calvin's rare illustrations compares the way purblind folk like me need glasses to put print and people in focus with the way we all need Scripture to bring into focus our genuine sense of the divine. Though Calvin stated this comparison in general terms only, he clearly had in mind specific biblical truths as the lens whereby clear focus is achieved. Everyone, Calvin thought, has inklings of the reality of God, but they are vague and smudged. Getting God in focus means thinking correctly about his character, his sovereignty, his salvation, his love, his Son, his Spirit, and all the realities of his work and ways; it also means thinking rightly about our own relationship to him as creatures either under sin or under grace, either living the responsive life of faith, hope, and love or living unresponsively, in barrenness and gloom of heart. How can we learn to think correctly about these things? Calvin's answer (mine, too) is: by learning of them from Scripture. Only as we thus learn shall we be able to say that God the Triune Creator, who is Father, Son, and Spirit, is more than a smudge in our minds.

To my point, now, and my reason for writing these pages. Great attention, as I said, is being given today to the Holy Spirit—who he is and what he does in the individual, the church, and the wider human community. Fellowship, body life, every-member ministry, Spirit baptism, gifts, guidance, prophecy, miracles, and the Spirit's work of revealing, renewing, and reviving, are themes on many lips and are discussed in many books. That is good: We should be glad that it is so, and something is wrong with us spiritually if we are not. But just as a shortsighted man fails to see all that he is looking at and just as anyone may get hold of the wrong end of the stick about anything, and so have only half the story, so we may (and I think often do) fall short of a biblical focus on the Spirit, whose work we celebrate so often. We really are too purblind and prejudiced in spiritual things to be able to see properly what we are looking at here.

Knowing and Experiencing God

We glibly assume that because we know something of the Spirit's work in our own lives, therefore we know all that matters about the Spirit himself, but the conclusion does not follow. The truth is that just as notional knowledge may outrun spiritual experience, so a person's spiritual experience may be ahead of his notional knowledge. Bible believers have often so stressed (rightly) the need for correct notions that they have overlooked this. But fact it is, as we may learn from the experience of Jesus' followers during his earthly ministry. Their understanding of spiritual things was faulty; their misunderstandings of Jesus were frequent; yet Jesus was able to touch and transform their lives beyond the limits of what had entered their minds, simply because they loved him, trusted him, wanted to learn from him, and honestly meant to obey him according to the light they had. Thus it was that eleven of the twelve were "made clean" (their sins were forgiven and their hearts renewed [John 15:3]) and others entered with them into Jesus' gift of pardon and peace (*see* Luke 5:20-24; 7:47-50; 19:5-10), before any single one of them had any grasp at all of the doctrine of atonement for sin through Jesus' coming cross. The gift was given and their lives were changed first; the understanding of what had happened to them came after.

So it is, too, when in good faith and openness to God's will, folk ask for more of the life of the Spirit. (Naturally! for seeking life from the Spirit and life from Jesus is in fact the same quest under two names, did we but know it.) To ask consciously for what Scripture teaches us to ask for is the ideal here, and since God is faithful to his word, we may confidently expect that, having asked for it, we shall receive it—though we may well find that when the good gift comes to us, there is more to it than ever we realized. Said the Lord Jesus: "Ask, and it will be given you. . . . If you . . . know how to give good gifts to your children, how much more will the heavenly Father give the Holy Spirit to those who ask him!" (Luke 11:9, 13). Many have been staggered at the wealth of God's answer in experience to this request.

But because God is gracious, he may also deepen our life in the Spirit even when our ideas about this life are nonexistent or quite wrong, provided only that we are truly and wholeheartedly seeking his face and wanting to come closer to him. The formula that applies here is the promise in Jeremiah 29:13, 14: ". . . When you seek me with all your heart, I will be found by you, says the Lord. . . ." Then comes the task of understanding by the light of Scripture what the Lord has actually done to us and how his specific work in our personal experience, tailored as it lovingly was to our particular temperamental and circumstantial needs at that time, should be related to the general biblical declarations of what he will do through the Spirit for all who are his. This task, as it seems to me, faces many of God's people just at present.

Now please do not misunderstand me! I am not saying that God blesses the ignorant and erring by reason of their ignorance and error. Nor am I saying that God does not care whether or not we know and grasp his revealed purposes. Nor do I suggest that ignorance and error are unimportant for spiritual health so long as one has an honest heart and a genuine passion for God. It is certain that God blesses believers precisely and invariably by blessing to them something of his truth and that misbelief as such is in its own nature spiritually barren and destructive. Yet anyone who deals with souls will again and again be amazed at the gracious generosity with which God blesses to needy ones what looks to us like a very tiny needle of truth hidden amid whole haystacks of mental error. As I have said, countless sinners truly experience the saving grace of Jesus Christ and the transforming power of the Holy Spirit while their notions about both are erratic and largely incorrect. (Where, indeed, would any of us be if God's blessing had been withheld till all our notions were right? Every Christian without exception experiences far more in the way of mercy and help than the quality of his notions warrants.) All the same, however, we would appreciate the Spirit's work much more, and maybe avoid some pitfalls concerning it, if our thoughts about the Spirit himself were clearer; and that is where this book tries to help.

My mind goes back to a wet afternoon twenty years ago when I made my way to the back-street cinema that we called the fleapit for my first sight of a famous Golden Silent that had come to town. This was *The General*, made in 1927, hailed by critics nowadays as Buster Keaton's masterpiece. I had recently discovered the sad, high-minded, disaster-prone, dithery, resourceful clown that was Keaton, and *The General* drew me like a magnet. I had read that the story was set in the American Civil War and, putting two and two together, I assumed that as in several of his other films, the title was telling me what Keaton's own role was going to be. Now I am not a war film buff, and I remember wondering as I walked to the cinema how fully what I was to see would grab me.

Well, *The General* certainly puts Keaton into uniform—lieutenant's uniform, to be precise—but to characterize it as a film in which Keaton is a soldier with leadership responsibilities would be inadequate and misleading to the last degree. For Keaton only gets his uniform in the final moments, and what unfolded before my wondering eyes for seventy magic minutes before that was not a Goon- or M.A.S.H.-type send-up of the military, nor anything like it, but the epic of an ancient steam locomotive—a dear, dignified, clumsy, cowcatchered 4-4-0—which, by letting itself be stolen, pitchforked its dauntless driver into the clever-crazy heroics of a marvelous one-man rescue operation, out of which came as a reward the military identity that was previously denied him and without which his girl had refused to look at him. *General* turned out to be the loco's name, and the story was Keaton's version of the Great Locomotive Chase of 1863, when the real *General* was snatched by northern saboteurs at Marietta, Georgia, but was pursued and recaptured when it ran out of fuel before it managed to reach northern territory. Being both a slapstick addict and a train nut, I was absolutely entranced.

I am suggesting, now, that some of the things that are said today concerning the work of the Holy Spirit and the true experience of the life of the Spirit that many enjoy reflect ideas about the Spirit that are no more adequate to the reality than was my own first guess at the subject matter of *The General*. Look with me at some of these ideas, and let me show you what I mean.

Power

To start with, some people see the doctrine of the Spirit as essentially about *power*, in the sense of God-given ability to do what you know you ought to do and indeed want to do, but feel that you lack the strength for. Examples include saying no to cravings (for sex, drink, drugs, tobacco, money, kicks, luxury, promotion, power, reputation, adulation, or whatever), being patient with folks who try your patience, loving the unlovable, controlling your temper, standing firm under pressure, speaking out boldly for Christ, trusting God in face of trouble. In thought and speech, preaching and prayer, the Spirit's enabling power for action of this kind is the theme on which these people constantly harp.

What ought we to say about their emphasis? Is it wrong? No, indeed, just the opposite. In itself it is magnificently right. For *power* (usually *dunamis,* from which comes the English word *dynamite,* sometimes *kratos* and *ischus*) is a great New Testament word, and empowering from Christ through the Spirit is indeed a momentous New Testament fact, one of the glories of the gospel and a mark of Christ's true followers everywhere. Observe these key texts, if you doubt me.

". . . Stay in the city," said Jesus to the apostles, whom he had commissioned to evangelize the world, "until you are clothed with *power* from on high." "But you shall receive *power* when the Holy Spirit has come upon you . . ." (Luke 24:49; Acts 1:8). When the Spirit had been poured out at Pentecost, "with great *power* the apostles gave their testimony to the resurrection of the Lord Jesus . . ." (Acts 4:33); and "Stephen, full of grace and *power,* did great wonders and signs . . ." (Acts 6:8; *see also* Peter's similar statement about Jesus, who was "anointed . . . with the Holy Spirit and with *power* . . ." [Acts 10:38]). In these verses Luke tells us that from the first the gospel was spread by the Spirit's power.

Paul prays for the Romans that ". . . by the *power* of the Holy Spirit you may abound in hope" (Romans 15:13). Then he speaks of "what Christ has wrought through me . . . by word and deed, by the *power* of signs and wonders, by the *power* of the Holy Spirit . . ." (Romans 15:18, 19). He reminds the Corinthians that at Corinth he preached Christ crucified ". . . in demonstration of the Spirit and of *power,* that your faith might . . . rest . . . in the *power* of God" (1 Corinthians 2:4, 5; *see also* 2 Corinthians 6:6–10; 10:4–6; 1 Thessalonians

1:5; 2:13). Of his thorn in the flesh he writes that Christ "said to me, 'My grace is sufficient for you, for my *power* is made perfect in weakness.' I will all the more gladly boast of my weaknesses," he continues, "that the *power* of Christ may rest upon me" (2 Corinthians 12:9; *see also* 4:7). He emphasizes to Timothy that God has given Christians ". . . a spirit of *power* and love and self-control," and censures those who are "lovers of pleasure rather than lovers of God, holding the form of religion but denying the *power* of it" (2 Timothy 1:7; 3:4, 5). Christ, he says, gives strength (*endunamoō, dunamoō, krataioō*), so that the Christian becomes able to do what left to himself he never could have done (Ephesians 3:16; 6:10; *see also* 1:19–23; Colossians 1:11; 1 Timothy 1:12; 2 Timothy 4:17; *see also* 2 Corinthians 12:10; 1 Peter 5:10). And his own triumphant cry from prison as he faces possible execution is: "I can do all things [meaning, all that God calls me to do] in him who *strengthens* me" (Philippians 4:13). There is no mistaking the thrust of all this. What we are being told is that supernatural living through supernatural empowering is at the very heart of New Testament Christianity, so that those who, while professing faith, do not experience and show forth this empowering are suspect by New Testament standards. And the empowering is always the work of the Holy Spirit, even when Christ only is named as its source, for Christ is the Spirit giver (John 1:33; 20:22; Acts 2:33). So power from Christ through the Spirit is a theme that should always be given prominence whenever and wherever Christianity is taught.

For more than three centuries evangelical believers have been making much of God's promise and provision of power for living, and we should be glad that they have. For not only is this, as we saw, a key theme in Scripture, it speaks to an obvious and universal human need. All who are realistic about themselves are from time to time overwhelmed with a sense of inadequacy. All Christians time and again are forced to cry, "Lord, *help* me, *strengthen* me, *enable* me, give me *power* to speak and act in the way that pleases you, *make* me equal to the demands and pressures which I face." We are called to fight evil in all its forms in and around us, and we need to learn that in this battle the Spirit's power alone gives victory, while self-reliance leads only to the discovery of one's impotence and the experience of defeat. Evangelical stress, therefore, on supernatural sanctity through the Spirit as something real and necessary has been and always will be timely teaching.

POWER FOR CHRISTIANS.   The power of the Spirit in human lives, first taught with emphasis by seventeenth-century Puritans, became a matter of debate among Evangelicals in the eighteenth century, when John Wesley began to teach that the Spirit will root sin out of men's hearts entirely in this life. This was the "scriptural holiness" that Wesley believed God had raised up Methodism to spread. Non-Wesleyans recoiled, seeing the claim as unbiblical and delusive, and they constantly warned their constituencies against it. By the second half of the nineteenth century, however, the pendulum of reaction was thought to have swung too far; and many felt, rightly or wrongly, that antiperfectionist zeal had left Christians simply unaware that God has power to deliver from sinful practices, to energize a calmly triumphant righteousness, and to give piercing efficacy to preachers' utterances. Quite suddenly the theme of power in human lives caught on as the topic for sermons, books, and informal discussion groups ("conversation meetings" as they were called) on both sides of the Atlantic. What was said by Phoebe Palmer, Asa Mahan, Robert Pearsall Smith and Hannah Whitall Smith, Evan Hopkins, Andrew Murray, R. A. Torrey, Charles G. Trumbull, Robert C. McQuilkin, F. B. Meyer, H. C. G. Moule, and others who spent their strength proclaiming the "secret" (their word) of power for believers was hailed as virtually a new revelation, which indeed the teachers themselves took it to be. A new evangelical movement was off and running.

The "secret" of what was sometimes called the Higher or Victorious Life has been most fully institutionalized in England's annual Keswick Convention week. There to this day there operates, like a jazz band's "head" arrangement, an agreed understanding that Monday's theme is sin, Tuesday's is Christ who saves from sin, Wednesday's is consecration, Thursday's is life in the Spirit, and Friday's is empowered service by the sanctified, especially in missions. A Keswick periodical was launched in 1874, called *The Christian's Pathway of Power*. After five years it changed its name to *The Life of Faith*, but this did not mean any change of character; faith is the pathway of power according to Keswick. Keswick's influence has been worldwide. "Keswicks" crop up all over the English-speaking world. "Keswick teaching has come to be regarded as one of the most potent spiritual forces in recent Church history."[1] Preachers "of Keswick type," specializing in convention addresses about power, have become a distinct evangelical ministerial species, alongside evangelists, Bible teachers, and speakers on prophetic subjects. Thus institutionalized and with its supporting constituency of those who appreciate the Keswick ethos—equable, cheerful, controlled, fastidious, very congenial to the middle class—the Keswick message of power for sanctity and service is plainly here to stay for some time yet.

Nor is this the only way in which the power theme has been developed in recent years. The power of Christ, not only to forgive sin, but also, by his Spirit, to deliver from enslaving evil is becoming again what it was in the first Christian centuries, a major ingredient in the church's evangelistic message. This is so both in the urban West, where the evil faced is usually the power of destructive habit, and also among tribal communities, where the evil is still often the power of malevolent demons recognized as such. Older evangelism, with its stress on law, guilt, judgment, and the glory of Christ's atoning death, certainly had strengths that today's evangelism lacks, but on the whole it made little of the power theme, and so was to that extent poorer.

Since God's promise and provision of power are realities, it must be judged a happy thing that the topic should be highlighted in the ways I have described. Emphasis on it in one form or another now marks virtually the whole of mainstream evangelical Christianity, along with the worldwide charismatic movement, and this is surely a hopeful sign for the future.

THE LIMITATIONS OF POWER.   Yet pleasure in today's power talk cannot be unmixed. For experience shows that when the power theme is made central to our thinking about the Spirit and is not anchored in a deeper view of the Spirit's ministry with a different center, unhappy disfigurements soon creep in. What sort of disfigurements? Well, take the following for starters. Pietistic concentration of interest on the felt ups and downs of the soul as it seeks power over this and that tends to produce an egoistic, introverted cast of mind that becomes indifferent to community concerns and social needs. The Spirit's work tends to be spoken of man centeredly, as if God's power is something made available for us to switch on and *use* (a frequent, telltale Keswick word) by a technique of thought and will for which *consecration and faith* is the approved name. Also, the idea gets around that God's power works in us automatically so far as we let it do so, so that in effect we regulate it by the degree of our consecration and faith at any one time. Another notion popping up is that inner passivity, waiting for God's power to carry us along, is a required state of heart ("let go and let God," as the too popular slogan has it). Then, too, in evangelizing, it is almost conventional in certain circles to offer "power for living" to the spiritually needy as a resource that, apparently, they will be privileged to harness and control once they have committed themselves to Christ.

But all this sounds more like an adaptation of yoga than like biblical Christianity. To start with, it blurs the distinction between manipulating divine power at one's own will (which is magic, exemplified by Simon Magus [Acts 8:18–24]) and experiencing it as one obeys God's will (which is religion, exemplified by Paul [2 Corinthians 12:9, 10]). Furthermore, it is not realistic. Evangelists' talk regularly implies that, once we become Christians, God's power in us will immediately cancel out defects of character and make our whole lives plain sailing. This however is so unbiblical as to be positively dishonest. Certainly God sometimes works wonders of sudden deliverance from this or that weakness at conversion, just as he sometimes does at other times; but every Christian's life is a constant fight against the pressures and pulls of the world, the flesh, and the devil; and his battle for Christlikeness (that is, habits of wisdom, devotion, love, and righteousness) is as grueling as it is unending. To suggest otherwise when evangelizing is a kind of confidence trick. Again Keswick talk regularly encourages us to expect at once too much and not enough—full freedom from the down drag of sin on a moment-by-moment basis (too much), yet without any progressive loosening of the grip of sin on our hearts at motivational level (not enough). This is bad theology, and is psychologically and spiritually unreal into the bargain. By saying as much in print in 1955 I gave great offense,[2] but my points would, I think, be more widely taken today.

The real need here, as we shall in due course see, is for deeper insight into what the doctrine of the Spirit is really about—insight in the light of which our twisted talk of inward power put at our disposal can be set straight. That part of the argument, however, will be held back till my preliminary survey is complete. At present we should simply note that the power theme does not quite take us to the heart of the matter and move on.

Performance

In the second place, there are those who see the doctrine of the Spirit as essentially about *performance*, in the sense of exercising spiritual gifts. For these folk, the Spirit's ministry seems both to start and to finish with the use of gifts—preaching, teaching, prophecy, tongues, healing, or whatever it may be. They see that, according to the New Testament, gifts (*charismata*) are God-given capacities to do things: specifically, to serve and edify others by words, deeds, or attitudes that express and communicate knowledge of Jesus Christ. They see also that, as "... the manifestation of the

Spirit . . ." (1 Corinthians 12:7), gifts are discerned in action:
Christians show what God enables them to do by doing it.
Thus they are led to think of performance as the essence of
life in the Spirit and to suppose that the more gifts a person
exhibits, the more Spirit filled he or she is likely to be.

THE MINISTRY OF THE BODY.   The first thing to say about this
view, or mind-set as perhaps we had better call it, is that here
again is an emphasis—this time, on the reality of gifts and
the importance of putting them to use—which is in itself entirely right. For centuries the churches assumed that only a
minority of Christians (good clergy and some few others) had
gifts for ministry, and they gave the whole subject of gifts
small attention. Prior to the twentieth century, only one full-
scale study of the gifts of the Spirit had been written in
English, penned by the Puritan John Owen in 1679, 1680. The
current stress on the universality of gifts and God's expectation of every-member ministry in the body of Christ was
long overdue, for New Testament teaching on both points is
explicit and clear. Here are the main statements.

"There are varieties of gifts [charismata], but the same
Spirit; and there are varieties of service [diakoniai], but the
same Lord; and there are varieties of working [energēmata],
but it is the same God who inspires them all *in every one*"
(1 Corinthians 12:4–6). "But grace was given *to each of us* according to the measure of Christ's gift. . . . we are to grow up
in every way into him who is the head, into Christ, from
whom the whole body . . . *when each part is working properly*,
makes bodily growth and upbuilds itself in love" (Ephesians
4:7, 15, 16). "As *each* has received a gift, employ it for one another, as good stewards of God's varied grace" (1 Peter 4:10).
"For as in one body we have many members [melē, 'limbs':
Members is always *limbs* in the New Testament], and all the
members do not have the same function, so we, though
many, are one body in Christ, and individually members one
of another. Having gifts that differ according to the grace
given to us, let us use them . . ." (Romans 12:4–6). It is not
only clergy and office bearers who are gifted; all Christians

are. Official ministers must recognize this and use their own gifts in preparing lay Christians to use theirs. "These were his [Christ's] gifts: some to be apostles, some prophets, some evangelists, some pastors and teachers, to equip God's people [Greek, *hagioi*, "the saints"] for work in his service, to the building up of the body of Christ" (Ephesians 4:11, 12 NEB).

The King James Version (alas) masks Paul's meaning here by making him say that Christ gave apostles, prophets, evangelists and pastor-teachers "for the perfecting of the saints, for the work of the ministry, for the edifying of the body of Christ," as if these three phrases are parallel statements of what the clergy are for. A sixteenth-century edition of Scripture, which omitted *not* from the seventh commandment (Exodus 20:14), very properly went down in history as the Wicked Bible; with equal propriety we could speak of the Wicked (or if you like alliteration, Calamitous) Comma that the King James Version put after *saints*. For by thus restricting "the ministry" to what official leaders do, this comma not only hides but actually reverses Paul's sense, setting clericalism where every-member ministry ought to be. (By *clericalism* I mean that combination of conspiracy and tyranny in which the minister claims and the congregation agrees that all spiritual ministry is his responsibility and not theirs: a notion both disreputable in principle and Spirit quenching in practice.)

The Plymouth Brethren proclaimed the universality of gifts and the rightness of every-member ministry from the middle of the last century on, but because their thesis was bound up with a reactionary polemic against trained and salaried clergy in supposedly apostate churches, little notice was taken of it. Recently, however, both the ecumenical and the charismatic movements have seized on this aspect of biblical truth and made it almost a Christian commonplace, with some happy results. One effect has been to create in many quarters an unprecedented willingness to experiment with new structural and liturgical forms for church life, so as to make room for the full use of all gifts for the benefit of the whole congregation. With that has come a new seriousness in checking traditional patterns of worship and order to make sure that they do not in fact inhibit gifts and so actually quench the Spirit. This is all to the good.

KEEPING PERFORMANCE IN FOCUS.   Unhappily, there is a debit side, too: Three big disfigurements have periodically marred the new approach.

First, magnifying lay ministry has led some laymen to undervalue and indeed discount the special responsibilities to which clergy are ordained and to forget the respect that is due to the minister's office and leadership.

Second, emphasis on God's habit of giving saints gifts that correspond to nothing of which they seemed capable before conversion (and make no mistake, that really is God's habit) has blinded some to the fact that the most significant gifts in the church's life (preaching, teaching, leadership, counsel, support) are ordinarily natural abilities sanctified.

Third, some have balanced their encouragement of extreme freedom in personal Christian performance by introducing extremely authoritarian forms of pastoral oversight, in some cases going beyond the worst forms of medieval priestcraft in taking control of Christians' consciences.

Plainly these developments are defects. But to call for their correction is not in any way to denigrate the principles of which they have been the less welcome by-products. The principles are right, and there is no high-quality church life without practical observance of them.

But something is deeply wrong, nonetheless, when attention centers on the manifesting of gifts (starting, perhaps, with tongues at a personal Pentecost) as if this were the Spirit's main ministry to individuals and hence the aspect of his work on which we should chiefly concentrate. What is wrong becomes clear the moment we look at 1 Corinthians. As the Corinthians were proud of their knowledge (8:1, 2), so they were cock-a-hoop, or, as some would say, gung ho, about their gifts. They despised fellow worshipers and visiting preachers who struck them as less gifted than themselves and tried to outdo one another in showing off their gifts whenever the church met. Paul rejoices that they are knowledgeable and gifted (1:4–7), but tells them that they are at the same time babyish and carnal, behaving in ways that for Christians are inconsistent and a cause for shame (3:1–4; 5:1–13; 6:1–8; 11:17–22). They were valuing gifts and freedom above righteousness, love, and service; and that scale of values, says Paul, is wrong. No church known to us received such wide-ranging apostolic rebuke as did that at Corinth.

The Corinthians thought themselves "men of the Spirit" (*pneumatikoi*, 14:37) by reason of their knowledge and gifts. Paul labors, however, to show them that the essential element in true spirituality (assuming Spirit-given understanding of the gospel, which is basic to everything) is ethical. "Do you not know that your body is a temple of the Holy Spirit within you, which you have from God? You are not your own; you were bought with a price. So glorify God in your body" (6:19, 20). The "still more excellent way," surpassing all the performances that the Corinthians most prized, is the way of love: ". . . patient and kind . . . not jealous or boastful . . . not arrogant or rude . . . not irritable or resentful. . . . Love bears all things, believes all things, hopes all things, endures all things" (13:4–7). Without love, says Paul, you can have the grandest gifts in the world, and still be—nothing (13:1–3)—that is, be spiritually dead. Paul suspected that some in the Corinthian church were in fact "nothing" in this sense. "Come to your right mind, and sin no more," he writes to them. "For some have no knowledge of God. I say this to your shame" (15:34; *see also* 2 Corinthians 13:5).

What the Corinthians had to realize, and what some today may need to relearn, is that, as the Puritan John Owen put it, there can be *gifts* without *graces*; that is, one may be capable of performances that benefit others spiritually and yet be a stranger oneself to the Spirit-wrought inner transformation that true knowledge of God brings. The manifestation of the Spirit in charismatic performance is not the same thing as the fruit of the Spirit in Christlike character (*see* Galatians 5:22, 23), and there may be much of the former with little or none of the latter. You can have many gifts and few graces; you can even have genuine gifts and no genuine graces at all, as did Balaam, Saul, and Judas. This, writes Owen, is because:

> *Spiritual gifts* are placed and seated in the *mind* or understanding only; whether they are ordinary or extraordinary they have no other hold nor residence in the soul. And they are in the mind as it is *notional* and theoretical, rather than as it is *practical*. They are *intellectual abilities* and no more. I speak of them which have any residence in us; for some *gifts*, as *miracles* and *tongues*, consisted only in a *transient operation* of an extraordinary power. Of all others *illumination* is the foundation, and spiritual light their matter. So the apostle declares in his order of expression, Heb.vi.4. [where Owen identifies "powers of the age to come" with spiritual gifts]. The will, and the affections, and the conscience, are unconcerned in them. Wherefore they *change not the heart* with power, although they may reform the life by the efficacy of light. And although God doth not ordinarily bestow them on flagitious persons, nor continue them with such as after the reception of them become flagitious; yet they may be in those who were unrenewed, and have nothing in them to preserve them absolutely from the worst of sins.[3]

So no one should treat his gifts as proof that he pleases God or as guaranteeing his salvation. Spiritual gifts do neither of these things.

All through the New Testament, when God's work in human lives is spoken of, the ethical has priority over the charismatic. Christlikeness (not in gifts, but in love, humility, submission to the providence of God, and sensitiveness to the claims of people) is seen as what really matters. This is particularly clear in Paul's prayers for believers. He asks, for instance, that the Colossians may be "strengthened with all power, according to . . . [God's] glorious might, for . . ." what? Ministerial exploits and triumphs through a superabundant display of gifts? No, "all endurance and patience with joy" (Colossians 1:11). Again, he asks that the Philippians' love may abound, ". . . with knowledge and all discernment, so that you . . ." what? May preach and argue with cogency, or heal the sick with authority, or speak in tongues with fluency? No, ". . . may be pure and blameless for the day of Christ, filled with the fruits of righteousness which come through Jesus Christ . . ." (Philippians 1:9–11; *see also* Ephesians 3:14–19).

This point touches not only those who are preoccupied with finding and using their gifts, but all who, betrayed perhaps by their own vigorous temperament, measure the Spirit's work in them by the number of Christian activities in which they invest themselves and the skill and success with which they manage to carry them out.

My argument is that any mind-set which treats the Spirit's gifts (ability and willingness to run around and do things) as more important than his fruit (Christlike character in personal life) is spiritually wrongheaded and needs correcting. The best corrective will be a view of the Spirit's work that sets activities and performances in a framework that displays them as acts of serving and honoring God and gives them value as such, rather than leaving us to suppose them valuable just because they are dramatic or eye-catching or impress people or fill vital roles in the church or transcend our former expectations from the person concerned. A framework of this kind will be offered shortly. Meantime, let us note that concentrating on gifts and activities does not take us to the heart of the truth about the Spirit, any more than concentrating on the experience of power does, and proceed with our review.

Purity

In the third place, there are those for whom the doctrine of the Spirit centers on *purifying* and *purgation*, that is, God's work of cleansing his children from sin's defilement and pollution by enabling them to resist temptation and do what is right. For these folk, the key thought is of the holiness that the Spirit imparts as he progressively sanctifies us, enabling us to mortify indwelling sin (that is, put it to death: Romans

8:14; *see also* Colossians 3:5) and changing us ". . . from one degree of glory to another. . ." (2 Corinthians 3:18). The heart of the matter for them is neither the experience of power as such nor the quantity or quality of Christians' public performances, but our inward conflict as we battle for holiness against sin and seek the Spirit's help to keep ourselves pure and undefiled.

Here is yet another emphasis that in itself is fully biblical. Unregenerate human beings are indeed, as Paul says, ". . . under the power of sin . . ." (Romans 3:9), and sin still "indwells" those who are born again (Romans 7:20, 23; *see also* Hebrews 12:1; 1 John 1:8). Sin, which is in essence an irrational energy of rebellion against God—a lawless habit of self-willed arrogance, moral and spiritual, expressing itself in egoism of all sorts—is something that God hates in all its forms (Isaiah 61:8; Jeremiah 44:4; Proverbs 6:16–19) and that defiles us in his sight. Therefore Scripture views it not only as guilt needing to be forgiven, but also as filth needing to be cleansed.

Accordingly, Isaiah looks for a day when "the Lord shall have *washed away the filth* of the daughters of Zion . . . by a spirit of judgment and by a spirit of burning" (Isaiah 4:4; *see also* the call to wash, 1:16; Jeremiah 4:14). Ezekiel reports God as saying: "I will sprinkle clean water upon you, and you shall be *clean from all your uncleannesses,* and from all your idols I will *cleanse* you" (36:25). Zechariah foretells that ". . . there shall be a fountain opened for the house of David and the inhabitants of Jerusalem to *cleanse* them from sin and *uncleanness*" (13:1). Malachi warns that God ". . . is like a refiner's fire and like fullers' soap; he will sit as a refiner and purifier of silver, and he will *purify* the sons of Levi and *refine* them like gold and silver . . ." (3:2, 3; *see also* Isaiah 1:25; Zechariah 13:9). Sinful behavior, say these passages, makes us, as it were, dirty before God; sinful behavior disgusts and repels God as we ourselves are disgusted and repelled if we find dirt where cleanliness ought to be; and God in the holiness of his grace is resolved not only to forgive our sinful behavior, but also to bring it to an end.

All purity laws and purification rituals in the Old Testament point to this divine work of purging out what pollutes. So do all New Testament references to salvation, which describe it as being washed and cleansed (John 13:10; 15:3; Acts 22:16; 1 Corinthians 6:11; Ephesians 5:25–27; Hebrews 9:13, 14; 10:22; 1 John 1:7–9), and refer to the Christian life as a matter of cleansing oneself from whatever makes one dirty in God's eyes (2 Corinthians 7:1; Ephesians 5:3–5; 2 Timothy 2:20–22; 1 John 3:3). So in particular is it reflected in Christian baptism, which is neither more nor less than a symbolic wash.

To highlight the work of the Spirit in making Christians aware and ashamed of sin's defilement and in stirring us to "... *cleanse* ourselves from every defilement of body and spirit, and make holiness perfect in the fear of God" (2 Corinthians 7:1) is thus to underscore a biblical emphasis— one that (be it said) needs a good deal of underscoring in a decadent age like ours, in which moral standards count for so little and the grace of shame is so much at a discount.

Moreover, it is equally right to stress that the Christian's present quest for purity of life means conscious tension and struggle and incomplete achievement all along the line. "For the desires of the flesh are against the Spirit, and the desires of the Spirit are against the flesh; for these are opposed to each other, to prevent you from doing what you would" (Galatians 5:17).

Whether or not we read Romans 7:14–25 as a cross section of healthy Christian experience and so as illustrating this point directly (some do, some don't; we shall discuss the matter later), there is no room for uncertainty as to what Paul is telling us here in Galatians about the reality of conflict in the Christian life. You must realize, he says, that there are two opposed sorts of desire in every Christian's makeup. The opposition between them appears at the level of motive. There are desires that express the natural anti-God egoism of fallen human nature, and there are desires that express the supernatural, God-honoring, God-loving motivation that is implanted by new birth. Now because he has in him these opposite motivational urgings, one holding him back whenever the other draws him forward, the Christian finds that his heart is never absolutely pure, nor does he ever do anything that is absolutely right, even though his constant goal is perfect service of God springing from what the hymn calls "loyal singleness of heart." In this sense he is being prevented every moment from doing what he wants to do. He lives with the knowledge that everything he has done might and should have been better: not only the lapses into which pride, weakness, and folly have betrayed him, but also his attempts to do what was right and good. After each such attempt and each particular action, he regularly sees specific ways in which it could have been improved, both motivationally and in performance. What felt at the time like the best he could do does not appear so in retrospect. He spends his life reaching after perfection and finding that his reach always exceeds his grasp.

This does not of course mean that he never achieves righteousness in any measure at all. Paul is envisioning a Christian life not of constant, total defeat, but of constant moral advance. ". . . Walk by [in] the Spirit, and do not gratify the desires of the flesh," is the direct summons of Galatians 5:16, a summons to which verse 17 is attached as a mere explanatory footnote. It is clear both here and wherever else Paul teaches Christian conduct that he expects the believer always to be moving forward in the formation of godly habits and the practice of active Christlikeness.

The Christian, Paul says, has been freed from slavery to sin so that now he may practice love and righteousness ". . . in the new life of the Spirit" (Romans 7:6); and what he now can do he now must do, for this holiness is the will of God (Galatians 5:13, 14; Romans 6:17–7:6; 1 Thessalonians 4:1–8). The Christian can and must mortify sin through the Spirit (Romans 8:13); he can and must walk in the Spirit, in a steady course of godliness and good works (Romans 8:4; Galatians 5:16, 25). This means that he will stop doing certain things that he did before and that unconverted folk still do, and he will start doing other things instead. The desires of the Spirit, felt in the believer's own spirit (that is, his consciousness) are to be followed, but the desires of the flesh are not to be indulged. The Christian's life must be one of righteousness as the expression of his repentance and rebirth. That is basic.

The point I am developing out of Paul's words in verse 17 is only this: The Christian who thus walks in the Spirit will keep discovering that nothing in his life is as good as it should be; that he has never fought as hard as he might have done against the clogging restraints and contrary pulls of his own inbred perversity; that there is an element of motivational sin, at least, in his best works; that his daily living is streaked with defilements, so that he has to depend every moment on God's pardoning mercy in Christ, or he would be lost; and that he needs to keep asking, in the light of his own felt weakness and inconstancy of heart, that the Spirit will energize him to the end to maintain the inward struggle. "You cannot achieve as much in the way of holiness as you want to achieve." Paul evidently sees this as belonging to the inside story of all human saintliness. Who, now, is going to say that he is wrong?

Certainly, since Clement and Origen mapped out the purging of the soul from the passions, and the desert fathers told of their fights against tormenting fantasies of wine, women, and song, and Augustine spelled out experientially the nature of sin and grace, the inescapability of conflict with temptation has been a fixed emphasis in Christian devotional teaching. Luther and Calvin made much of it, and Lutherans and Calvinists, the latter especially, have followed in their footsteps. Over many centuries the truth, realism, and healthiness of this point have been both called in question and vindicated in discussion over and over again, and no serious challenge can be brought against it now. Stress on the reality of struggle as by God's grace one's life is progressively cleansed and purged is fully scriptural and entirely proper.

PITFALLS OF THE MORAL-STRUGGLE DOCTRINE. But for all that, experience shows that pitfalls surround those who make moral struggle central in their thinking about the Holy Spirit.

Their tendency is to grow *legalistic*, making tight rules for themselves and others about abstaining from things indifferent, imposing rigid and restrictive behavior patterns as bulwarks against worldliness and attaching great importance to observing these man-made taboos. They become *Pharisaic*, more concerned to avoid what defiles and adhere to principle without compromise than to practice the love of Christ. They become *scrupulous*, unreasonably fearful of pollution where none threatens and obstinately unwilling to be reassured. They become *joyless*, being so preoccupied with thoughts of how grim and unrelenting the battle is. They become *morbid*, always introspective and dwelling on the rottenness of their hearts in a way that breeds only gloom and apathy. They become *pessimistic* about the possibility of moral progress, both for themselves and for others; they settle for low expectations of deliverance from sin, as if the best they can hope for is to be kept from getting worse. Such attitudes are, however, spiritual neuroses, distorting, disfiguring, diminishing and so in reality dishonoring the sanctifying work of God's Spirit in our lives.

Granted, these states of mind are usually products of more than one factor. Accidents of temperament and early training, meticulous mental habits turned inward by shyness or insecurity, a low self-image and perhaps actual self-hatred often go toward the making of them; so do certain in-turned types of ecclesiastical culture and community. But inadequate views of the Spirit always prove to underlie them, too, and that is my point now. These folk, like the other two groups we looked at, need a different focus for their thinking about the Spirit, to move them on from the somber spiritual egoism that I have just described. In a moment I will say what I think that focus should be.

Presentation

A fourth approach that must now be looked at views the Holy Spirit's ministry as essentially one of *presentation*; that is, in simplest terms, making us aware of things. This is the view of Bishop J. V. Taylor in *The Go-between God*.

Taylor sees the Spirit (*ruach* in Hebrew, *pneuma* in Greek, each meaning "wind blowing" or "breath blown") as the biblical name for a divine "current of communication" that produces awareness of objects, of oneself, of others, and of God as significant realities demanding choices that in some way involve self-sacrifice. It is by this awareness-choice-sacrifice behavior pattern that the influence of the Spirit, the "life-giving Go-Between"[4] who operates (so Taylor urges) in and through all nature, history, human life, and world religion, may be known. The awareness, an immediate inkling of meaning and claim, is seen as both rational and emotional. The resultant choice and sacrifice are shaped each time by that of which one has become aware and to which one is responding. The Spirit's constant work since Pentecost has been to make individuals aware of deity in Jesus so that they will reproduce in their own lives the spirit of Jesus' self-sacrifice for sins at Calvary. In evoking the responses for which this awareness calls, the Spirit acts most potently in like-minded groups where all may heighten the awareness of each and each may heighten the awareness of all. Taylor works this out in a series of reflections on the actual life of older and younger churches, which bodies he sees as both tokens and means of the divine mission around which all his thinking is ultimately organized.

Taylor is a gifted theologian, whereas most exponents of the other positions which we have reviewed have been pastors promoting what scholars fastidiously call "popular piety"; so it is not surprising that his level of reflection should be deeper than theirs. Much in his book is impressive. To start with, his viewpoint is consistently God-centered. Not only does his key thought (the "current of communication") spring, according to the classic Trinitarian insight, from the Spirit's "eternal employ between the Father and the Son, holding each in awareness of the other,"[5] he also sees further into the nature of the Spirit's free lordship than do those who think of the Spirit as God's power given to us to use or to make us perform and as released in us automatically once we remove the blockages. Taylor sees that the Spirit is not given to us as a kind of pep pill and that it is not for us to harness and control him. So he never slips into the shallowness of those who talk as if we let the Spirit loose in ourselves by means of decisions and acts of will that are not themselves his doing. In all that Taylor says about the Spirit as communicator and quickener, he never forgets that we are men—sinful, silly, varied, mixed-up human creatures—and that the Spirit is our divine Lord, whose work within us passes our understanding. Nor does he allow us the self-absorption of concentrating on our own inward battle with sin, for he sees the Spirit as constantly directing attention upward and outward to God, to Jesus Christ, and to others.

Hence, while Taylor underscores each man's individuality before God (awareness being an individual matter), his overall approach is consistently group-, church-, and community-oriented and in no way individualistic. Yet with this he negates in principle all the restrictions that culture and convention would set on Spirit-led community, observing that as Jesus fitted into no established cultural mold in his own time, so the Spirit smashes any within which we try to confine him today.

Taylor also shrewdly theologizes charismatic "manifestations of spontaneity and unrational response"—ventures in healing, glossolalia, and prophecy in particular—in terms of the wholeness of man who is so much more than conscious analytical reason and whose total being is the sphere of the Spirit's work. Yet with this he warns us against the egoism that is both a root and a fruit of immaturity and as such always threatens the charismatic ethos with corruption. Again Taylor shows wisdom (though not, perhaps, quite all that was needed) in plumbing the dangerous truth that the Spirit's moral guidance will grow more creative as maturity increases, taking us beyond (though never, I think, outside) the realm of biblically based formal rules.

These are genuine excellences.

DEFECTS IN TAYLOR'S ACCOUNT.   Two shortcomings, however, go with these strengths—shortcomings that should be seen as Taylor's failures to carry through his biblical approach with full biblical rigor.

First, he says too little about the word *that the Spirit presents.* In discussing this theme, having cited two references to God's *words* (Isaiah 59:21; Numbers 23:5), he goes straight on to speak of the Johannine and patristic *Word,* the personal divine Logos, as if words and Word were one.[6] But both biblical usage and common sense assure us that they are not. Words that witness to, among other things, the personal Word are obviously distinct from that Word. (Karl Barth, whom Taylor may be following here, certainly claimed that these are two of the three forms of the one Word of God, but that claim itself was a theological conundrum: Nowhere in the Bible is any such thing said, and at half a century's distance it looks as if this was an unnoticed lurch on Barth's part into the kind of beyond-the-Bible speculation that he professed to abhor.)

What was needed to complete Taylor's account of Spirit-born awareness was an analysis of how the Spirit authenticates the revealed words of God, his teachings and messages both as received and relayed by prophets and apostles and then as written in the form of Holy Scripture; and of how as interpreter the Spirit brings us to the place where we actually grasp what God is hereby saying to us. But Taylor offers nothing on these questions.

Second, Taylor says too little about the Christ *whom the Spirit presents.* Surprisingly, he gives no systematic review of how Paul and John, the two great New Testament theologians of the Spirit, set forth the Spirit's many-sided mediation of Christ, and this greatly weakens his exposition. His own references to the Spirit making us aware of Christ, while centering admirably on the Jesus of history, fail to lay equal stress on Jesus' present reign and future return, his constant intercession for us, the reality of his friendship now, and the Christian's sure hope of being with him forever. The effect of these omissions is to dilute radically the meaning of awareness of Christ.

"It does not matter," Taylor writes, "whether the Christ who fills our vision is the historical Jesus, or the living Saviour, or the Christ of the Body and the Blood, or the Logos and Lord of the universe, or the Christ in my neighbor and in his poor. These are only aspects of his being. In whatever aspect he is most real to us, what matters is that we adore him."[7] That is finely said; but it would have been finer doctrine had Taylor added something about the need to bring together all these aspects, and indeed more, if our vision of Christ is to be worthy of him and adequate to the reality of what, according to the Scriptures, he is to us.

In the last analysis, it does matter how we habitually think of Christ; our spiritual health really does depend in great measure on whether or not our vision of him is adequate. For to know Christ is not just to know his cosmic status and earthly history; rather it is, as Melanchthon said long ago, to know his benefits—that is, to know how much he has to give us in his character as messenger, mediator, and personal embodiment of the saving grace of God. But if your vision of Christ himself is deficient, your knowledge of his benefits will of necessity be deficient, too.

I do not mean by this that no one ever receives more from Jesus than he knows about before receiving it. What I said earlier about the generosity of the God who can do, and does, for those who love him ". . . far more abundantly [NIV has "immeasurably more"] than all that we ask or think" (Ephesians 3:20) should be recalled here. Jesus Christ is what he is to believers (divine-human Saviour, Lord, mediator, shepherd, advocate, prophet, priest, king, atoning sacrifice, life, hope, and so forth), irrespective of how much or how little of this multiple relationship they have with him is clear to their minds. An apostolic theologian like Paul, for instance, had it all far clearer in his mind than did the penitent thief of Luke 23:39–43; yet Jesus' saving ministry was as rich to the one as to the other, and we may be sure that at this very moment the two of them, the apostle and the bandit, are together before the throne, their differences in theological expertise on earth making no difference whatsoever to their enjoyment of Christ in heaven. ". . . The same Lord . . . bestows his riches upon all who call upon him" (Romans 10:12)—not just upon Gentiles alongside Jews, but also upon the theologically unskilled alongside the theologically learned. No one should question that.

But this is my point of concern: The less men know about Christ, the sooner it will be necessary to raise the question whether their response to the Jesus of whom they have only hazy and distorted ideas can really be viewed as Christian faith. The further folk depart or stand aloof from biblical categories of thought about Jesus (those listed above being perhaps the basic ones), the less real knowledge of Christ can they have, till they reach the point where, though they talk about him much (as Moslems, Marxists, and theosophists, for instance, will do), they do not really know him at all. For the biblical categories are all concerned with Christ as the answer to questions that the Bible itself teaches us to pose about our relationship to God, questions that arise from the reality of divine holiness and our sin; and the further one stands from those categories, and therefore from those questions, the less knowledge of the *real* Christ and the *real* God can one have, in the nature of the case. A person who thought that England is ruled today by an ex-go-go dancer named Elizabeth who legislates at her discretion from a wood hut in Polynesia could justly be said to know nothing of the real queen, and similarly it takes more to constitute real, valid saving knowledge of Jesus than simply being able to mouth his name.

To put the matter another way: The givenness of Jesus Christ is bound up with the givenness of New Testament theology, which is (so I urge, following its own claim as mainstream Christian tradition has always done) nothing less than the Father's own witness through the Spirit to the Son. Surely there is no real Jesus save the Jesus of that theology. And New Testament theology, whether in Paul, John, Luke, Matthew, Peter, the writer to the Hebrews, or whoever, is essentially proclamation that Jesus Christ saves men from the bondage to false gods, false beliefs, false ways, false hopes, and false posturings before the Creator, into which all non-Christian religions and philosophies, impressive as they often are, are locked. New Testament proclamation diagnoses this whole kaleidoscope of falseness and falsehood as rooted in actual if unwitting suppression of general revelation, misdirection of man's worshiping instincts, and ignorance or rejection of the gospel God has sent. Romans 1:18–3:20, to look no further, is decisive on that; and certainly Emil Brunner was correct when he wrote: "In all religion there is a recollection of the Divine Truth which has been lost; in all religion, there is a longing after the divine light and the divine love; but in all religion also there yawns an abyss of demonic distortion of the Truth, and of man's effort to escape from God."[8]

But if so, then the antithesis between the God-taught truth of the gospel and all other ideas of what is ultimately real and true must always be lovingly yet firmly pointed up and may never out of lax benevolence or courtesy be watered down. Otherwise, the New Testament account of the ". . . unsearchable riches of Christ" (Ephesians 3:8), who saves from the guilt, power, and ultimately the fruits and presence of sin, will have to be watered down, too, so as to fit into alien molds of thought. And to do that would be to relativize the gospel in a radical and ruinous way. For though within these alien frames of reference some New Testament thoughts might be given some weight, the absolute validity, definitive status, and unqualified authority of New Testament theology as such would all the time be denied—denied, that is, by the very fact of not letting it criticize and amend the frames of reference themselves: Hindu, Buddhist, Jewish, Moslem, Marxist, or whatever they might be. For it is simply not true that all religions and ideologies ask the same basic questions about either God or man or look in the same direction for answers.

A vast difference exists between dialogue that explores the antithesis between Christianity and other faiths, the antithesis that ultimately requires negation of the one in order to affirm the other, and the sort of dialogue that looks for Christ in, or seeks to graft him onto, some other faith as it stands. It has to be said that despite Taylor's talk of the conversion, transformation, death, and resurrection of ethnic and post-Christian faiths through meeting Christ as presented by the Spirit,[9] it is not at all clear that what he is after is the first of these rather than the second. This haziness is in fact a third weakness in Taylor's book, brought on by the two weaknesses already pinpointed—namely, his omitting to reckon with the reality of "God's Word written"[10] and to observe that knowledge of Christ must be measured, among other tests, by how much of the New Testament teaching about Christ is or is not embraced.

The above, however, is no criticism of Taylor's key thought of the Spirit as the divine Go-between who presents realities, compels choices, and evokes sacrificial responses. To find the New Testament key thought in terms of which we should understand the Spirit's ministry to Christians yesterday and today, we do not need to move far beyond the point at which Taylor stops. He has led us almost to our goal.

Tracing Our Path

Glance back for a moment at our path so far.

We started by noting that though the Holy Spirit is much spoken of today, and his influence is truly claimed for many different sorts of Christian experience, different key ideas about his essential ministry dominate different Christian minds. This shows (so I urged) that the Spirit is not always being seen in proper focus. Many think about the Spirit in a way that, though not wholly false, is certainly smudgy and not true enough. Hence spring all sorts of inadequacy and practical imbalance, sometimes threatening to stifle the Spirit whom in our incompetence we are seeking to honor. Getting the Spirit into better focus is, therefore, an urgent matter.

To take the measure of the contemporary situation, we looked at four key ideas round which currently influential concepts of the Spirit's ministry have been organized: *power* for living, *performance* in service, *purity* of motive and action, and *presentation* for decision. This list of "sweet *p*'s" (a preacher's ploy for pointedness. Pardonable? Perhaps) is not, indeed, exhaustive. It could at once be lengthened by adding *perception*, and *push* (or *pull*), and *personhood*. For as we move out from the circles where living Christianity is found today

(the circles on which our sights have been trained so far), we
find folk who do in fact think that the Spirit's central and
characteristic work is just to enhance awareness (perception)
as such, so that any heightened state of consciousness,
whether religious (Christian, Hindu, cultic, ecstatic, mystical)
aesthetic (being "sent" by music, sex, poetry, sunsets, drugs),
or idealistic (as in passionate patriotism, romance, or devotion to a group or a cause), is, so to speak, the Spirit's signa-
ture. We meet others who, forgetting what nature and Satan
can do with the inordinate instincts and repressed reasonings
and sick fantasies of mixed-up specimens of fallen humanity
like ourselves, equate the Spirit's moving with inner urges
(pushes or pulls) as such, especially when these are linked
with visual and auditory images (visions, voices, dreams) that
come suddenly and strongly and recur insistently. We run
across yet others who will claim that to make folk realize the
mystery of their own individuality (personhood) and the
worth of other persons and the demands of truly personal relationships, is the Spirit's essential work, which he carries on
among men of all religions and of none.

It would certainly be wrong to say that the Spirit of God
never heightens consciousness, or ever communicates by
inner urges of the now-do-this sort, or causes unbelievers
better to appreciate personal values, and I am not venturing
such denials. I would in fact argue against them all. But the
idea that any one of these operations might constitute the
Spirit's essential ministry today seems very wide of the mark.
Central to the Spirit's ministry since Christ came, as we shall
see, is the furthering of fellowship with him. Heightening
perception and sensitivity in secular and pagan contexts is no
doubt something that in common grace the Spirit does, but it
is not the heart of his work, nor ever was.

As for inner urges, it is surely enough to point out that
some people have inner urges, strong and recurring, sometimes reinforced by voices, visions, and dreams, to rape, to
take revenge, to inflict pain, to molest children sexually, and
to kill themselves. Is any of that the leading of the Spirit? The
question answers itself. Obsessiveness (which is what we are

really talking about here) is no sure sign of a divine origin for thoughts; Satan can spawn obsessive impulses equally well, just as he can nourish and manipulate those our disordered natures spontaneously produce. So sudden, obsessive thoughts need to be very carefully checked (preferably by consulting others) before we dare conclude that they come to us from the Spirit of God. Their obsessiveness, indeed, indicates that they probably do not.

Presence

We return, then, to the world of living Christianity, where everyone at least looks in the right direction by linking the Spirit's work one way or another with the new life in Christ. Once more we pose the question: What is the essence, heart, and core of the Spirit's work today? What is the central, focal element in his many-sided ministry? Is there one basic activity to which his work of empowering, enabling, purifying, and presenting must be related in order to be fully understood? Is there a single divine strategy that unites all these facets of his life-giving action as means to one end?

I think there is, and now I offer my view of it—a view that I focus (still pursuing my path of *p*'s) in terms of the idea of *presence*. By this I mean that the Spirit makes known the personal presence in and with the Christian and the church of the risen, reigning Saviour, the Jesus of history, who is the Christ of faith. Scripture shows (as I maintain) that since the Pentecost of Acts 2 this, essentially, is what the Spirit is doing all the time as he empowers, enables, purges, and leads generation after generation of sinners to face the reality of God. And he does it in order that Christ may be known, loved, trusted, honored and praised, which is the Spirit's aim and purpose throughout as it is the aim and purpose of God the Father, too. This is what, in the last analysis, the Spirit's new covenant ministry is all about.

The presence of which I speak here is not the divine *omnipresence* of traditional theology, which texts like Psalm 139;

Jeremiah 23:23, 24; Amos 9:2–5 and Acts 17:26–28 define for us as God's awareness of everything everywhere as he upholds it in its own being and activity. Omnipresence is an important truth, and what I am saying here assumes it, but when I use the word *presence* I have in view something different. I mean by this word what the Bible writers meant when they spoke of God being present with his people—namely, God acting in particular situations to bless faithful folk and thus make them know his love and help and draw forth their worship. Granted, God would sometimes "visit" and "draw near" for judgment (look at Malachi 3:5, for instance); that is, he would act in a way that made men realize his displeasure at their doings, as indeed he does still; but usually in Scripture God's coming to his people and granting them his presence meant their blessing.

Often this was expressed by saying that God was "with" them. "The Lord was *with* Joseph, and he became a successful man"—"a lucky fellow," as Tyndale put it (Genesis 39:2). When Moses panicked at the thought of returning to Egypt, where there was a price on his head, and of bearding Pharaoh in his den, God said: "But I will be *with* you"—a promise that was meant to shame out of existence all the butterflies in Moses' stomach (Exodus 3:12; *see also* 33:14–16). God repeated the same promise to Joshua when the latter took on the leadership after Moses' death: ". . . As I was *with* Moses, so I will be *with* you. . . . Be strong and of good courage . . . for the Lord your God is *with* you wherever you go" (Joshua 1:5, 9; *see also* Deuteronomy 31:6, 8). Israel was reassured in the same terms: "When you pass through the waters I will be *with* you. . . . Fear not, for I am *with* you . . ." (Isaiah 43:2, 5). Matthew takes up this thought of God being present with his people to bless them when he starts his gospel by proclaiming Jesus' birth as fulfillment of Isaiah's Emmanuel prophecy (*Emmanuel* means "God is *with* us") and again when he ends it by recording Jesus' promise to all his disciple-making followers: ". . . Lo, I am *with* you always . . ." (Matthew 1:23; 28:20). For Jesus, the author and bringer of salvation, is himself God incarnate, and the presence of Christ is precisely the presence of God.

The truth of the matter is this. The distinctive, constant, basic ministry of the Holy Spirit under the new covenant is so to mediate Christ's presence to believers—that is, to give them such knowledge of his presence with them as their Saviour, Lord, and God—that three things keep happening.

First, personal fellowship *with Jesus,* that is, the to-and-fro of discipleship with devotion, which started in Palestine, for Jesus' first followers, before his passion, becomes a reality of experience, even though Jesus is now not here on earth in bodily form, but is enthroned in heaven's glory. (This is where the thought of presentation properly belongs: The Spirit presents the living Lord Jesus to us as Maker and Friend so that we may choose the path of sacrificial response to his love and his call.)

Second, personal transformation *of character into Jesus' likeness* starts to take place as, looking to Jesus, their model, for strength, believers worship and adore him and learn to lay out and, indeed, lay down their lives for him and for others. (This is where the themes of power, performance, and purgation properly come in. They mark out what it means to move beyond our natural selfishness into the Christlike path of righteousness, service, and conquest of evil.)

Third, the Spirit-given certainty *of being loved, redeemed, and adopted* through Christ into the Father's family, so as to be "heirs of God and fellow heirs with Christ" (Romans 8:17), makes gratitude, delight, hope, and confidence—in a word, *assurance*—blossom in believers' hearts. (This is the proper way to understand many of the Christian's postconversion mountaintop experiences. The inward coming of the Son and the Father that Jesus promised in John 14:21–23 takes place through the Spirit, and its effect is to intensify assurance.)

By these phenomena of experience, Spirit-given knowledge of Christ's presence—"elusive, intangible, unpredictable, untamed, inaccessible to empirical verification, outwardly invisible but inwardly irresistible," to borrow Samuel Terrien's description[11]—shows itself.

AN AWARENESS OF GOD. Throughout the Bible, knowing God's presence appears as a twofold awareness. It is awareness, first, that God is *there*: the objectively real Creator, Upholder, Master, and Mover of all that exists in space and time; the God who holds one, for good or ill, completely in his hands. Second, it is awareness that God is *here*, having come close to address, question, and search us, to bring us low by exposing our weakness, sin and guilt, yet therewith to raise us up by his word of pardon and promise. In the days before it was revealed that God is, in John Donne's words, "three-personed," knowledge of the God who was present was undifferentiated. Now, however, through the revelation given in the Incarnation and elucidated in the New Testament, knowledge of God has become knowledge of Father, Son, and Spirit; and knowledge of God's presence has become confrontation by and communion with the Son, and with the Father through the Son, in virtue of the Spirit's activity. Knowing Christ's presence thus means finding in oneself this double awareness of God as real and close, centered upon the man from Galilee whom Thomas called "My Lord and my God!" (John 20:28). Paul was describing this knowledge when he wrote that ". . . the God who said, 'Let light shine out of darkness,' . . . has shone in our hearts to give the light of the knowledge of the glory of God in the face of Christ" (2 Corinthians 4:6).

That it is the special ministry of the Spirit since Pentecost to mediate Christ's active presence is clear in the New Testament. There, as exegetes often point out, the Spirit is always viewed as the Spirit of Jesus Christ, God's Son (Acts 16:7; Romans 8:9; Galatians 4:6; Philippians 1:19; 1 Peter 1:11). The Spirit who indwells us is the Spirit who was in and upon Jesus (Luke 3:22; 4:1, 14, 18; 10:21; John 1:32; 3:34; Acts 10:38). Jesus, the Spirit bearer, is also the Spirit giver (John 1:33; 15:26; 16:7; 20:22; *see also* 7:37–39; Acts 2:33; 1 John 2:20, 27), and the coming of the Spirit to the disciples after Jesus had been taken from them was in a real sense his return to them (John 14:16, 18–21). The indwelling of the Spirit of God, who is the Spirit of Christ, is described as the indwelling of Christ himself (*see* Romans 8:9–11), just as the personal message of the exalted Christ is "what the Spirit says to the churches" (*see* Revelation 2:1, 7, 8, 11, 12, 17, 18, 29; 3:1, 6, 7, 13, 14, 22).

Again, having said in 2 Corinthians 3:16, "when a man turns to the Lord the veil [over his mind] is removed" (a verbal echo of Exodus 34:34, which tells how Moses removed his veil when he spoke with God), Paul goes on:

> Now the Lord [to whom that last statement referred] is the Spirit [so that "turn to the Lord" meant "embrace the new covenant, in and by which the Spirit is given" (*see* verse 6)], and where the Spirit of the Lord [Jesus] is, there is freedom. And we all, with unveiled face, beholding [or *reflecting:* Both renderings are possible and profoundly true] the glory of the Lord [Jesus], are being changed into his likeness from one degree of glory to another; for this comes from the Lord who is the Spirit.
>
> 2 Corinthians 3:17, 18

What these passages show is not, as some have thought, that the New Testament writers saw no clear personal distinction between the Son and the Spirit, but rather that they saw the Spirit's post-Pentecostal task as essentially that of mediating the presence, word, and activity of the enthroned Christ. It is by grasping this basic New Testament perspective that we get the Spirit in focus.

Program

This book takes the thought of the Spirit as charged and committed to mediate the presence of Christ as the clue to understanding some of the main facets of his ministry. Many existing surveys of the Spirit's work fall short, in my view, through not integrating their material in this way. It is not enough to give a surface-level account of how the Spirit was manifested in New Testament times and of what New Testament writers said about those manifestations, without going on to ask how their statements fitted with their total view of God, his work, and his truth—in other words, their total the-

ology—for failure here sentences us, more or less drastically,
to man-centered, experience-based, criterionless thoughts
about the Spirit in our own lives. That is why so many otherwise excellent books on the Spirit have not helped their readers as much as was expected, nor as much as those readers
thought they were being helped at the time. For the help we
need nowadays in order to live in the Spirit is not exhortation
to open our lives to him—we have enough and to spare of
that already—rather, it is a thought-out theological perspective on the Spirit's work, which will give us a coherent view
of what his free, unfettered, multiform moving in churches,
small groups, and personal lives (which is so marked a feature of Christianity today) is really all about and all in aid of.
My hope is that by developing the thought of the Spirit as
mediating Christ's presence and fellowship—which is central
to New Testament teaching on the Spirit—I may be able to
provide such a theological perspective, in outline at any rate.

Biblically my aim and viewpoint can be expressed like
this: On the night of his betrayal Jesus said of the Spirit: "He
will glorify me ..." that is, "he shall make me glorious in
men's eyes by making them aware of the glory that is mine
already and that will be enhanced when I have gone back to
the Father via the cross and resurrection and ascension to be
enthroned in my kingdom" (John 16:14). That basic definition
(as I take it to be) of what the Spirit was and is sent to do
gives us a comprehensive directional frame of reference
within which the whole of the Spirit's new covenant ministry
should be seen, and apart from which no feature of that ministry can be adequately understood.

Jesus then told how the glorifying was to be done: "For he
will take what is mine and declare it to you." What did Jesus
mean by "what is *mine*"? He must have meant, at least,
"everything that is real and true about me as God incarnate,
as the Father's agent in creation, providence and grace, as this
world's rightful lord, and as the one who actually is master of
it [*see* 17:2] whether men acknowledge me or not." But surely
he also meant, "all that is real and true about me as your divine lover, your mediator, your surety in the new covenant,

your prophet, priest and king, your Saviour from the guilt and power of sin and from the world's corruptions and the devil's clutches; and all that is true of me as your shepherd, husband, and friend, your life and your hope, the author and finisher of your faith, the lord of your own personal history, and the one who will some day bring you to be with me and share my glory, who am thus both your path and your prize." So the words "what is *mine*" come to mean "what is *yours*, by virtue of my relationship to you and yours to me."

From the crooner era in which I was brought up I recall a ballad, "All the things you are," which ended thus: ". . . and someday I'll know that moment divine When all the things you are are mine." The Spirit glorifies Jesus in Christian eyes by convincing us that all he is and has in his glory is really and truly for us—"unto our glory," to borrow Paul's phrase in 1 Corinthians 2:7 (KJV)—and to know this is something even more divine than the romantic moment crooned of in the song.

"He . . . will declare it *to you*," said Jesus. Did this mean apostles only or all Christians with them? Primarily apostles, to whom direct revelations of these things were to be given; but secondarily all believers, to whom the Spirit would teach the same things out of the witness to them, spoken and written, which apostles would bear. Apostolic spiritual understanding was to be shared with all God's people, as indeed it still is.

Verse 15 was then spoken as, in effect, a footnote. In order that the full scope and implications of the word *mine* in the previous sentence should not be missed, Jesus went on to say: "All that the Father has is *mine*; therefore I said that he will take what is *mine* and declare it to you." The footnote was spoken to warn against supposing that what Jesus is and does is in any way exceeded by what the Father is and does, or (putting it the other way round) that the Father's attributes, claims, powers, plans, prospects, and glories are in any way greater or extend further than his. "*All* that the Father has is mine"; coequality of Son with Father is a fact; the Father intends ". . . that all may honor the Son, even as they honor the Father . . ." (John 5:23). It is on joyful assent to this divine purpose that all true Christian belief, worship, and practice ultimately rest.

In the following pages I shall seek to interpret the Spirit's ministry from this point of view. I shall present it in terms of his furthering the Father's pleasure by leading us to glorify the Son in adoration as we respond to the Spirit's glorifying of him by declaration. I maintain that no account of the Holy Spirit—no *pneumatology*, to use the technical word—is fully Christian till it exhibits all his many-sided work from the standpoint of, on the one hand, the Father's purpose that the Son be known, loved, honored, praised, and have preeminence in everything, and on the other hand, the Son's promise to make himself present with his people, here and hereafter, by giving his Spirit to them. My present agenda is to point out some of the main elements in a properly Christian pneumatology, meaning by that an account that builds consistently on the thoughts which Jesus himself expresses in John 14:16–23 and 16:14, 15 and will not be drawn away from them. I hope the program is acceptable. I think it is needed, and I now go to it.

2

The Holy Spirit in the Bible[1]

THE KEY thought of this book is now before you. It is not a new thought; it is as old as the New Testament. To state it is no more than to recall Christians to their roots. The thought is simply this: The essence of the Holy Spirit's ministry, at this or any time in the Christian era, is to mediate the presence of our Lord Jesus Christ. Under this ministry I as a Christian writer and you as a Christian reader live already, though our thoughts about it may be lagging behind the reality.

Jesus' presence in my formula should be thought of not in spatial, but rather in relational terms. What I am pointing to when I use this phrase is an awareness of three things. The first is that Jesus of Nazareth, the Christ of the Scriptures, once crucified, now glorified, is *here*, personally approaching and addressing me. The second is that he is *active*, powerfully enlightening, animating, and transforming me along with others as he stirs our sluggishness, sharpens our insight, soothes our guilty consciences, sweetens our tempers, supports us under pressure, and strengthens us for righteousness. The third is that in himself as in his work he is *glorious*, meriting all the worship, adoration, love, and loyalty of which we are capable. Mediating Jesus' presence, therefore, is a matter of the Spirit doing whatever is necessary for the creating, sustaining, deepening, and expressing of this awareness in human lives. The themes that come in as one spells this out are familiar enough: communication from God in Christ and communion with God through Christ; the interpreting of Holy Scripture and the illuminating of human hearts; the regenerating and sanctifying of sinners; the actualizing of gifts and good works; the Spirit bearing witness to our adoption and helping our human weakness; the supernatural engendering of faith, prayer, hope, love, and all the many facets of Christlike character; and so forth. Nothing is new here save that I am highlighting the Christ centeredness of all these deeds of the Spirit in a way that is not always done. The present chapter seeks to show that in doing so I am only following the lead of the Bible itself.

We had best start, I think, by looking at the name *Spirit* and noting what it signifies.

The Spirit of God

For most people nowadays *Spirit* is a vague and colorless word. The thought it is most likely to bring to mind is of a human mood or attitude (high or low *spirits*, good *spirits*, animal *spirits*, a cheerful or downcast *spirit*, a *spirit* of mischief or of kindness, "that's the *spirit*," and so forth). Once upon a time *spirit* was the class name for nonhuman and disembodied intelligences of many sorts (angels, demons, fairies, elves, sprites, ghosts, souls departed, local gods inhabiting mountains, stones, and trees); thus when in 1691 the elderly Puritan Richard Baxter wrote his quaint book affirming the reality of these things he called it *The Certainty of the Worlds of Spirits*. But belief in such spirits has waned, at least in the West. Many now mean by *spirits* nothing more than what my dictionary primly calls "distilled liquor, containing much alcohol" and would view belief in other sorts of spirits as indicating a lack of philosophical sobriety at least. All in all, our culture gives us virtually no help when the Spirit of God is the theme of our study.

In fact, *Spirit*, like all biblical terms that refer to God, is a picture-word with a vivid, precise, and colorful meaning. It pictures breath breathed or panted out, as when you blow out the candles on your birthday cake or blow up balloons or puff and blow as you run. *Spirit* in this sense was what the big bad wolf was threatening the little pigs with when he told them, "I'll huff, and I'll puff, and I'll blow your house down!" The picture is of air made to move vigorously, even violently, and the thought that the picture expresses is of energy let loose, executive force invading, power in exercise, life demonstrated by activity.

Both the Hebrew and Greek words rendered *spirit* in our Bibles (*ruach* and *pneuma*) carry this basic thought, and both have the same range of association. They are used of (1) the divine Spirit, personal and purposeful, invisible and irresistible; (2) the individual human consciousness (in which sense *spirit* becomes synonymous with *soul*, as for instance in Luke 1:46, 47); and (3) the wind that when aroused whirls leaves, uproots trees, and blows buildings over. (For examples of this latter use, see (a) Ezekiel 37:1–14, the dry-bones vision, where *ruach* is breath, wind, and Spirit of God in quick succession, and (b) the use of *pneuma* for the wind as well as for God's Spirit in John 3:8.) I wish that our language had a word that would carry all these associations. *Puff* and *blow* are two English words (the only ones, I think) that refer to both the outbreathing of air from human lungs and the stirring of the wind, but English has no term that will cover, along with this, the intellectual, volitional, and emotional individuality of God and of his rational creatures. *Spirit* in English, by contrast, denotes conscious personhood in action and reaction, but cannot be used of either breath or wind. This is doubtless one reason why it does not suggest to us power in action in the way that *ruach* and *pneuma* did to people in Bible times.

Power in action is in fact the basic biblical thought whenever God's Spirit is mentioned. In the Old Testament, "the Spirit of God" is always God at work, changing things. In the course of just under a hundred references (minimum count, eighty-eight; maximum ninety-seven; scholars differ), the Spirit of God is said to:

1. Mold *creation* into shape and animate created beings (Genesis 1:2; 2:7; Psalms 33:6; Job 26:13; 33:4)
2. Control the course of what we call *nature and history* (Psalms 104:29, 30; Isaiah 34:16; 40:7)
3. Reveal *God's truth and will* to his messengers by both direct communication and/or distilled insight (Numbers 24:2; 2 Samuel 23:2; 2 Chronicles 12:18; 15:1; Nehemiah 9:30; Job 32:8; Isaiah 61:1–4; Ezekiel 2:2; 11:24; 37:1; Micah 3:8; Zechariah 7:12)
4. Teach God's people through these revelations *the way of faithfulness and fruitfulness* (Nehemiah 9:20; Psalms 143:10; Isaiah 48:16; 63:10–14)
5. *Elicit personal response to God*—knowledge of God in the Bible's own sense—in the form of faith, repentance, obedience, righteousness, openness to God's instruction, and fellowship with him through praise and prayer (Psalms 51:10–12; Isaiah 11:2, 44:3; Ezekiel 11:19; 36:25–27; 37:14, 39:29; Joel 2:28, 29; Zechariah 12:10)
6. Equip individuals for *leadership* (Genesis 41:38, Joseph; Numbers 11:17, Moses; 11:16–29, seventy elders; 27:18, Deuteronomy 34:9, Joshua; Judges 3:10, Othniel; 6:34, Gideon; 11:29, Jephthah; 13:25, 14:19, 15:14, Samson; 1 Samuel 10:10, 11:6, *see also* 19:20–23, Saul; 16:13, David; 2 Kings 2:9–15, Elijah and Elisha; Isaiah 11:1–5, 42:1–4, the Messiah)
7. Equip individuals with *skill and strength* for creative achievements (Exodus 31:1–11, 35:30–35, Bezalel and Oholiab; *see also* 1 Kings 7:14, Hiram, for artistic craftsmanship; Haggai 2:5, Zechariah 4:6, for temple building)

In short, the Spirit in the Old Testament is God active as *creator, controller, revealer, quickener,* and *enabler;* and in all this God makes himself present to men in the dynamic, demanding way in which the Lord Jesus is now made present to Christian believers. When the psalmist asks: "Whither shall I go from thy Spirit? Or whither shall I flee from thy presence?" (139:7), the two questions expound each other; both mean the same thing. However, the Spirit's distinct personhood was no part of this revelation. In the Old Testament, God's *Spirit* (breath!) is on the same footing logically as are his *hand* and *arm*, two anthropomorphisms signifying his almighty power, and as is his *zeal*, a personification signifying his firmness of purpose. You could truly say that references to God's *Spirit* signify God at work in resolute omnipotence, his *arm* and *zeal* acting together, but it would not be true to say that these references express any thought on the writers' part of a plurality of persons within the unity of the Godhead. The truth of the Trinity is a New Testament revelation.

But should anyone think that according to Scripture God was unipersonal during the Old Testament period and only became tripersonal when Jesus was born, he would be wrong. What is in question here is not the mode of God's being from eternity, but the manner of its revelation in history. I am not saying that the third person of the Godhead did not exist or was not active in Old Testament times; the New Testament writers assure us that he did and was. I am only saying that his distinct personhood is not expressed by the Old Testament writers; though God's triunity is an eternal fact, only through Christ was it made known.

And now I add this: The right way for followers of Jesus Christ to read the Old Testament is in the light of all that was revealed in and through Christ and that now lies before us in the New Testament. Following Jesus' identification of himself as the reference point and fulfiller of the Scriptures (*see* Matthew 5:17; 26:54–56; Luke 18:31; 22:37; 24:25–27, 44–47; John 5:39, 45–47), the apostles laid claim to the whole Old Testament as God-given instruction for Christians (*see* Romans 15:4; 1 Corinthians 10:11; 2 Timothy 3:15–17; 2 Peter 1:19–21; 3:16); and as they constantly read divine truth and wisdom out of it, so they constantly found their knowledge of Christ and Christian realities reflected in it. In the New Testament use of the Old we see this happening. Apostolic Christians, then, should read Old Testament references to the work of the Spirit of God in the light of the New Testament revelation of the Spirit's distinct personhood, just as they should read Old Testament references to the one God, the Lord Yahweh, Creator, Saviour and Sanctifier, the only right object of worship, in the light of the New Testament disclosure that God is triune. There is nothing arbitrary about doing this; the rightness of the procedure follows directly from recognizing that the God of both Testaments is one.

To be sure, this procedure is not what modern scholars call historical exegesis. Historical exegesis stops at asking what the human writer meant his intended readers to gather from what he said. Reading the Old Testament by the light of the New is better described as theological interpretation— "canonical interpretation," to use the current phrase—which is a matter of asking what the Holy Spirit, who inspired each writer, means Christians today to find in his words as they read them with all New Testament truth and all the rest of the Christian Bible as their context. Historical exegesis assures us that Old Testament statements about God's almighty breath were not intended by their writers to imply personal distinctions within the deity. Christian theological interpretation, however, requires us to follow the Lord Jesus and his apostles in recognizing that the third person of the Godhead was active in Old Testament times and that Old Testament statements about God's almighty breath do in fact refer to the personal Spirit's activity. The lead here is given by such passages as Mark 12:36 and Acts 1:16; 4:25, where David is said to have spoken by the Holy Spirit, in echo of 2 Samuel 23:2; Luke 4:18-21, where Jesus, filled with the power of the personal Holy Spirit (*see* 3:22; 4:1, 14; *see also* 1:35, 41, 67), claims that his preaching fulfills Isaiah's witness to his own anointing by the Spirit in chapter 61:1-4 of his prophecy; John 3:5-10, where the teaching on new birth "of water and the Spirit" clearly looks back to Ezekiel 36:25-27; 37:1-14 and Nicodemus, the teacher of Israel, is chided (verse 10) for not picking up the reference; Acts 28:25 and Hebrews 3:7; 10:15-17, where Old Testament teaching that has a New Testament application is ascribed to the Holy Spirit as its source; and—most decisive of all—Acts 2:16–18, where Peter identifies the Pentecostal outpouring of the personal Holy Spirit as that which was predicted in the words ". . . I will pour out my spirit . . ." in Joel 2:28, 29.

I proceed, therefore, on the basis that Old Testament references to the Spirit of God are in fact witnessing to the work of the personal Holy Spirit of the New Testament.

The Personhood of the Spirit

THE SPIRIT AS PARACLETE. In the New Testament, the Holy Spirit is set forth as the third divine person, linked with yet distinct from the Father and the Son, just as the Father and the Son are distinct from each other. He is "the Paraclete" (John 14:16, 25; 15:26; 16:7)—a rich word for which there is no adequate English translation, since it means by turns Comforter (in the sense of Strengthener), Counselor, Helper, Supporter, Adviser, Advocate, Ally, Senior Friend—and only a person could fulfill such roles. More precisely, he is "another" Paraclete (14:16), second in line (we may say) to the Lord Jesus, continuing Jesus' own ministry—and only a person, one like Jesus, could do that. John underlines the point by repeatedly using a masculine pronoun (*ekeinos*, "he") to render Jesus' references to the Spirit, when Greek grammar called for a neuter one (*ekeino*, "it") to agree with the neuter noun "Spirit" (*pneuma*): John wants his readers to be in no doubt that the Spirit is *he* not *it*. This masculine pronoun, which appears in 14:26; 15:26; 16:8, 13, 14 is the more striking because in 14:17, where the Spirit is first introduced, John had used the grammatically correct neuter pronouns (*ho* and *auto*), thus ensuring that his subsequent shift to the masculine would be perceived not as incompetent Greek, but as magisterial theology.

Again the Holy Spirit is said to hear, speak, witness, convince, glorify Christ, lead, guide, teach, command, forbid, desire, give speech, give help, and intercede for Christians with inarticulate groans, himself crying to God in their prayers (*see* John 14:26; 15:26; 16:7–15; Acts 2:4; 8:29; 13:2;

16:6, 7; Romans 8:14, 16, 26, 27; Galatians 4:6; 5:17, 18). Also, he can be lied to and grieved (Acts 5:3, 4; Ephesians 4:30). Only of a person could such things be said. The conclusion is that the Spirit is not just an influence; he, like the Father and the Son, is an individual person.

THE SPIRIT AS DEITY.   Moreover, the Holy Spirit is set forth as a divine person. His individuality is within the unity of the Godhead. The very word *holy* suggests his deity, and several passages are explicit about it. Jesus declares that the name of God, into which those who become his disciples are to be baptized (*name* in the singular, note, for there is only one God) is a tripersonal name: "the name of the Father and of the Son and of the Holy Spirit" (Matthew 28:19). (Karl Barth sweetly called this God's "Christian name!") Again, John begins his letter to the seven churches by wishing them grace and peace ". . . from him who is and who was and who is to come, and from the seven spirits who are before his throne, and from Jesus Christ . . ." (Revelation 1:4, 5). In the number symbolism of Revelation, seven signifies divine complete-ness, and the "seven spirits" certainly signify the Holy Spirit in the fullness of his power and work (*see* 3:1; 4:5; 5:6). When the Father is put first and the Son third and the Spirit be-tween them, as here, no room remains for doubt as to the Spirit's coequality with them. Confirming this, a series of "triadic" passages link Father, Son, and Spirit together in the inseparable unity of a single plan of grace (*see* 1 Corinthians 12:4–6; 2 Corinthians 13:14; Ephesians 1:3–13; 2:18; 3:14–19; 4:4–6; 2 Thessalonians 2:13, 14; 1 Peter 1:2). The conclusion is that the Spirit is no mere powerful creature, like an angel; he, with the Father and the Son, is God Almighty.

So I plead: Never think or speak of the Holy Spirit in less than personal terms! My heart sinks and I wince, when I hear Christians, as I sometimes do, calling the third divine person "it" rather than "he." This is the spiritual equivalent of a Freudian lapse, such as I fell into on the occasion when in a chapel message to students at Regent College I meant to say "Remember, this place is a kind of seminary," and actually came out with "Remember, this place is a kind of cemetery."

Though I brought the house down quite spectacularly, I was neither saying quite what I meant nor meaning quite what I said. I hope it is a similar slip of the Christian tongue when saints call the Spirit "it," and that they do not mean what they say. For you cannot understand the Spirit's ministry till you have grasped the fact of his personhood, and it is where no strong sense or clear grasp of the Spirit's work is found that his personhood comes to be denied. (Look at liberal and radical Protestantism, Judaism, Islam, Unitarianism, and Christian Science if you need proof of that.) One does not want to see any wavering at this point among biblical Christians. A major way in which Pentecostalism has benefited the church is by making it so much harder than it was to call the Spirit anything less than "he." The surest method, however, of establishing believers in the truth of the Spirit's personhood is actually to set before them the New Testament witness to his work, so to this we now turn.

The Holy Spirit and Christ

A century of academic debate about the historical trustworthiness of John's gospel has made it unfashionable to start with it when exploring New Testament themes. The convention is rather to work up to the study of John's witness via Matthew, Mark, Luke's two volumes, and sometimes Peter and Paul, too, as if you could only hope to see what John is saying by standing on the shoulders of these other writers. But as one who sees no good reason to doubt either the authenticity or the intrinsic clarity of what John records, I propose to make his gospel my jumping-off point for elucidating the Spirit's new covenant ministry; for it is in John's gospel, from Jesus' own lips, that the vital clue for understanding that ministry is given. On this topic, at any rate, we need to stand on John's shoulders if we are fully to understand what we are told about the Spirit by Matthew, Mark, Luke, Peter, and Paul.

THE PROMISE OF THE SPIRIT. On the night of his betrayal, so John tells us, Jesus talked at length to eleven of his followers about their future discipleship in the light of his own imminent departure to glory (chapters 13–16). He referred several times to the Paraclete, whom he identified as the Spirit of truth (14:17; 15:26; 16:13) and the Holy Spirit (14:26). The Paraclete, he said, would be sent by the Father at his (the Son's) personal request, following his own departure (14:16, 26), and so could be said to be sent by the Son as the Father's agent (15:26; 16:7). He would be sent, said Jesus, "in my name" (14:26), that is as Jesus' courier, spokesman, and representative; he would stay with Jesus' disciples "for ever" (14:16); and through his coming to them Jesus himself, their glorified Lord, would actually return to them (14:18–23). In his new covenant ministry (for this is what Jesus was talking about) the Spirit would be self-effacing, directing all attention away from himself to Christ and drawing folk into the faith, hope, love, obedience, adoration, and dedication, which constitute communion with Christ. This, be it said, remains the criterion by which the authenticity of supposedly "spiritual" movements—the ecumenical movement, the charismatic movement, the liturgical movement, the small-group movement, the lay apostolate movement, the world missionary movement, and so on—and also of supposedly "spiritual" experiences, may be gauged.

THE SPIRIT AND CHRIST'S PRESENCE. So the Spirit would make the presence of Christ and fellowship with him and his Father realities of experience for those who, by obeying his words, showed that they loved him (14:21–23). "If a man loves me, he will keep my word, and my Father will love him and we will come to him and make our home with him." This is the charter for that quality of Christian experience to which John himself testified when he wrote, ". . . our fellowship is with the Father and with his Son Jesus Christ" (1 John 1:3), and it comes as Christ's challenge to us all to seek this experienced fellowship and settle for nothing less.

THE TEACHING OF GOD'S SPIRIT. Again, the Spirit would teach, as Jesus had taught for the three precious years of his ministry on earth; and the Spirit's way of teaching would be to make disciples recall and comprehend what Jesus himself had said (14:26; *see also* 16:13, where Jesus' phrase "all the truth," like "all things" in 14:26, means not "all there is to know about anything," but "all you need to know *about me*," and "the things that are to come" means not "what awaits you" but "what awaits *me*"—the cross, the resurrection, the reign, the return, the restoring of all things). This is the test that will show how much of the Spirit there is in each of the various types of supposedly Christian theology that jostle for our attention in these days.

THE WITNESS OF THE SPIRIT. Finally, the Spirit would attest Christ in the manner of a witness, causing folk to know that though crucified as a criminal, he was not in any way a sinner, that he was in fact vindicated as righteous by his return to the Father's glory, that he began to fulfill his role as the world's judge by the judgment, carried out on the cross, which dethroned the world's dark lord (*see also* 12:31), and that failure to acknowledge him in these terms is the sin of unbelief (15:27; 16:8–11). The witnessing Spirit would hereby act as humanity's prosecutor, working in heart after heart the verdict "I was wrong; I am guilty; I need forgiveness" as he brings home the enormity of rejecting Jesus or at least not taking him seriously enough (16:8). This is a promise of the Spirit's aid in evangelism. His way of convincing and convicting is through Christian persuading as the Church relays the apostolic message; his witness is a matter of his opening the inward ear and applying to the individual conscience the truths that witnessing Christians set before the mind (see 15:27; 17:20).

Thus the Spirit would glorify the glorified Saviour (16:14), acting both as interpreter to make clear the truth about him and as illuminator to ensure that benighted minds receive it. Jesus, the Lord Christ, would be the focal point of the Spirit's ministry, first to last.

THE FLOODLIGHT MINISTRY. The Holy Spirit's distinctive new covenant role, then, is to fulfill what we may call a floodlight ministry in relation to the Lord Jesus Christ. So far as this role was concerned, the Spirit "was not yet" (7:39, literal Greek) while Jesus was on earth; only when the Father had glorified him (see 17:1, 5) could the Spirit's work of making men aware of Jesus' glory begin.

I remember walking to a church one winter evening to preach on the words "he shall glorify me," seeing the building floodlit as I turned a corner, and realizing that this was exactly the illustration my message needed. When floodlighting is well done, the floodlights are so placed that you do not see them; you are not in fact supposed to see where the light is coming from; what you are meant to see is just the building on which the floodlights are trained. The intended effect is to make it visible when otherwise it would not be seen for the darkness, and to maximize its dignity by throwing all its details into relief so that you see it properly. This perfectly illustrates the Spirit's new covenant role. He is, so to speak, the hidden floodlight shining on the Saviour.

Or think of it this way. It is as if the Spirit stands behind us, throwing light over our shoulder, on Jesus, who stands facing us. The Spirit's message to us is never, "Look at me; listen to me; come to me; get to know me," but always, "Look at *him*, and see his glory; listen to *him*, and hear his word; go to *him*, and have life; get to know *him*, and taste his gift of joy and peace." The Spirit, we might say, is the matchmaker, the celestial marriage broker, whose role it is to bring us and Christ together and ensure that we stay together. As the second Paraclete, the Spirit leads us constantly to the original Paraclete, who himself draws near, as we saw above, through the second Paraclete's coming to us (14:18). Thus, by enabling us to discern the first Paraclete, and by moving us to stretch out our hands to him as he comes from his throne to meet us, the Holy Spirit glorifies Christ, according to Christ's own word.

The Holy Spirit and Christians

This teaching by Jesus, as has already been said, is the clue to interpreting everything the New Testament tells us about the Spirit's ministry to Christians. Too often that ministry is related only to our lacks and needs, and not thought through in terms of the truth we have been learning— namely, that the Spirit is here to glorify Christ and that his main and constant task is to mediate Jesus' presence to us, making us aware of all that Jesus is, so that we will trust him to be all that to us. The result is a view of the Spirit's ministry that is Christian centered instead of being Christ centered: man centered, in other words, rather than God centered.

One reason for this man-centered view, no doubt, is that in the epistles, where the Spirit's ministry to individuals is most fully discussed, very little is said about the disciple's communion with and love for Jesus his Master (for it is clearly assumed that readers of the epistles will already know about that), while in the gospels, where response to all that Jesus is is most fully set forth and illustrated, very little apart from John 14–16 is said about the Spirit. But we ought to remember that as the gospels were written for folk who already knew much of the doctrine of the epistles, so the epistles were written to folk who already knew many of the stories of the gospels and who would therefore be able to fill out in their minds the brief and often formal references to faith in Christ, and love for Christ, which again and again are all that the epistles allow themselves. We should, indeed, be doing the same ourselves, never letting ourselves forget that mediating the presence of Christ was and remains the main task the Spirit is here to perform under the new covenant. The following paragraphs seek to show how remembering this fact will affect some of our usual ways of thinking.

NEW BIRTH.   It is, to start with, often and truly said that the great change that starts our Christian lives, the change that Jesus' two-word parable pictures as "new birth" or being "born again" (John 3:3–8; see also 1 Peter 1:23; James 1:18), is "of the Spirit" (verse 6). I have already hinted at my view that the "water" of verse 5 does not refer to anything external that is complementary to the inward work of the Spirit, not to John's baptism or to Christian baptism or to the waters of natural birth, as some have supposed, but rather to the cleansing aspect of inward renewal as such, as that is pictured in Ezekiel 36:25–27. (No problem then arises from the non-mention of water in verse 6, for the water was never more than an illustration of one aspect of the Spirit's renewing action.) It is also familiar ground that Paul calls this process "regeneration" (Titus 3:5) and "new creation" (2 Corinthians 5:17; Galatians 6:17) and explains it in terms of life-changing union with Christ in his death and resurrection (Romans 6:3–11; Colossians 2:12–15). Paul affirms, as does Christ himself, that the process of becoming a Christian reaches completion through faith, which means looking to Christ and trusting his shed blood and the promise of pardon that it sealed (*see* Romans 4:16–25; 10:8–13; Colossians 2:12; John 3:15–21; 5:24; 6:47, 53–58). Paul tells us, too, that the Spirit draws us into a personal expression of dependence on and discipleship under Jesus (1 Corinthians 12:3) and by this means unites us to him as members (that is, limbs, organs) of the one body that is his church (verse 13), so that henceforth by faith we live a supernatural life in his power. All this is correct and is commonplace among Bible believers.

Yet often our thoughts about the new birth are too *subjective*, by which I mean, not too personal (that could hardly be), but too turned in, with all our interest focused on the individual who believes rather than on the Christ who saves. This is bad thinking, and it produces two bad results.

The first is that our minds get possessed by a standard expectation of emotional experience in conversion (so much sorrow for sin, so much agony of search, so much excess of joy). We deduce this expectation from conversion stories known to us, probably starting with those of Paul, Augustine, Luther, Bunyan, Wesley, and our own, and then we use it as a yardstick for judging whether or not our contemporaries are converted. This is sad and silly. Conversion experiences, even those that are sudden and dateable (and perhaps only a minority of them are), vary too much to fit any standard expectations, and the effect of using this yardstick is that we are often found dismissing as unconverted many who show abundant signs of present convertedness, while continuing to treat as converted folk who look as if the standard experience to which they once testified has now completely worn off. The truth is, as the Puritans and Jonathan Edwards knew, that no emotional state or sequence as such, no isolated experience considered on its own, can be an unambiguous index of new birth, and we shall make endless errors if we think and judge otherwise. Only a life of present convertedness can justify confidence that a person was converted at some point in his or her past.

The second bad result is that in our evangelistic presentations Christ appears not as the center of attention and himself the key to life's meaning, but as a figure—sometimes a very smudgy figure—brought in as the answer to some preset egocentric questions of our own (How may I find peace of conscience? peace of heart and mind when under pressure? happiness? joy? power for living?). The necessity of faithful discipleship to Jesus, and the demands of it, are not stressed (some even think that as a matter of principle they should not be), and so the cost of following Jesus is not counted. In consequence, our evangelism reaps large crops of still unconverted folk who think they can cast Jesus for the role of P. G. Wodehouse's Jeeves, calling him in and making use of him as Saviour and Helper, while declining to have him as Lord. Also, it brings in great numbers who, misled by the glowing one-sidedness of our message, have assumed that Christ can be relied on to shield those who are his from all major trouble. The first group become dead wood in our churches, if they do not drift away entirely. The second group experience traumatic upsets—traumatic, because they expected the opposite.

I quote this testimony at random from the Christian press: "My husband . . . and I were youth directors in our church . . . when our 2½ year old son accidentally drowned. We had lived for the Lord and never lost anyone. *We thought we would be spared such things.* I went through four years numb, not understanding, not accepting my anger, continuing to try to be strong. I really was not talking to anyone about the pain and finally went into deep depression. . . ." The nurture that leaves Christians with false expectations of the kind confessed here and with no resources save the stiff upper lip for coping when trouble strikes, is defective to the point of cruelty. Where do these expectations come from? Are they just wishful thinking, or have they been induced by external factors? It seems very plain that the salesmanlike man centeredness of so much of our evangelism, cracking up the benefits and minimizing the burdens of the Christian life and thereby fixing the lines on which converts will subsequently think, is one root cause to which they ought to be traced.

How could we purge our evangelism of its excessive and damaging subjectivity? The short answer is: by learning to keep in step with the Spirit's new covenant ministry and to focus more directly on Jesus Christ himself as Saviour God, as model human being, as coming Judge, as Lover of the weak, poor, and unlovely, and as Leader along the path of cross bearing that he himself trod. Then we could correct the standard-experience stereotype of conversion, stressing that conversion is essentially not feelings at all, but personal commitment to this Christ. Then, too, we could correct the habit of treating conversion experiences in isolation as signs of Christian authenticity, by stressing that the only proof of past conversion is present convertedness. Also we could then correct the irreverent idea that Jesus the Saviour is there to be used, by stressing that as God incarnate he must be worshiped both by words of praise and by works of service.

In addition, we could then correct the bed-of-roses idea of the Christian life, by stressing that while, as Richard Baxter put it,

> Christ leads me through no darker rooms
> Than he went through before,

Christ's way was the way of a resurrection experience following a death experience, and we must expect to find that he is constantly taking us along that same road in one or other of its thousand different forms.

Finally, we could then correct woolliness of view as to what Christian commitment involves, by stressing the need for constant meditation on the four gospels, over and above the rest of our Bible reading; for gospel study enables us both to keep our Lord in clear view and to hold before our minds the relational frame of discipleship to him. The doctrines on which our discipleship rests are clearest in the epistles, but the nature of discipleship itself is most vividly portrayed in the gospels. Some Christians seem to prefer the epistles to the gospels and talk of graduating from the gospels to the epistles as if this were a mark of growing up spiritually; but really this attitude is a very bad sign, suggesting that we are more interested in theological notions than in fellowship with the Lord Jesus in person. We should think, rather, of the theology of the epistles as preparing us to understand better the disciple relationship with Christ that is set forth in the gospels, and we should never let ourselves forget that the four gospels are, as has often and rightly been said, the most wonderful books on earth.

Surely it is clear that if we could achieve all these corrections it would be great gain.

KNOWING AND LOVING GOD. Certain truths about the Christian life are also common knowledge among biblical Christians. It is familiar ground, for instance, that everyone who believes "receives" the Holy Spirit (Acts 2:38; Galatians 3:2). The Spirit, thus given, is a "seal"—that is a mark of ownership, indicating that the believer belongs to God (2 Corinthians 1:22; Ephesians 1:13). Thereafter the Spirit "indwells" him or her (Romans 8:11): That is to say, he is like a houseguest, noting and caring about and being involved in everything that happens in one's heart and life. Fulfilling his role as "a gracious, willing guest," he acts as a change agent, transforming us into Jesus' moral likeness, "... from one degree of glory to another ..." (2 Corinthians 3:18). There is nothing novel here; this is all standard teaching.

Sanctification is the usual word for the process of change. The way of sanctification, from our point of view, is to "walk in [by] the Spirit" (Galatians 5:16). That means saying no to "desires of the flesh" (sinful lusts of body and mind) and allowing the Spirit to bring forth in us his "fruit," which is defined for us as a nine-point profile of Christlikeness (verses 22, 23). Imitating Jesus in humility, love, avoidance of sin, and the practice of righteousness (John 13:12–15, 34, 35; 15:12, 13; Ephesians 5:1, 2; Philippians 2:5–8; 1 Peter 2:21–25; Hebrews 12:1–4) is another way in which the life of sanctity is formulated. Jesus himself defines it repeatedly in terms of doing the things he says, and he sums up the life that pleases God as one of love to God and one's neighbor (Mark 12:29–31; Luke 10:25–37). Among Evangelicals, at any rate, this ground also is well mapped and is often gone over.

When, however, experiential aspects of life in the Spirit come up for treatment (as distinct from convictional, volitional, and disciplinary aspects), it is a different story. Here we move into new country, where Evangelicals for the most part seem to be at a loss. In this terrain of direct perceptions of God—perceptions of his greatness and goodness, his eternity and infinity, his truth, his love, and his glory, all as related to Christ and through Christ to us—understanding was once much richer than is commonly found today. This is a place where we have some relearning to do. Of such perceptions the following at least may be said. They presuppose and arise through biblical understanding, and they are to be identified by biblical criteria and interpreted by biblical theology. Nonetheless, they are in themselves immediate and sovereign. They are not under our control; they can neither be demanded nor predicted; they simply happen as God wills. Ordinarily (so far as that word has meaning here, where everything is tailored to the individual) these perceptions are given through the Spirit to the loving and obedient disciple in fulfillment of Christ's promise that the Father and the Son would come to him, stay with him, and show themselves to him (John 14:18, 20–23). The perceptions themselves (better so called than "experiences," although each truly is what we mean by "an experience") bring great joy because they communicate God's great love. They belong to the inner life, as distinct from that of the outward senses by which we know men and things. They are to be distinguished from our knowledge of people and things, though it seems always to be via that knowledge, in memory if not in the moment of its being given, that perceptions of God occur. Any idea that the condition of perceiving God is reduced or dissolved self-awareness should be dismissed as a confusion.

But that very confusion is widespread, and there is, as a result, much prejudice against any attempt to reemphasize the experiential side of Christianity. It seems clear that the realized communion with God of which I am speaking is commonly equated with the so-called mysticism of Hindu holy men, who are pantheists and for whom accordingly the transcending and abolishing of conscious selfhood, as being in fact an illusion, is the main item on the agenda. It is obvious that for Christians to seek the Hindu goal would be practical heresy, if not apostasy. Why then should devoted "mystical" believers, some past and some present, be suspected of doing just this? The answer seems to be: because of the words they use. The paradoxical truth, as I read the story, is that they have come under suspicion because some of the language in which they have spontaneously expressed their awareness of and response to their God has been the language of love between the sexes. That is in fact the fittest language for the purpose, since the love of man and woman really is the closest analogy in creation to the relationship with himself that the heavenly Lover intended for us. Human love was, indeed, always meant to help lovers on into just that. In love experiences, both human and divine, one is intensely self-aware. But the height of self-awareness in sexual love is to see yourself as having become part of the other person to the point where the two of you are a single new entity (which is probably what "one flesh" in Genesis 2:24 points to). That sense of things is expressed, for instance, in Shakespeare's "Number there in love was slain"[2] and in Wagner's lines:

TRISTAN: *You are Tristan.   I am Isolde—no longer Tristan.*
ISOLDE: *You are Isolde.   I am Tristan—no longer Isolde.*
BOTH: *Gone all naming* (Ohne Nennen) . . . *always, ever,*
             One confessed . . .[3]

This, however, is individuality enhanced by empathy, not diminished by being depersonalized.

The use by devoted Christians of comparable love language—strong talk, that is, about two being one—to express their sense of being loved by and loving God has sometimes, as I said, been held to show that they have tuned in to the Hindu wavelength. That, however, is nonsense. In Hinduism there is no personal God, no personal distinction between God and myself, and no love fellowship to enjoy with the divine; and separate selfhood, as was noted above, is thought of as an illusion to be dispelled. But the Christian saint contemplates the Father and the Son, who, though eternally distinct from him—he being a mere creature—are nonetheless eternally bound to him by bonds of redeeming love. It is the heightened self-awareness of love receiving and responding to love that his language of identity with God expresses. He is as far from the Hindu sense of things as he could possibly be. Anyone who studies Christian mystical spirituality will soon see that this is true.[4] But prejudice against the language of realized fellowship with God remains strong, and it cannot be expected that the reality will be well understood while this is so.

There is another reason, too, why the experiential reality of perceiving God is unfamiliar country today. The pace and preoccupations of urbanized, mechanized, collectivized, secularized modern life are such that any sort of inner life (apart from the existentialist *Angst* of society's misfits and the casualties of the rat race) is very hard to maintain. To make prayer your life priority, as countless Christians of former days did outside as well as inside the monastery, is stupendously difficult in a world that runs you off your feet and will not let you slow down. And if you attempt it, you will certainly seem eccentric to your peers, for nowadays involvement in a stream of programmed activities is decidedly "in," and the older ideal of a quiet, contemplative life is just as decidedly "out." That there is widespread hunger today for more intimacy, warmth, and affection in our fellowship with God is clear from the current renewal of interest in the experiential writings of the Puritans and the contemplative tradition of prayer as expounded by men like Thomas Merton. But the concept of Christian life as sanctified rush and bustle still dominates, and as a result the experiential side of Christian holiness remains very much a closed book.

Though twentieth-century men like Alexander Whyte and A. W. Tozer have greatly valued and largely drawn on authors who wrote of experiential fellowship with God, and though the great Puritans and especially that late-flowering Puritan Jonathan Edwards, along with Wesley's designated successor John Fletcher, have made classic contributions to the literature of this subject,[5] Evangelicals in our time have tended to give it a wide berth. This, it seems, is partly because of the observable unorthodoxy, or at least doctrinal indifference, of some of its exponents (odd fish like George Fox, Jacob Boehme, and William Blake, for instance), partly because it sometimes opened the door to fanatical and antinomian attitudes, partly because it was thought to be anti-intellectual, partly because it was viewed as a Roman Catholic preserve and likely therefore to be unhealthy, and partly because evangelical devotion is so firmly oriented to listening for God to speak in and through the text of Scripture that anything beyond this is at once suspect. Whatever the causes, however, the result is that on those aspects of God's sanctifying action that directly involve experiential awareness of God most of us nowadays have little or nothing to say. So not much is heard about the Spirit as the "anointing," through which believers are made sure of the reality of Jesus Christ as proclaimed by the apostles (1 John 2:27, *also* 20). Nor is much offered concerning the Spirit as the witness who assures believers that they are sons and heirs of God through Christ and with Christ (Romans 8:15–17; Galatians 4:6). We do not seem able to explain in what sense the Spirit is the "earnest"—that is, the down payment, the first installment guaranteeing the rest, the "first fruits" (Romans 8:23)—of the heavenly life that the believer inherits (2 Corinthians 1:22; Ephesians 1:14). Nor are we any clearer about the meaning of prayer in the Spirit (Ephesians 6:18; Jude 20) and love in the Spirit (Colossians 1:8; Romans 15:30). Indeed, that is one of the understatements of the year; the present-day silence on these subjects is almost deafening. The plain fact is that today's biblical Christians, wherever else they are strong, are weak on the inner life—and it shows.

A full treatment of these themes is not possible here, even were I capable of it. All I can do now is put on record my conviction that the key that lays them open to our understanding is the Spirit's work specified in John 16:14: his work of making Jesus Christ, our crucified, risen, reigning Saviour, real and glorious to us moment by moment.

The Anointing, the Witness, and the Earnest

I claim, then, that John is referring to this ministry of the Spirit, when as he rejects Gnostic misbelief about Jesus, he declares that "the anointing which you received from him . . . teaches you about everything" (everything, he means, concerning Jesus and his glory), and leads us to "abide in him" (that is, maintain not just a true confession about him, but a disciple relationship to him as the living Lord). I contend that when John calls the Spirit "the witness," literally "the witnessing one" (the first of three witnesses, in fact, the second and third being "the water and the blood," the facts of Jesus' baptism and death), he has in view the Spirit's ministry of making us sure that the apostles' Christ is real and is ours (1 John 5:7, 8). I hold that the breathtaking certainty of mind, confidence of manner, and evident rapture of heart, with which Augustine, Bernard, Luther, Calvin, Owen, Whitefield, Spurgeon, and many more, including crowds of hymn writers, have celebrated and commended the Lord Jesus is the direct fruit of this ministry. I believe that all in whose lives the Spirit fulfills this ministry will speak of Christ the same way. And I maintain that apart from this God-given certainty concerning the Christ of the New Testament and this God-taught habit of abiding in him by faith and love and obedience and adoration, there is no authentic Christian living and no genuine sanctification—for indeed, where these things are lacking, there is in reality no new birth.

I hold, too, that the Spirit's way of witnessing to the truth that as believers we are sons and heirs of God (Romans 8:15–17) is first to make us realize that as Christ on earth loved us and died for us, so in glory now he loves us and lives for us as the Mediator whose endless life guarantees us endless glory with him. The Spirit makes us see the love of Christ toward us, as measured by the cross, and to see along with Christ's love the love of the Father who gave his Son up for us (Romans 8:32). The line of thought is given in Romans 5:5–8, and as the Spirit leads us along it, over and over, ". . . God's love . . . [is] poured into our hearts. . . ."

Then, together with that, the Spirit also makes us see that through Christ, in Christ, and with Christ, we are now God's children; and hereby he leads us, spontaneously and instinctively—for there are spiritual instincts as well as natural ones—to think of God as Father, and so to address him (Romans 8:15; Galatians 4:6). Paul's *Abba* both times that he speaks of this underlines the intimacy and confidence of heart that are involved, for *Abba*, Jesus' own regular address to God, was a term of informality unprecedented in the history of prayer; it was the Aramaic equivalent of "dad."

To know that God is your Father and that he loves you, his adopted child, no less than he loves his only begotten Son and to know that enjoyment of God's love and glory for all eternity are pledged to you brings inward delight that is sometimes overwhelming; and this also is the Spirit's doing. For the "joy in the Holy Spirit," in terms of which Paul defines the kingdom of God in Romans 14:17, is the "rejoicing in God" spoken of in Romans 5:2, 11, and it is the Spirit's witness to God's love for us that calls forth this joy.

I should add that the Spirit's witness is not ordinarily "an experience" in the sense in which orgasm, or shock, or bewilderment, or being "sent" by beauty in music or nature, or eating curry are experiences—dateable, memorable items in our flow of consciousness, standing out from what went before and what came after, and relatively short-lived. There are, to be sure, "experiences" in which the Spirit's witness becomes suddenly strong. Such was the famous experience of Blaise Pascal on November 23, 1654, the record of which he began thus:

> From about half-past ten in the evening till about
>   half-past twelve
>   FIRE
> God of Abraham, God of Isaac, God of Jacob, not of the
>   philosophers and scholars (*savants*).
> Certainty.   Certainty (*certitude*).   Feeling (*sentiment*).   Joy.
> Peace.[6]

Such, too, was John Wesley's equally famous experience on May 24, 1738, when he "went very unwillingly to a society in Aldersgate Street, where one was reading Luther's preface to the Epistle to the Romans. About a quarter before nine, while he was describing the change which God works in the heart through faith in Christ, I felt my heart strangely warmed. I felt I did trust in Christ, Christ alone, for salvation; and an assurance was given me, that he had taken away *my* sins, even *mine*, and saved *me* from the law of sin and death." But what such "experiences" do is intensify a quality of experience that is real in some measure for every believer from the first. Paul speaks of the Spirit's witness in the present tense ("the Spirit himself testifies with our spirit that we are God's children," [Romans 8:16 NIV]), implying that it is a continuous operation that imparts permanent confidence in God. Though not felt always as vividly as it is sometimes, and though overshadowed from time to time by feelings of doubt and despair, this confidence remains constant and in the final analysis insuperable. The Spirit himself sees to that!

Then also I hold that the Holy Spirit given to us is the "earnest" of our inheritance in this precise sense: that by enabling us to see the glory of Christ glorified, and to live in fellowship with him as our Mediator and with his Father as our Father, the Spirit introduces us to the inmost essence of the life of heaven. To think of heaven as a place and a state cannot be wrong, for the Bible writers do it; nonetheless, what makes heaven to be heaven, and what must always be at the heart of our thoughts about heaven, is the actual relationship with the Father and the Son that is perfected there. It is of this that the Spirit's present ministry to us is the first installment. To see God and to be forever with Christ in an experiential deepening of our present love relation to both is the true definition of heaven (*see* Matthew 5:8; 2 Corinthians 5:6–8; 1 Thessalonians 4:7; Revelation 22:3–5). And by means of the ministry to us of the indwelling Spirit heaven begins for us here and now, as through Christ and in Christ we are made sharers with Christ in his resurrection life. "You have died," writes Paul to believers, "and your life is hid with Christ in God" (Colossians 3:3; *see* 2:11–14; Romans 6:3–11; Ephesians 2:1–7). This "life" is eternal life, heaven's life, which never starts anywhere else but here.

Along with this, I hold that praying in the Spirit includes four elements. First it is a matter of seeking, claiming, and making use of access to God through Christ (Ephesians 2:18). Then the Christian adores and thanks God for his acceptance through Christ and for the knowledge that through Christ his prayers are heard. Third, he asks for the Spirit's help to see and do what brings glory to Christ, knowing that both the Spirit and Christ himself intercede for him as he struggles to pray for rightness in his own life (Romans 8:26, 27, 34). Finally, the Spirit leads the believer to concentrate on God and his glory in Christ with a sustained, singleminded simplicity of attention and intensity of desire that no one ever knows save as it is supernaturally wrought.

Prayer in the Spirit is prayer from the heart, springing from awareness of God, of self, of others, of needs, and of Christ. Whether it comes forth verbalized, as in the prayers and praises recorded in Scripture, or unverbalized, as when the contemplative gazes Godward in love or the charismatic slips into glossolalia, is immaterial. He (or she) whose heart seeks God through Christ prays in the Spirit.

As for love in the Spirit, that is surely the gratitude to God and the goodwill toward men that are generated by knowing the love of the Father, who gave the Son, and of the Son, who gave himself for our salvation. Modeling itself on this divine love, love in the Spirit takes form as a habit of self-giving service in which some element of one's life is constantly being laid down and let go for someone else's sake (*see* John 15:12, 13). Paul draws its profile in 1 Corinthians 13:4–7. It has at its heart an outgoing altruism, a desire to see others made great, good, holy, and happy—a passion that this fallen world finds incomprehensible and which in itself is altogether supernatural. *Agapē*, the regular New Testament word for it, was not used in this sense before Christianity appeared, and no wonder: The thing itself only became known through Christ. Now *agapē* is the identifying mark of those who, among the many who claim to know God, really and genuinely do (1 John 3:14–16; 4:7–11). It is no natural gift or development, but the supernatural fruit of the Spirit (*see* Galatians 5:22), the issue of a heart that through the Spirit sees and knows the love of God.

The Inward Journey

I wish I could discuss these matters fully (which I have certainly not done in the foregoing paragraphs), but I have to leave them here, with just this final comment. The journey of our lives is a double journey. There is an outward journey into external confrontations, discoveries, and relationships, and there is an inner journey into self-knowledge and the discovery of what for me as an individual constitutes self-expression, self-fulfillment, freedom, and contentment within. For the Christian, the outward journey takes the form of learning to relate positively and purposefully to the world and other people—that is, to all God's creatures—for God the Creator's sake, and the inward journey takes the form of gaining and deepening our acquaintance with God himself and with Jesus the Son.

Now in the hustling, bustling West today, life has become radically unbalanced, with education, business interests, the media, the knowledge explosion, and our go-getting community ethos all uniting to send folk off on the outward journey as fast as they can go and with that to distract them from ever bothering about its inward counterpart. In Western Christianity the story is the same, so that most of us without realizing it are nowadays unbalanced activists, conforming most unhappily in this respect to the world around us. Like the Pharisees, who were also great activists (*see* Matthew 23:15!), we are found to be harsh and legalistic, living busy, complacent lives of conforming to convention and caring much more, as it seems, for programs than for people. When we accuse businessmen of selling their souls to their firms and sacrificing their integrity on the altars of their organizations, it is the pot calling the kettle black. Perhaps there are no truths about the Spirit that Christian people more urgently need to learn today than those that relate to the inner life of fellowship with God, that life which I call the inward journey. (You could also call it the upward journey—that adjective would fit equally well.)

You see, then, why I am sorry to have to leave this part of the discussion and move on. But there are other matters about which I must now say something.

Spiritual Gifts

I said a little about spiritual gifts in chapter 1, but fuller discussion is called for here.

We ought to be glad—I hope you are—that Paul's emphasis on the universality of spiritual gifts to Christians, with its corollary that every-member ministry in the body of Christ should be the rule everywhere, has been received so widely in recent years. After more than a millennium in which most of the church was caught in the clutches of clericalism (Methodist bodies, Plymouth Brethren, and the Salvation Army being honorable exceptions), this is an immense change for the better. Though lay passivity persists in many churches and though many clergy still foster it because they would feel threatened by anything else, mainstream Christian opinion has now moved on from indulging lay ministry as an option for the specially keen to specifying it as a necessary part of everyone's discipleship. Challenging Christians to know their gifts and find their ministry once seemed to be an exotic speciality of pietistic Protestant hothouses, but that has changed. The thrust of Romans 12:3–13; 1 Corinthians 12; and Ephesians 4:7–15 is appreciated, and Catholics and Protestants, liberals and conservatives, charismatics, ecumenicals, and Evangelicals of all denominations nowadays agree that all Christians have gifts and tasks of their own within the church's total ministry. Good news!

WHAT IS A SPIRITUAL GIFT?   But our thinking about gifts is shallow. We say, rightly, that they come from the Spirit (Paul calls them "manifestations of the Spirit" [see 1 Corinthians 12:4–11]). However, we go on to think of them in terms either of what we call "giftedness" (that is, human ability to do things skillfully and well) or of supernatural novelty as such (power to speak in tongues, to heal, to receive messages straight from God to give to others, or whatever). We have not formed the habit of defining gifts in terms of Christ the head of the body, and his present work from heaven in our midst. In this we are unscriptural. At the start of 1 Corinthians Paul gives thanks "... because of the grace of God which was given you *in Christ Jesus,* that in every way you were enriched *in him* with all speech and all knowledge ... so that you are not lacking in any spiritual gift [*charisma*] ..." (1:4, 7). Paul's wording makes it clear that spiritual gifts are given in Christ; they are enrichments received from Christ. First Corinthians 12 assumes the Christ-oriented perspective that 1:4–7 established. It is vital that we should see this, or we shall be confusing natural with spiritual gifts to the end of our days.

Nowhere does Paul or any other New Testament writer define a spiritual gift for us, but Paul's assertion that the use of gifts *edifies* ("builds up," 1 Corinthians 14:3–5, 12, 26, *see also* 17; Ephesians 4:12, 16) shows what his idea of a gift was.

For Paul, it is only through Christ, in Christ, by learning Christ and responding to Christ that anyone is ever edified. Our latter-day secular use of this word is far wider and looser than Paul's; for him, edification is precisely a matter of growing in the depth and fullness of one's understanding of Christ and all else in relation to him and in the quality of one's personal relationship with him, and it is not anything else. So spiritual gifts must be defined in terms of Christ, as actualized powers of expressing, celebrating, displaying and so communicating Christ in one way or another, either by word or by deed. They would not be edifying otherwise.

USE OF SPIRITUAL GIFTS.   We should observe that, over and above the common but rather unclear distinction between "ordinary" and "extraordinary" gifts, or "natural" and "supernatural" as the two sets are sometimes called, there is a further distinction to be drawn between gifts of speech and of Samaritanship (loving helpful response to others' physical and material needs). From Paul's flitting to and fro between the two categories in Romans 12:6–8, where prophecy, teaching, and exhorting, items one, three, and four in his list are gifts of speech and serving [*diakonia*], giving, leading, and showing mercy, items two, five, six, and seven, are gifts of Samaritanship, we should learn that he saw no ultimate theological difference between them, however much they might differ as forms of human activity.

The truth we must grasp here is that our exercise of spiritual gifts is nothing more nor less than Christ himself ministering through his body to his body, to the Father, and to all mankind. From heaven Christ uses Christians as his mouth, his hands, his feet, even his smile; it is through us, his people, that he speaks and acts, meets, loves, and saves here and now in this world. This seems (though the point is disputed) to be part of the meaning of Paul's picture of the church as Christ's body, in which every believer is a "member" in the sense of a limb or organ: The head is the command center for the body, and the limbs move at the head's direction.

Christ "came and preached peace to you who were far off

...," wrote Paul to the Ephesian Christians and others (Ephesians 2:17; I take the letter to be a circular, with Ephesus as one of its destinations). How did Christ do that? Not in his own risen body, but by using the preaching and teaching gifts he gave to folk like Paul himself. To the Philippians, again, Paul wrote: "And my God will supply every need of yours according to his riches in glory in Christ Jesus" (Philippians 4:19). How would God do that? Partly, at least, by Christ's work through the Spirit actualizing gifts of Samaritanship among the Philippians themselves. When Christians speak one to another in Christ's name (*see* 2 Thessalonians 3:6) and practice care for others because they are Christians (*see* Mark 9:41), Christ in person blesses through them. As Christ says categorically of the practice of care that ". . . whatever you did for one of the least of these brothers of mine, you did for me" (Matthew 25:40 NIV), so we may say just as categorically that when other Christians bring us understanding and encouragement and relief of need in any form at all, Christ himself ministers to us, bringing us these benefits through them (*see* 2 Corinthians 13:3; Romans 15:18).

THE BLESSING OF GIFTS.   I defined gifts (*charismata*) as "actualized powers" of showing Christ forth, and the adjective seems important. Ability to speak or act in a particular way—*performing* ability, as we may call it—is only a *charisma* if and as God uses it to edify. Some natural abilities that God has given he never uses in this way, while sometimes he edifies through performances that to competent judges seem substandard. This is characteristic: God highlights the weakness of those whom he saves and uses, so that nothing will rival or obscure his glory (1 Corinthians 1:27–29; 2 Corinthians 4:7; *see also* 12:9). When, therefore, Christians are said to "have gifts" (Romans 12:6), the meaning is not that they are in any respect outstandingly brilliant or efficient (they may be, they may not; it varies), but rather that God has observably used them to edification in specific ways already, and this warrants the expectation that he will do the same again. We need to draw a clear distinction between man's capacity to perform and God's prerogative to bless, for it is God's use of our abilities rather than the abilities themselves that constitute *charismata*. If no regular, identifiable spiritual benefit for others or ourselves results from what we do, we should not think of our capacity to do it as a spiritual gift.

This principle was assumed in the original admissions procedure at C. H. Spurgeon's Pastors' College. Evidence was sought that candidates had already preached and taught to the blessing of others. In the absence of such evidence, the applicant, however able otherwise, was judged to lack gifts for the pastorate and was turned down.

Pentecostals and charismatics claim that God has renewed among them the so-called sign gifts of the New Testament (tongues, interpretation, prophecy, healing). Later in this book I shall say why I do not accept the claim as it stands; but supposing that I am wrong and it is true, still my principle applies, no less than it applies to Christians with skills in, say, teaching or administration. Glossolalia and power to relieve bodily malfunctions by laying on hands might, for instance, be found—in fact, I think, are found—outside the church as well as inside it; and within it these abilities are not necessarily spiritual gifts to all who have them. For you cannot define a *charisma* as performance alone; the definition must include the relational factor of God-given edification in Christ through the performance. Where this is lacking, a supposed "gift" will be a carnal rather than a spiritual manifestation, even though its form may correspond to a genuine manifestation of the Spirit in someone else. Some ex-Pentecostals and charismatics tell us that their own former glossolalia now seems to them to have been carnal, and one can agree with them without having to conclude that the same is true of all glossolalia everywhere. What constitutes and identifies a *charisma* is not the form of the action, but the blessing of God.

The Meaning of Pentecost

We can now answer with precision the much disputed question of the significance of the Pentecostal outpouring of the Spirit recorded in Acts 2.

Was this the Spirit's first appearance in this world? In the obvious sense of the question, no. We have already seen something of his activity in the Old Testament period, and there are in addition abundant references to his work in Jesus' own earthly life and ministry. When Jesus announced to his disciples the coming mission of the Counselor-Comforter, ". . . the Spirit of truth, whom the world cannot receive," he at once added, "you know him, for he dwells with you, and will be in you" (John 14:17). Those present tenses, "you know" and "he dwells," could be idiomatic, meaning that this state of affairs will begin very shortly (John uses the present tense for what will be in the immediate future in other places, too); but Jesus may equally, and perhaps more probably, have meant "you know the Spirit already (though maybe you don't yet know that you know him), for he dwells with you here and now, inasmuch as he indwells me." The contrast of tenses and prepositions ("he *dwells with* you, and *will be in* you") is hard to explain on any other basis, and the Spirit's presence in and with Jesus throughout his earthly course is underlined constantly in the records. Jesus' miraculous conception was by the Spirit (Matthew 1:18, 20; Luke 1:35). At his baptism the sign of the descending dove marked him out as God's anointed one, the Spirit-filled Spirit bearer (Matthew 3:16; Mark 1:10; Luke 3:21, 22; *see also* 4:1, 14; Acts 10:38; John 1:32–34, *see also* 6:27, which probably refers to the baptismal anointing, and 3:34, ". . . to him God gives the Spirit without limit" [NIV]). Jesus was "led by the Spirit" to his ordeal of temptation (*see* Luke 4:1; Matthew 4:1; Mark 1:12). He preached in the Spirit's power (Luke 4:18). He exorcized demons by the Spirit (Matthew 12:28). He ". . . rejoiced in the Holy Spirit . . ." (Luke 10:21). ". . . Through the eternal Spirit . . ." he offered himself to God on the cross as a pure sacrifice (Hebrews 9:14); he was ". . . made alive by the Spirit" (1 Peter 3:18 NIV) in resurrection; and it was "through the Holy Spirit" that he gave his disciples their marching orders before his ascension (Acts 1:2). The incarnate Son of God was thus the archetypal "man of the Spirit"—we are left no room for doubt about that! So here is a further dimension of the Spirit's pre-Pentecost ministry.

A PROBLEM TEXT: JOHN 20:22.   It is a central thought for John that the Spirit bearer is also the Spirit giver, the one who "baptizes with" the Spirit and "sends" the Spirit to his disciples (John 1:42; 15:26; 16:7); and John records how, on resurrection day itself, at his first appearance to the disciples in Jerusalem, Jesus, having commissioned them—". . . As the Father has sent me, even so I send you"—then at once ". . . breathed on them, and said to them, 'Receive the Holy Spirit' " (20:21, 22). The gesture was one of sharply blowing out air from his lungs in their direction. It has been urged that this was the moment when the Spirit was actually given to them for their regeneration. But that can hardly be right, for three good reasons.

First, Jesus' words, ". . . you are clean . . ." (John 13:10; 15:3) imply that they were regenerate before the passion. "Clean" (pure, because washed and purged from sin's guilt and defilement) is, as we have seen already, one half of the verbal picture of regeneration that Jesus drew for Nicodemus when he spoke of being "born of water and the Spirit" (3:5). What Jesus said to Nicodemus was an oblique, or maybe not so oblique, invitation to faith (to which Nicodemus seems to have responded [*see* 7:50; 19:39]), and Jesus' whole line of teaching indicates clearly enough that there is no faith without regeneration, just as there is no regeneration without faith. Believers were regenerated, then, during Jesus' three years of ministry, including eleven out of Jesus' chosen twelve.

Second, Jesus' gesture of outbreathing is linked in the context not with regeneration, but with the commission that he had just announced ("I send you") and the promise of discernment and authority in applying the gospel, which at once follows ("If you forgive the sins of any, they are forgiven; if you retain the sins of any, they are retained" [20:23]). Receiving the Spirit as equipment for this evangelistic and pastoral task is evidently what Jesus' sign is about.

Third, Jesus' gift of the Spirit could not be given till he was *glorified*, which means "ascended, exalted, enthroned."

First he must "go to the Father" (13:1; 14:28; 16:10; 17:11; 20:17), returning to the place of honor with the Father that had always been his (17:5). Then he would send the Spirit from the Father (*see* 15:26) to glorify him in his disciples' eyes by revealing to them the glory which their Saviour-King, vindicated and enthroned, now enjoys (16:14). John made a comment earlier in the gospel, underlining the fact that this must be the order. Jesus had said: ". . . If any one thirst, let him come to me and drink. He who believes in me, as the scripture has said, 'Out of his heart shall flow rivers of living water.' " (The Scripture that Jesus referred to was apparently the vision of the restored temple in Ezekiel 47:1–12, which Jesus saw as a type of the Christian believer.) Having reported these words, John stepped into his own story to explain them. "Now this he said about the Spirit, which those who believed on him were to receive; for as yet the Spirit had not been given, *because Jesus was not yet glorified*" (7:37–39). John's Greek reads literally "the Spirit *was not yet*," that is, did not yet exist in the new role that he would later fulfill. So we might say that Charles III and Queen Diana of England do not yet exist, though one day they will. I am not convinced by those scholars who would persuade me that John means us to think of Christ as already glorified on the evening of resurrection day, and I conclude instead that John expects us to remember 7:37–39 and to infer from it as we read 20:21–23 that the promised gift of the Spirit could not in the nature of the case actually have been given at that time.

This argument tells not only against those who see John 20:22 as the moment of the disciples' new birth, but also against those who see it as John's alternative to Luke's story of Pentecost in Acts 2, an alternative that puts the start of the Spirit's new covenant ministry forty days earlier than Luke does. That also looks like a mistake.

So it seems every way more natural and sensible to understand Jesus' breathing on the disciples as most commentators have always understood it—that is, as an acted prophecy—and to take his words ("receive the Holy Spirit") as a promise that very soon the disciples would begin to experience the Spirit's new ministry, which would fit and equip them to meet all the demands of their new task.

THE ESSENCE OF PENTECOST.   How then should we understand what happened on Pentecost morning, forty days later? We should not see the essence of this epoch-making event in the tornado sound, the sight of human tongues afire over each person's head, and the gift of language (these were secondary matters, what we might call the trimmings). We should see the essence of it, rather, in the fact that at nine o'clock that morning the Holy Spirit's new covenant ministry began, giving each disciple a clear understanding of Jesus' place in God's plan, a robust sense of identity and authority as Jesus' person in this world, and an unlimited boldness in proclaiming Jesus' power from his throne—the new elements that are so amazing in Peter's sermon when we recall what sort of man he had been before. Jesus had promised that when the Spirit came he would empower the disciples for witness (Acts 1:5, 8), and Luke evidently means us to see in Peter, whose failures he had diligently chronicled in his gospel, a model instance of that promise being fulfilled. And he means us also to understand that this new covenant "gift of the Holy Spirit"—in other words, experiential enjoyment of this new ministry whereby the Spirit glorifies Jesus to, in, and through his people—is promised to all who repent and are baptized, from the moment their discipleship starts (2:38; *see also* 16:31–33).

Whatever we make of God's postponing of tongues and prophecy at Samaria till Peter and John arrived (8:12–17) and his producing these phenomena in the twelve Ephesian disciples after their Christian baptism (19:1–6)—and these are matters on which Luke is poker-faced; it is not clear that he has any personal theology about them to offer—the expectation that the Spirit's full ministry to Christians would begin at conversion is clear throughout Acts, not least in the two stories just mentioned. Without raising here the special question of whether all or any of the "sign gifts" that followed Pentecost should be looked for today (we come back

to that in a later chapter), we may confidently say that since
nine o'clock on that momentous morning the Holy Spirit has
been active to fulfill in one way or another to all Jesus' followers the full ministry that Jesus foretold in John 14–16 and
that the whole New Testament celebrates; and so he is today.

~There is a seminary whose president was chosen from the
faculty and took office on the understanding that he would
continue to teach the courses he was teaching already. Thus
as president he gained new responsibilities without losing
any. So, too, the Holy Spirit's ministry was enlarged at Pentecost, without being in any way diminished from what it
was before. Prior to Pentecost, as we saw, the Spirit sustained
creation and natural life, renewed hearts, gave spiritual understanding, and bestowed gifts for service both in leadership and in other ways, and all this he still does. The
difference since Pentecost is that all his present ministry to
Christian believers relates not to Christ who was to come, as
was the case when he ministered to Old Testament saints (*see*,
for hints of this, John 8:56–59; 1 Corinthians 10:4; Hebrews
11:26; 1 Peter 1:10); nor does it relate any more to Christ
present on earth, as it did when Simeon and Anna recognized him (Luke 2:25–38), and during his three years of public ministry; it relates now to Christ who has come and has
died and risen and now reigns in glory. It is primarily in
these terms that the newness of God's new era, so far as the
Spirit is concerned, ought to be defined, just as it is primarily
in terms of fellowship with this Christ that the newness of
life which Christians have enjoyed since Pentecost ought to
be explained.

SPIRIT BAPTISM AND SPIRIT FILLING TODAY.　What should we
say, then, of the often-heard view, based on Acts 2, that God
means every Christian's life to be a two-stage, two-level affair, in which conversion is followed by a second event
(called Spirit baptism on the basis of Acts 1:5 or Spirit filling
on the basis of 2:4), which raises one's spiritual life to new
heights? We should say that though individual Christians
need, and again and again are given, "second touches" of this

kind (and third, and fourth, and any number more), the idea that this is God's program for all Christians as such is mistaken. God means all Christians as such to enjoy the full inward blessing of Pentecost (not the outward trimmings necessarily, but the communion of heart with Christ and all that flows from it) right from the moment of their conversion.

The only reason why the first disciples had to be taken through a two-stage, two-level pattern of experience was that they became believers before Pentecost. But for folk like you and me, who became Christians nearly two thousand years after Pentecost, the revealed program is that fullest enjoyment of the Spirit's new covenant ministry should be ours from the word "go." This is already clear in the New Testament, where Paul explains Spirit baptism as something that happened to the Corinthians—and, by parity of reasoning, happens to all other post-Pentecost converts—at conversion (1 Corinthians 12:13). He describes Spirit filledness in terms of a life-style that all Christians should have been practicing from conversion (see Ephesians 5:18–21; one sentence in Greek, as in KJV and ASV). If it has not worked out that way for any of us, the reason is not that God never meant it to, but rather that somehow, whether we realize it or not, we have been quenching God's Spirit (see 1 Thessalonians 5:19), which is a state of affairs that has to be changed.

To be sure, Christians are meant to grow spiritually through, and within, and under, the fullness of the Spirit's new covenant ministry (see Ephesians 4:15; 1 Thessalonians 3:12; 2 Thessalonians 1:3; 2 Peter 3:18), and that will involve for each of us many new kinds of spiritual experience, and therewith many deepenings and enrichments of the old kinds. But spiritual growth is not what I am talking about here.

The Spirit and Ourselves

If what has been said in this chapter is right, two questions about the Spirit that we often ask today are wrong.

First, we ask: Do you know the Holy Spirit? We should

not be asking that. We should instead be asking: Do you know Jesus Christ? Do you know enough about him? Do you know him well? Those are the questions the Spirit himself desires us to ask. For he is self-effacing, as we saw. His ministry is a floodlight ministry in relation to Jesus, a matter of spotlighting Jesus' glory before our spiritual eyes and of matchmaking between us and him. He does not call attention to himself or present himself to us for direct fellowship as the Father and the Son do; his role and his joy is to further our fellowship with them both by glorifying the Son as the object for our faith and then witnessing to our adoption through the Son into the Father's family.

Should our interest shift from knowing the Son to knowing the Spirit, two evils would at once result. On the one hand, like the Colossian angel worshipers, we should impoverish ourselves by ". . . not holding fast to the Head, from whom the whole body, nourished and knit together through its joints and ligaments, grows with a growth that is from God" (Colossians 2:19). On the other hand, we should enmesh ourselves in a world of spurious "spiritual" feelings and fancies that are not Christ related and do not correspond to anything that actually exists except Satan's web of deceptions and his endless perversions of truth and goodness. We should not take one step down this road. Questions about the Holy Spirit that are not forms and facets of the basic question, How may I and all Christians—and indeed all the world—come to know Jesus Christ and know him better? ought not to be asked. This is a basic mental discipline that the Bible imposes upon us. In golf it would be described as keeping your eye on the ball.

Second, we ask: Do you have the Holy Spirit? That question, too, should not be put to a Christian, for as we have seen, every Christian has the Spirit from the moment of his or her believing. ". . . If anyone does not have the Spirit of Christ, he does not belong to Christ" (Romans 8:9 NIV). In that case, however, what a person must do is not go on a search for the Spirit, but rather come to Christ in faith and repentance, and then the Spirit will be given him. "Repent, and be baptized . . . and you shall receive the gift of the Holy Spirit. For the promise [of forgiveness and the Spirit] is to . . . every one whom the Lord our God calls to him" (Acts 2:38). A person receives the Spirit by receiving Christ, not in any other way, and the idea that one can have the Spirit and be "spiritual" apart from personal encounter with the risen Lord is a damaging error.

No, the question we should ask instead, both of ourselves and of each other, is: Does the Holy Spirit have you? Does he have all of you, or only some parts of you? Do you grieve him (*see* Ephesians 4:30), or are you led by him (*see* Romans 8:12–14; Galatians 5:18–24)? Do you rely on him to enable you for all those responses to Christ to which he prompts you? Do you reckon with the fact that ". . . your body is a temple of the Holy Spirit, who is in you, whom you have received from God? . . ." (1 Corinthians 6:19 NIV). Do you revere his work within you and cooperate with it or obstruct it by thoughtlessness and carelessness, indiscipline and self-indulgence? Here again, the specific questions must be understood Christ centeredly; they are all in reality ways of asking whether Christ your Saviour is Lord of your life. But to ask them in relation to the Spirit, who indwells us in order to transform us and who works constantly in our hearts and minds to bring us close to Christ and keep us there and who is himself as close as can be to any foul thinking or behavior in which we allow ourselves to engage, is to give them a force and a concreteness that otherwise they might not have. In the world of projecting pictures onto screens this would be called sharpening the focus.

We shall pursue the theme of Christian holiness in our next two chapters.

3

Mapping the Spirit's Path: The Way of Holiness

FOR BETTER or for worse, *sex* has become for most of us an electric word. By that I mean that it compels attention, jarring us awake; it grabs scanning eyes and casual ears; it carries an emotional charge, and makes an emotional impact on us. Why is this? Because sex is a theme of endless interest to normal adults. (You found yourself reading this paragraph with more than ordinary alertness, did you not? That's just what I mean.)

A Christian Priority

For healthy Christians, *holiness* is a similarly electric word. Why? Because God has implanted a passion for holiness deep in every born-again heart. Holiness, which means being near God, like God, given to God, and pleasing God, is something believers want more than anything else in this world. One reason for their interest in the Holy Spirit is their awareness that making us holy is one of his main tasks. It is natural and normal for Christians to want to understand and prove the Spirit's sanctifying power; any believer who was apathetic about seeking sanctity would be very much out of sorts. Those who find in themselves this proper Christian concern are the persons to whom this chapter is addressed.

Holiness, we should realize, is a weighty biblical term.

Having at its root the thought of separation or apartness, it signifies, first, all that marks out God as set apart from men and, second, all that should mark out Christians as set apart for God. Its second reference is the one that concerns us here. Look at these Scriptures:

> But as He who called you is *holy*, be *holy* yourselves in all your conduct; since it is written, "You shall be *holy*, for I am *holy*."
>
> 1 Peter 1:15, 16, quoting Leviticus 11:44, 45

> This is the will of God, your *sanctification*. . . . God has not called us for uncleanness, but in *holiness*. . . . [*Sanctification* and *holiness* are the same Greek word.] May the God of peace himself *sanctify* you wholly [that is, make you completely holy]; and may your spirit and soul and body be kept sound and blameless at the coming of our Lord Jesus Christ.
>
> 1 Thessalonians 4:3, 7; 5:23

> . . . [God] chose us in him [Christ] before the foundation of the world, that we should be *holy* and *blameless* before him. . . . Christ loved the church and gave himself up for her, that he might *sanctify* her, having cleansed her by the washing of water with the word, that he might present the church to himself in splendor, without spot or wrinkle or any such thing, that she might be *holy* and without blemish. . . . We are his [God's] workmanship, created in Christ Jesus for good works, which God prepared beforehand, that we should walk in them.
>
> Ephesians 1:4; 5:25, 26; 2:10

> I appeal to you therefore, brethren, by the mercies of God, to present your bodies as a living sacrifice, *holy* and acceptable to God, which is your spiritual worship.
>
> Romans 12:1

> . . . Let us cleanse ourselves from every defilement of body and spirit, and make *holiness* perfect in the fear of God.
>
> 2 Corinthians 7:1

These texts show us at once that holiness is both God's gift and his command; we should therefore pray for it and seek to practice it each day of our lives. Holiness was the goal of our election and redemption, and holiness remains God's basic requirement of us and the goal of all his providential dealings with us.

How should we define the believer's holiness? The holiness of a holy man, we may say, is the distinctive quality of his living, viewed both as the expression of his being set apart for God and as the outworking of his inward renewal by God's grace. With rumbling rhetoric, the Puritan John Owen explicates this by defining sanctification as the work of the Christian's God transforming him and holiness as the life-style of the person being thus transformed. These are helpful definitions, so I quote them in full. Owen writes:

> Sanctification is an immediate work of the Spirit of God on the souls of believers, purifying and cleansing of their natures from the pollution and uncleanness of sin, renewing in them the image of God, and thereby enabling them, from a spiritual and habitual principle of grace, to yield obedience unto God, according unto the tenor and terms of the new covenant, by virtue of the life and death of Jesus Christ. . . . Hence it follows that our holiness, which is the fruit and effect of this work, the work as terminated in us, as it compriseth the renewed principle or image of God wrought in us, so it consists in a holy obedience unto God by Jesus Christ, according to the terms of the covenant of grace, from the principle of a new nature.[1]

Holiness, thus viewed, is the fruit of the Spirit, displayed as the Christian walks by the Spirit (Galatians 5:16, 22, 25). Holiness is consecrated closeness to God. Holiness is in essence obeying God, living to God and for God, imitating God, keeping his law, taking his side against sin, doing righteousness, performing good works, following Christ's teaching and example, worshiping God in the Spirit, loving and serving God and men out of reverence for Christ. In relation to God, holiness takes the form of a single-minded passion to please by love and loyalty, devotion and praise. In relation to sin, it takes the form of a resistance movement, a discipline of not gratifying the desires of the flesh, but of putting to death the deeds of the body (Galatians 5:16; Romans 8:13). Holiness is, in a word, God-taught, Spirit-wrought Christ-likeness, the sum and substance of committed discipleship, the demonstration of faith working by love, the responsive outflow in righteousness of supernatural life from the hearts of those who are born again. Such holiness is the theme of this chapter.

A Neglected Priority

The pursuit of holiness is very evidently a Christian priority, but it is one believers today commonly neglect. That, alas, is all too easy to see.

Look, for instance, at *the man centeredness of our godliness.*

Self-Centered Godliness. Modern Christians tend to make satisfaction their religion. We show much more concern for self-fulfillment than for pleasing our God. Typical of Christianity today, at any rate in the English-speaking world, is its massive rash of how-to books for believers, directing us to more successful relationships, more joy in sex, becoming more of a person, realizing our possibilities, getting more excitement each day, reducing our weight, improving our diet, managing our money, licking our families into happier shape, and whatnot. For people whose prime passion is to glorify God, these are doubtless legitimate concerns; but the how-to books regularly explore them in a self-absorbed way that treats our enjoyment of life rather than the glory of God as the center of interest. Granted, they spread a thin layer of Bible teaching over the mixture of popular psychology and common sense they offer, but their overall approach clearly reflects the narcissism—"selfism" or "me-ism" as it is sometimes called—that is the way of the world in the modern West.

Now self-absorption, however religious in its cast of mind, is the opposite of holiness. Holiness means godliness, and godliness is rooted in God centeredness, and those who think of God as existing for their benefit rather than of themselves as existing for his praise do not qualify as holy men and women. Their mind-set has to be described in very different terms. It is an ungodly sort of godliness that has self at its center.

THE PERILS OF ACTIVISM.   Or look at *the activism of our activity.* Modern Christians tend to make busyness their religion. We admire and imitate, and so become, Christian workaholics, supposing that the busiest believers are always the best. Those who love the Lord will indeed be busy for him, no doubt about that; but the spirit of our busyness is constantly wrong. We run round doing things for God and leave ourselves no time for prayer. Yet that does not bother us, for we have forgotten the old adage that if you are too busy to pray, you really are too busy. But we do not feel the need to pray, because we have grown self-confident and self-reliant in our work. We take for granted that our skills and resources and the fine quality of our programs will of themselves bring forth fruit; we have forgotten that apart from Christ—Christ trusted, obeyed, looked to, relied on—we can achieve nothing (*see* John 15:5). This is activism: activity gone to seed through not being grounded on sustained self-distrust and dependence on God. But activism is not holiness, nor is it the fruit of holiness, and the activist's preoccupation with his own plans and schemes and know-how tends to keep him from either seeking holiness or increasing in it.

It seems however that the activist spirit has infected us all. When, for instance, we think of the pastor's role and choose men to minister in our churches, we habitually rate skills above sanctity and dynamism above devotion, as if we did not know that power in ministry stems from the man behind the ministry rather than from the particular things he can do. Perhaps we really do not know this, though our fathers knew it; but if not, then it is high time that we learned it. The corrective we need comes from Scottish minister and revival preacher Robert Murray McCheyne, who a century and a half ago began a sentence thus: "My people's greatest need is. . . ." Now, how would you expect a pastor to complete that sentence? By specifying a program or some particular skill he would bring or a new way of looking at things or what? In fact, McCheyne ended it with the words, ". . . *my personal holiness.*" "Take time to be holy," said the old hymn, and it looks as if we all need to learn afresh to do that. For self-reliant busyness, so far from being a form or expression of holiness, is actually a negation of it and a distraction from it. This spirit also has to be described in very different terms. It is an unholy sort of holiness that has self-reliance at its root.

Nor is this the worst. As holiness is a neglected priority throughout the modern church generally, so it is specifically a fading glory in today's evangelical world. Historically, holiness has been a leading mark of evangelical people, just as it has been a central emphasis among their teachers. Think of Luther's stress on faith producing good works and of Calvin's insistence on the third use of the law as code and spur for God's children. Think of the Puritans demanding a changed life as evidence of regeneration and hammering away at the need for everything in personal and community life to be holiness to the Lord. Think of the Dutch and German Pietists stressing the need for a pure heart expressed in a pure life and of John Wesley proclaiming that "scriptural holiness" was Methodism's main message. Think of the so-called holiness revival of the second half of the nineteenth century and of the classic volume by J. C. Ryle, *Holiness* (still in print and selling well after 100 years), and of the thrust of the thought of such latter-day teachers as Oswald Chambers, Andrew Murray, A. W. Tozer, Watchman Nee, and John White. In the past, the uncompromising evangelical quest for holiness was awesome in its intensity. Yet that which was formerly a priority and a passion has become a secondary matter for us who bear the evangelical name today. Why? For four reasons, at least, it seems.

HOLINESS IN ECLIPSE.   *First, Evangelicals today are preoccupied with controversy.* We fight to defend the biblical faith from diminution and distortion. We work to develop evangelical scholarship to stem and, if possible, to turn the liberal-radical-subjectivist tide. We struggle to mobilize outreach in mission and evangelism. We expend energy to combat the superstition that the essence of holiness is abstinence from activities, supposedly "worldly," which in fact are lawful, worthwhile, educative, and truly recreational; and to answer positively the question, "What liberty in Christ do believers have, and how may they best use it?" These preoccupations, proper enough in themselves, keep us from pursuing holiness as zealously as our fathers did.

Second, Evangelicals today are disillusioned with what has long been put to them as "holiness teaching" (higher life, deeper life, victorious life, Keswick, entire sanctification, or any other version of the "second-blessing" theme). What they have heard now strikes them as sterile, superficial, stunting real growth and irrelevant to today's perplexities and conflicts about Christian living. An inner-city pastor, asked what he thought of the "higher life" on which this kind of teaching dwells, said in my hearing, "It's all right, if you've got the time and money for it"—a comment that raised a laugh, but in which, so I thought, some disillusionment was clearly breaking surface.

Third, evangelical talent today is preempted so that when holiness is discussed, it is often not dealt with as weightily as it deserves. In Reformation and Puritan days, theological and pastoral leaders of outstanding mental gifts—Martin Luther, John Calvin, John Owen, Richard Baxter, Thomas Goodwin, John Howe, Richard Sibbes, William Gurnall, Thomas Watson, Thomas Brooks, for starters—thought and taught constantly and at length about holiness. But in the twentieth century, most of the best evangelical brains have been put to work in other fields. The result is that much of our best modern theology (there are exceptions) is superficial about holiness, while modern treatments of holiness often lack the biblical insight, theological depth, and human understanding that are needed in order to do the subject justice. The most distinguished evangelical theologians have not always been the most ardent exponents of holiness, and the most ardent evangelical exponents of holiness have not always been the most reliable or judicious theologians.

Fourth, and most disturbing of all, Evangelicals today are evidently insensitive to the holiness of God himself. Though we routinely affirm the reality of divine wrath against our sins, save as Christ's shed blood covers them, we do not think much about God's revealed hatred of sin in his own adopted family, nor do we "tremble at his word" as our forebears did, fearful lest they offend him (*see* Isaiah 66:2; Ezra 10:3), nor do we display that abhorrence of ungodly things that Jude had in mind when he spoke of "hating even the garment spotted by the flesh" (Jude 23). It is our habit to think of the Father, the Son, and the Holy Spirit as pally rather than pure, and to dismiss as sub-Christian any idea that God's first concern in his dealings with us might be to train us in righteousness as a step toward future joy, rather than to load us with present pleasures. We are not in tune with the biblical perception of sin as pollution—*dirt*, to use a four-letter word—in the eyes of God, and when we find Scripture telling us that there are ways of behaving that God positively hates (*see*, for example, Psalms 5:4–6; 7:11–13; Proverbs 6:16; Isaiah 1:14; 61:8; Amos 5:21; Luke 16:15) we treat it as imaginative exaggeration. No wonder, then, that the quest for holiness among us has so largely petered out.

This relative eclipse of holiness as a main evangelical concern is little short of tragic, and I hope it will not long continue, particularly in a day of such striking evangelical advance in numbers, in institutional resources, in mission strategy, in academic achievement, in public standing, and in many other respects. We need to be very clear in our minds that none of these advances are going to count for much in the long run unless renewal in holiness accompanies them. A generation ago, on both sides of the Atlantic, the vision of Evangelicals outthinking liberals grabbed leading Christian minds. That vision has borne much fruit over the years, and I for one am thankful that it still remains alive and motivates many; long may it continue to do so! But it is high time that a comparable vision of Evangelicals outliving nonevangelicals made a similar grab for our attention and began to motivate us to explore the realities of holiness afresh at the deepest level of scholarship, pastoral insight, and personal experiment.

In this century, Roman Catholics, high Anglicans, and medievalists of all persuasions have produced many profound and perceptive treatments of the spiritual life—faith, prayer, peace, love; self-knowledge, self-denial, self-discipline, cross bearing; inward detachment with intercessory involvement; and so forth—which, whether or not fully sound in their understanding of the gospel, have qualities of spiritual sensitiveness and moral integrity that modern evangelical writing on holiness has not begun to match. That grieves me, and if what I write has the effect of alerting other Evangelicals to what needs to be done here, I shall rejoice.

HOLINESS OPPOSING WORLDLINESS.   Flooding Christian communities today is the anarchic worldliness of the post-Christian West. The gigantic corporate immoralism called "permissiveness" has broken over us like a tidal wave. Churches most closely in touch with their heritage have baled out more of the invading tide than others have been able to do, but none have been very successful here, certainly not among their younger members. Christian moral standards on the sexual, family, social, financial, commercial, and personal fronts have spectacularly broken down, and "new moralities" currently offered prove to be the old pagan immorality, traveling under various assumed names. "The place for the ship is in the sea," said D. L. Moody, "but God help the ship if the sea gets into it." That is an uncomfortable word to hear, for the waves of worldliness have got into the contemporary church and waterlogged it to a very damaging degree.

Christians are called to oppose the world. But how, in this case, can that be done? Credible opposition to secular ideologies can be shown by speaking and writing, but credible opposition to unholiness can only be shown by holy living (*see* Ephesians 5:3–14). Ecumenical goals for the church are defined nowadays in terms of the quest for social, racial, and economic justice, but it would be far healthier if our first aim was agreed to be personal and relational holiness in every believer's life. Much as the modern West needs the impact of Christian truth, it needs the impact of Christian holiness even more, both to demonstrate that godliness is the true humanness and to keep community life from rotting to destruction. The pursuit of holiness is thus no mere private hobby, nor merely a path for a select few, but a vital element in Christian mission strategy today. The world's greatest need is the personal holiness of Christian people.

Magisterial treatments of holiness for our time are in short supply. In their absence, I venture to cast my own mite into the treasury by offering some foundational, Bible-based reflections on a stopgap basis to function as reference points for the rest of what I have to say.

Some Biblical Basics

Here are seven principles about holiness that no reader of the New Testament will, I think, find dubious and that have always been common ground among Evangelicals in their discussions of our theme.

1. THE NATURE OF HOLINESS IS TRANSFORMATION THROUGH CONSECRATION. The New Testament has two words for holiness. The first, *hagiasmos* (also translated "sanctification," and connected with the adjective *hagios*, translated "saint," and the verb *hagiazō*, translated "sanctify"), is a relational word, signifying the state of being separated and set apart for God—on the human side, consecrated for service; on the divine side, accepted for use. The second word is *hosiotēs*, with its adjective *hosios*. This signifies an intrinsic moral and spiritual quality, that of being both righteous and pure, inwardly and outwardly, before God. The full idea of holiness is

reached by putting these concepts together. Relational holiness comes first; it is realized through that sustained energy of consecration and dedication of oneself to one's Saviour God which is the other side of the Christian's lifelong practice of repentance. Moral and spiritual purification then follows, both as the matching of our characters to our new position of privilege as God's adopted sons and also as the perfecting of the committed relationship itself from our side.

We need to realize that while God's acceptance of each Christian believer is perfect from the start, our repentance always needs to be extended further as long as we are in this world. Repentance means turning from as much as you know of your sin to give as much as you know of yourself to as much as you know of your God, and as our knowledge grows at these three points so our practice of repentance has to be enlarged.

So the substance of our holiness is the active expression of our knowledge of the grace that separated us sinners to God through Christ our Saviour and is now transforming us into Christ's image. As Paul puts it in Philippians 2:12, 13, by our obedience to God's revealed commands we "work out" (actualize and express) the salvation that God has wrought in us, doing so "with fear and trembling," that is, not panic and fright, but reverent awe at what God is up to in our lives as he works within us by his Spirit to make us will and work for his good pleasure. For the quality of life that results, *holiness* is the proper biblical name.

Let us be clear, then, that the positional holiness of consecration and acceptance underlies the personal transformation that is normally what we have in mind when we speak of sanctification ("The work of God's free grace, whereby we are renewed in the whole man after the image of God and are enabled more and more to die unto sin and to live unto righteousness," as answer 35 of the Westminster Shorter Catechism defines it). All the Christian's human involvements and commitments in this world must be consciously based on his awareness of having been separated from everything and everyone in creation to belong to his Creator alone. Ordered, costly, unstinting commitment for the Lord's sake to spouse, children, parents, employers, employees, and all one's other neighbors, on the basis of being radically detached from them all to belong to God—Father, Son and Spirit—and to no one else, is the unvarying shape of the authentically holy life. Other lives may be exceedingly religious, but to the extent that they fail to fit this description, they are not holy to the Lord.

It is worth pausing for a moment to note the glorious paradox this truth entails—namely, that thoroughgoing detachment from all creatures to love the Creator most of all makes possible, through prayer and the Spirit's power, a more thoroughgoing involvement with people and their needs and a heartier giving of oneself to help them than would ever have been possible otherwise. The common idea that holy folk stand somewhat aloof from others could not be more wrong. "I could not love thee, dear, so much Loved I not honour more," said the poet; and the Christian is able to show superhuman love to others, only and precisely because he has learned to love Jesus more than he loves them (*see* John 21:25). This is how detachment for God comes to energize that commitment to fellow human beings which is integral to true holiness. But we cannot develop the point here, important though it is.

2. THE CONTEXT OF HOLINESS IS JUSTIFICATION THROUGH JESUS CHRIST. God's free gift of justification, that is, pardon and acceptance here and now through Christ's perfect obedience culminating in his substitutionary sin bearing for us on the cross, is the basis on which the entire sanctifying process rests. It is out of our union by the Spirit, through faith, with the Christ who died for us and whom first we trust for justification (Romans 3–5), that our subsequent life of holiness is lived (Romans 6–8). Holy people glory, not in their holiness, but in Christ's cross; for the holiest saint is never more than a justified sinner and never sees himself in any other way. John Bradford—by common consent among those who knew him, the saintliest of the English Reformers—constantly described himself when signing his letters as a hard-hearted sinner. A Puritan in his last illness testified: "Never did I so feel my

need of the blood of Christ—and never was I enabled to
make such good use of it." John Wesley on his deathbed was
heard to whisper: "No way into the holiest but by the blood
of Jesus." It looks as if Paul himself, as he advanced in years,
and presumably in holiness, too, grew downward into an increasingly vivid and humbling sense of his own unworthiness; for whereas in 1 Corinthians (c. 54 A.D.) he called
himself the least of the apostles and in Ephesians (c. 61 A.D.)
the very least of all the saints, in 1 Timothy (c. 65 A.D.) he
describes himself as the foremost of sinners (see 1 Corinthians 15:9; Ephesians 3:8; 1 Timothy 1:15).

This may, of course, be reading too much into three isolated phrases; yet in any case, it is the most natural thing in
the world for a Christian at any time to see himself as the
foremost of sinners, and the apostle's phrase should cause us
no surprise. Why is this a natural judgment for any Christian
to pass on himself? Just because he knows the inside story of
his own life—the moral defeats, hypocrisies, lapses into
meanness, pride, dishonesty, envy, lust, exploitative thinking, and cowardice at motivational level, and all the rest of
his private shame—in a way that he does not know the inside
story of anyone else. Increase in holiness means, among
other things, an increased sensitivity to what God is, and
hence a clearer estimate of one's own sinfulness and particular shortcomings, and hence an intensified realization of
one's constant need of God's pardoning and cleansing mercy.
All growth in grace is growth downward in this respect.

We need, then, to remember that any ideas of self-
satisfied or self-righteous holiness or of a divinely imparted
righteousness that in any way reduces our need for
Christ's imputed righteousness are delusive and ungodly
will-o'-the-wisps. They are, indeed, contradictions in terms.
The correct name for them is Pharisaism; they are not in any
sense Christian holiness.

3. THE ROOT OF HOLINESS IS COCRUCIFIXION AND CORESUR-
RECTION WITH JESUS CHRIST.   In Romans 6, Paul explains that

all who have faith in Christ are new creatures in him. They have been crucified with him; this means that an end has been put to the sin-dominated lives they were living before. Also, they have been raised with him to walk in newness of life; this means that the power that wrought Jesus' resurrection is now at work in them, causing them to live differently because in truth they are different at the center of their being in what Paul in Romans 7:22 calls "my inmost self" and Peter in 1 Peter 3:4 calls "the hidden person of the heart." They have been changed by the dethroning in them of that allergic negative reaction to the law of God, which is called sin, and the creating in them of what Luis Palau in the title of one of his books calls a "heart after God"—a deep, sustained desire to know God, draw near to God, seek God, find God, love God, honor God, serve God, please God. This is now the controlling motive around which the whole of their lives must now be rebuilt. This is the change wrought by what John Wesley and his apostolic namesake, following Jesus himself, called the "new birth" (*see* John 1:12; 3:3, 5, 7–21).

We need then, to realize and remember that the believer's holiness is a matter of learning to be in action what he already is in heart. In other words, it is a matter of living out the life and expressing the disposition and instincts (that is, the new nature) that God wrought in him by creating him anew in Christ. Holiness is the *naturalness* of the spiritually risen man, just as sin is the naturalness of the spiritually dead man, and in pursuing holiness by obeying God the Christian actually follows the deepest urge of his own renewed being. His Godward—better, Fatherward—love, loyalty, and devotion form the motivational image in him of the risen Christ, who lives to God (*see* Romans 6:10, 11); we could call it his Christ nature or his Christ instinct.

In one who has not been united to Christ in his dying and rising, motivational holiness is so unnatural as to be impossible, because at motivational level sin has the dominion all the time. "The mind that is set on the flesh is hostile to God; it does not submit to God's law, indeed it cannot" (Romans 8:7). Loving God with heart, mind, soul, and strength is altogether beyond the unregenerate man's capacity. But in one who is thus united to Christ, by faith from the human side and by the Spirit from the divine side, motivational holiness is spontaneous and natural, and the unnatural thing is for him to do violence to his renewed nature by yielding to the desires of the flesh (*see* Galatians 5:16–26)—which explains why backsliders are always so miserable inside. Any idea of holiness as manful refusal to do all that one most wants to do must be dismissed as the unregenerate mind's misunderstanding. True holiness, springing as it does from what the Puritans called the "gospel mystery" of the sanctifying work of God, is the Christian's true fulfillment, for it is the doing of that which, deep down, he now most wants to do, according to the urging of his new, dominant instincts in Christ. The fact that few Christians seem to be sufficiently in touch with themselves to appreciate this does not alter its truth.

4. THE AGENT OF HOLINESS IS THE HOLY SPIRIT.   I spoke in an earlier chapter of the way in which the indwelling Spirit of God, in his role as the Spirit of Christ, induces holiness. When Paul says that God works in Christians to make them will and work for his good pleasure, the Apostle is certainly thinking of the Spirit's power active in what Augustine distinguished as *prevenient* grace (which creates in us a purpose of obedience) followed by *cooperative* grace (which sustains us in the practice of obedience). By the Spirit's enabling, Christians resolve to do particular things that are right, and actually do them, and thus form habits of doing right things, and out of these habits comes a character that is right. "Sow an action, reap a habit; sow a habit, reap a character," says the proverb, and as this is true in natural life, so it is in the life of grace. Paul describes the process of character formation by this means as one of being changed into Christ's likeness from one degree of glory to another (2 Corinthians 3:18) and calls the character itself the fruit of the Spirit—which on inspection proves to be neither more nor less than the profile of Jesus Christ himself in his disciples, as was said before (Galatians 5:22–24). This should by now be familiar ground.

Yet we need to remember two things here, both of which sometimes get forgotten. The first is that the Spirit works through *means*—through the objective means of grace, namely, biblical truth, prayer, fellowship, worship, and the Lord's Supper, and with them through the subjective means of grace whereby we open ourselves to change, namely, thinking, listening, questioning oneself, examining oneself, admonishing oneself, sharing what is in one's heart with others, and weighing any response they make. The Spirit shows his power in us, not by constantly interrupting our use of these means with visions, impressions, or prophecies, which serve up to us ready-made insights on a plate, so to speak (such communications come only rarely, and to some believers not at all), but rather by making these regular means effective to change us for the better and for the wiser as we go along. Holiness teaching that skips over disciplined persistence in the well-doing that forms holy habits is thus weak; habit forming is the Spirit's ordinary way of leading us on in holiness. The fruit of the Spirit itself is, from one standpoint, a series of habits of action and reaction: love, joy, peace, patience, kindness, goodness, faithfulness, gentleness, self-control are all of them habitual dispositions, that is, accustomed ways of thinking, feeling, and behaving. Habits are all-important in holy life, particularly those biblically prescribed habits that we find it difficult and even painful to form.

The second thing to remember balances the first and is just as important. It is that holy habits, though formed in the natural manner I have described, by self-discipline and effort, are not natural products. The discipline and effort must be blessed by the Holy Spirit, or they would achieve nothing. So all our attempts to get our lives in shape need to be soaked in constant prayer that acknowledges our inability to change ourselves and in thanksgiving recognizes that as Harriet Auber put it:

Every virtue we possess, And every victory won,
And every thought of holiness Are his [the Spirit's] alone.

Holiness by habit forming is not self-sanctification by self-effort, but is simply a matter of understanding the Spirit's method and then keeping in step with him.

5. THE EXPERIENCE OF HOLINESS IS ONE OF CONFLICT.   "The desires of the flesh are against the Spirit, and the desires of the Spirit are against the flesh; for these are opposed to each other, to prevent you from doing what you would" (Galatians 5:17). These words alert us to the reality of tension, the necessity of effort, and the incompleteness of achievement that mark the life of holiness in this world. The desires of the Spirit in Paul's sentence are the inclinations of our renewed heart; the desires of the flesh are the contrary inclinations of ". . . sin which dwells within me" (Romans 7:20). The anti-God energy that indwelling sin repeatedly looses in the form of temptations, delusions, and distractions keeps total perfection beyond our grasp. By total perfection I mean what Wesley called "angelical" perfection, in which everything is as right and wise and wholehearted and God honoring as it could possibly be. The born-again believer who is in good spiritual health aims each day at perfect obedience, perfect righteousness, perfect pleasing of his heavenly Father; it is his nature to do so, as we have seen. Does he ever achieve it? Not in this world. In this respect he cannot do what he would.

How then does he see his own daily life? He knows that angelical perfection is promised for heaven, and he is resolved to get as close to it here and now as he can. He knows that he is being led and helped toward it; he can testify that God already enables him to resist sin and practice righteousness in ways in which, left to himself, he never could have done. (Any professed Christian who did not have such a testimony would make it doubtful whether he was yet born again.) Still, however, the believer faces active opposition to his being holy from the world, the flesh, and the devil. He fights back and wins victories against all three; yet he regularly falls short of angelical perfection, and none of his battles bring him to the end of the war.

The holy life is always, as the title of John White's little classic puts it, "the fight." When Paul in all exuberance declared, ". . . One thing I do, forgetting what lies behind and straining forward to what lies ahead, I press on toward the goal for the prize of the upward call of God in Christ Jesus" (Philippians 3:13, 14), he was referring to this constant battling (which he pictured as running a race, because of the sustained determination and exertion it involves). The Christian pushes on against constant opposition without, plus moments and moods of reluctance within that seem to come from nowhere, but which under Paul's tutelage he learns to identify as anti-Spirit desires of the flesh. He finds that, as Alexander Whyte trenchantly put it a century ago when deflating some rhapsodic unrealities about a life raised above temptation, "Aye, it's a sair fecht [sore fight—fierce battle] all the way."

So we need to remember that any idea of getting beyond conflict, outward or inward, in our pursuit of holiness in this world is an escapist dream that can only have disillusioning and demoralizing effects on us as waking experience daily disproves it. What we must realize, rather, is that any real holiness in us will be under hostile fire all the time, just as our Lord's was. "Consider him," wrote the writer to the Hebrews, "who endured from sinners such hostility against himself, so that you may not grow weary or fainthearted. In your struggle against sin you have not yet resisted to the point of shedding your blood"—but you may have to one day, as did Jesus before you, for there are no holds barred in this struggle (Hebrews 12:3, 4). Therefore we should lay to heart Jesus' words to the disciples who slept in Gethsemane: "Watch [be awake, alert, and on guard] and pray that you may not enter into temptation [which will surely come]; the spirit [the renewed you] is willing, but the flesh [here meaning not indwelling sin as such, but human nature, through which indwelling sin works] is weak" (Matthew 26:41). It is as certain as anything can be that without watchful prayer and a prayerful watch, we shall not be able to stand firm against the world, indwelling sin, and the evil one, but will fall victim to their wiles and blandishments instead.

6. THE RULE OF HOLINESS IS GOD'S REVEALED LAW.   The gospel, says Paul, is a summons to ". . . be renewed in the spirit of your minds, and put on the new nature, created after the likeness of God in true righteousness and holiness" (Ephesians 4:23, 24). *Righteousness* and *holiness* (which here is *hosiotēs*, purity both inward and outward) belong together: They are essentially the same thing, viewed from different angles. Holiness is righteousness viewed as the expression of our being consecrated to God. Righteousness is holiness viewed as the practice of conforming to God's law. The two are one.

The word *law* in Scripture means several different things, but here I use it in its basic sense of God's requirements in human lives. These requirements are embodied in the precepts and prohibitions of the Decalogue; expounded and applied by the prophets, the apostles, and Christ himself; and displayed in the biblical biographies of men and women who pleased God, with Christ himself, whose life from this standpoint could be described as the law incarnate, standing at the head of the list. As Paul tells us, the law in this sense is holy, just, good, and spiritual (Romans 7:12, 14). Its requirements express and reflect the Creator's own character, and conformity to it is that aspect of God's image in man—that is to say, of Godlikeness—which was lost through the Fall and is now being restored in us by grace. The standards that the law sets do not change, anymore than does God himself, and the height of holiness was, is, and always will be the fulfilling of this given rule of righteousness.

Taking God's law as our rule must not be confused with *legalism*. Legalism, we know, is a mistake Christians must avoid. Legalism means two things: first, supposing that all the law's requirements can be spelled out in a code of standard practice for all situations, a code which says nothing about the motives, purpose, and spirit of the person acting; second, supposing that formal observance of the code operates in some way as a system of salvation by which we earn our passage to glory or at least gain a degree of divine favor that we would not otherwise enjoy. Both aspects of legalism marked the Pharisees whom we meet in the gospels and the Judaizers who invaded the churches of Galatia. The former is however decisively exploded by Jesus' insistence that law keeping and law breaking are matters of desire and purpose before ever they become matters of deed and performance. And the latter is destroyed by Paul's gospel of present justification by faith alone, through Christ alone, without works of law.

Evangelical Christians today are often more successful in avoiding the second facet of legalism than the first. Clear as we are on the formula of forgiveness and acceptance by faith, we make up rules for ourselves and others, beyond what Scripture requires, and treat those who keep them as belonging to a spiritual elite. But this curtailing of personal Christian liberty by group pressure is not the way of holiness, and one can only be glad that there has been something of a reaction against it in our day.

Yet there is no wisdom in jumping out of the frying pan into the fire, and if in our flight from legalism we fell into lawless license, our last state might well be worse than our first. Christians must never cease to make law keeping their ideal, as Jesus himself stressed in the Sermon on the Mount. "For truly, I say to you, till heaven and earth pass away, not an iota, not a dot, will pass from the law . . ." (He spoke hyperbolically, for emphasis, as he and other teachers in the Bible are often found doing; what he meant was that the moral law embodied in the Decalogue and expounded throughout the Old Testament would not be in any way diminished.) "Whoever then relaxes one of the least of these commandments and teaches men so, shall be called least in the kingdom of heaven; but he who does them and teaches them shall be called great in the kingdom of heaven" (Matthew 5:18, 19). You cannot be a good quality disciple, says Jesus, without also being a conscientious law keeper.

To be sure, the Christian keeps the law nonlegalistically, from life rather than for life, not for gain but out of gratitude (*see* Romans 12:1). He obeys God not as a sinner trying to win salvation, but as a son of God rejoicing in the gift of salvation that is already his. He never forgets, however, that like Paul he is "not free from God's law but . . . under Christ's law" (1 Corinthians 9:21), so he seeks to please his Master by keeping the Master's commands. This, the proof of love (*see* John 14:15), is also the path of true holiness, a path which we must be careful to follow without any cutting of corners. For moral carelessness is spiritual carnality (*see* 1 Corinthians 3:1–3 KJV), and is holiness negated rather than fulfilled.

*7. THE HEART OF HOLINESS IS THE SPIRIT OF LOVE.   This point is so clear and familiar as to need little exposition. Love to God and man, says Jesus, is the whole burden of the law (Matthew 22:35–40). Love, says Paul, is the first fruit of the Spirit, and without love the would-be Christian is nothing (Galatians 5:22; 1 Corinthians 13:1–3). Love looks (not away from, but) beyond rules and principles to persons and seeks their welfare and glory. Love is not essentially a feeling of affection, but a way of behaving, and if it starts as a feeling, it must become more than a feeling if it is truly to be love. Love *does* something; it *gives*; that is how it establishes its identity. "By this we know love, that he [Jesus] laid down his life for us; and we ought to lay down our lives for the brethren. But if anyone has the world's goods and sees his brother in need, yet closes his heart against him, how does God's love abide in him? Little children, let us not love in word or speech but in deed and in truth" (1 John 3:16–18). Again: "Beloved, let us love one another; for love is of God . . . In this is love, not that we loved God but that he loved us and sent his Son to be the expiation for our sins. Beloved, if God so loved us, we also ought to love one another" (4:7, 10, 11).

As Jesus was law incarnate, so he was love incarnate, and following his way of self-giving is holiness in its purest and most perfect expression. Hard, harsh, cold-hearted holiness is a contradiction in terms. Love to God as prescribed in Matthew 22:37, citing Deuteronomy 6:5, and as voiced in Psalm 18, and love to neighbor as defined in 1 Corinthians

13:4–7 and illustrated in Jesus' story of the Samaritan (Luke 10:29–37) is, by contrast, the very heartbeat of holiness. On the costliness of such love I will not dwell, though in fact it is very costly to practice; suffice it here to have made the point that without love anything purporting to be holiness is in God's sight nothing: In other words, it is a hollow sham. We do well to examine ourselves often at this point.

On-Site Reconstruction

> And don't believe in anything
> That can't be told in coloured pictures.

Such was G. K. Chesterton's final advice to an intelligent child. Its serious point, and the genuine wisdom behind it, are surely plain. Ideas that are too insubstantial to illustrate are likely to be unreal abstractions or just mental muddles. Authentic insights are specific and so can be pictured in ways that help both to explain them and to verify them. And good mental pictures—*models*, to use the modern word—by involving that half of our mind which we call imagination, will take our understanding further than rational analysis on its own can ever go. This is evidently one reason why Jesus taught in parables and why all communicators do well to cultivate a style of presentation that is as imaginative as it is analytical. So did writers like C. S. Lewis and preachers like C. H. Spurgeon, and so will J. I. Packer if he has any sense, particularly when the doctrine of holiness is under discussion.

Why? Because bad pictures grab the imagination, too, and prepossess the mind with wrong notions, and in recent times this particular doctrine has suffered from bad pictures more than most. It has been verbalized and illustrated in ways that suggest that we can turn on the Spirit's power to work automatically in our lives; that holy persons are borne along in a state of psychological passivity; that they may uncritically trust their present thoughts and feelings as coming from God, once they have handed over their thought lives and emotional lives to their Lord; and that while Christ lives his divine life in their physical bodies, their personal self-hood is, or should be, in abeyance. Unbiblical phrases, loosely used, about letting go and letting God, surrendering your will, dying to self, laying yourself on the altar, and having Christ take you over, have become the only vocabulary some people possess for thinking and talking about what Scripture calls "repentance" and "obedience" in the Christian life (on repentance, see 2 Corinthians 7:9–11; 12:21; 2 Timothy 2:25; Revelation 2:5, 16; 3:3, 19; and on obedience, Romans 1:5; 6:16–19; 16:19; 2 Corinthians 10:5, 6; Galatians 5:7; Philippians 2:12, 13; 1 Peter 1:2, 22; see also 1 John 1:6). No wonder our thinking goes astray when wrong notions and bad pictures are cluttering our minds. So having tried to straighten out the basic notions, I need now to look around for an adequate illustration of the life of holiness. The best I can do is the following, which was suggested to me by experiences over the years, first at London's Heathrow Airport and later at Vancouver's Regent College—both of which are intricate administrative complexes using buildings whose reconstruction never seems to stop.

Imagine a site occupied by a functioning business. On this site the following operation is under way. The buildings out of which the firm works are being pulled down one by one, and where they stood new and better buildings are being put up, making use of materials that originally belonged to what was demolished. While this goes on, business continues as usual, though with various temporary arrangements that call for patience (as when at Heathrow one used to be funneled through a series of tents to buses that took one to planes standing a mile away from the terminal; very British, one felt, but not the ideal way to run an airport). The constant changes are wearisome to those who have to keep the business going and who are not always told in advance why each successive disruption of their routine is necessary. But in fact the architect has made a master plan for all stages of the rebuilding, and a most competent clerk of works directs and oversees each next step, and on a day-to-day basis there always proves to be a way of keeping everything going (it was planned so). Thus each day those involved in the business can truly feel that they have fulfilled their responsibility of serving the public, even if not always in the perfectly satisfactory manner they would have desired.

My parable is this. The site and the business that goes on there represent your life. God is constantly at work on that site, demolishing your bad habits and forming Christlike habits in their place. The Father has a master plan for this progressive operation. Christ, through the Spirit, is executing this plan on a day-to-day basis. Though it involves frequent disruptions of routine and periodic bewilderments as to what God is up to now, the overall effect of the work as it continues is to increase your capacity to serve God and others. (All the same, you may be, and perhaps should be, more conscious each moment of flaws in what you currently do than of now being able to do more than once you could.) The plan itself, as it applies to Christians in the mass, is described in Ephesians 5:25–27 thus: ". . . Christ loved the church and gave himself up for her, that he might sanctify her, having cleansed her by the washing of water with the word, that he might present the church to himself in splendor, without spot or wrinkle or any such thing, that she might be holy and without blemish."

In the midst of the turmoil of our ongoing personal reconstruction and conscious of present shortcomings and frustrations in serving God, ". . . we ourselves, who have the first fruits of the Spirit, groan inwardly as we wait for adoption as sons, the redemption of our bodies" (Romans 8:23). Sanctification is not usually a comfortable process, and inner ease is not to be expected while it goes on. This work of reconstructing us, viewed from another standpoint, is an infliction of God's moral discipline and training, and "for the moment all discipline seems painful rather than pleasant"; yet "later it yields the peaceful fruit of righteousness to those who have been trained by it." Thus God ". . . disciplines us for our good, that we may share his holiness" (Hebrews 12:11, 10).

"I know some Christians," writes Peter Williamson, "who display signs with the initials P.B.P.G.I.F.W.M.Y. This means 'Please be patient—God isn't finished with me yet!' This is completely right. We are in the middle of a process through which we are being made over into the image and likeness of God. . . . Paul writes: 'My little children, with whom I am again in travail until Christ be formed in you!' (Galatians 4:19). . . . Paul sees the life of Christ as something that needs to be formed in Christians. It doesn't come all at once. It takes work and time. We are somewhere in the middle of the process."[2] Precisely.

Keeping in Step With the Spirit

Twice Paul speaks of being "led" by the Spirit (Romans 8:14; Galatians 5:18). Both times the reference is to resisting one's own sinful impulses as the flip side of one's practice of righteousness (see the contexts, Romans 8:12–14 and Galatians 5:16–18). *Leads* is rightly taken to mean "guides," but the guidance in view here is not a revealing to the mind of divine directives hitherto unknown; it is, rather, an impelling of our wills to pursue and practice and hold fast that sanctity whose terms we know already. Thus to be led and guided, says Paul, is the mark of a Christian. "All who are led by the Spirit of God are sons of God," shown and known to be such by the direction of their lives. "If you are led by the Spirit you are not under the law"; your life shows you to be sharers in the new creation, now living under grace (Galatians 6:15; *see also* Romans 6:14). If a person was not being so led, it would be altogether uncertain whether he (or she) was a believer at all. And you certainly cannot keep in step with the Holy Spirit in respect of ministry if by your failure to pursue righteousness you are grieving him (*see* Ephesians 4:30) in the matter of sanctity. First things first!

I began this chapter by highlighting holiness as a Christian priority. I come back to this point as I close.

Remember that holiness was God's purpose for all his people when he planned their salvation: "even as he chose us in him [Christ] before the foundation of the world, that we should be holy and blameless before him" (Ephesians 1:4).

Remember that holiness was Christ's purpose for all of us when he died for us: He ". . . loved the church and gave himself up for her, that he might sanctify her, having cleansed her . . ." (Ephesians 5:25; the NIV rendering, "make her holy, cleansing her," is better).

Remember that it was for holiness that we were raised to life in Christ: "For we are his workmanship, created in Christ Jesus for good works, which God prepared beforehand, that we should walk in them" (Ephesians 2:10).

Remember that the gospel that calls us to Christ summons us also to holiness: "For the grace of God that brings salvation has appeared to all men. It teaches us to say 'No' to ungodliness and worldly passions, and to live self-controlled, upright and godly lives . . ." (Titus 2:11, 12 NIV). When you learned ". . . the truth that is in Jesus. You were taught, with regard to your former way of life, to put off your old self, which is being corrupted by its deceitful desires; to be made new in the attitude of your minds; and to put on the new self, created to be like God in true righteousness and holiness" (Ephesians 4:21–24 NIV).

Remember that holiness, which is another name for the life of deliverance from sin, is itself a part of the salvation that Jesus brings us: ". . . he will save his people from their sins" (Matthew 1:21).

Remember that ". . . without holiness no one will see the Lord" (Hebrews 12:14 NIV), not because a Christian's final acceptance has to be earned by holy living, but because, just as only through a sound eye can one ever see a view, so only through a pure heart can one ever see God (we have that on Jesus' authority [see Matthew 5:8]).

Remember, too, that holiness makes for the happiness of fellowship with God, which the unholy will miss. The answer to the question, "Lord, who may dwell in your sanctuary? Who may live on your holy hill?" is "He whose walk is blameless and who does what is righteous . . ." (Psalms 15:1, 2 NIV).

Remember also that holiness is the precondition of usefulness to God: "If any one purifies himself from what is ignoble, then he will be a vessel for noble use, consecrated and useful to the master of the house, ready for any good work" (2 Timothy 2:21).

Finally, remember that holiness is in any case the only way of life that is natural and fulfilling to anyone who is born again and that unholy children of God may expect not only inward discontent, because they are doing violence to their new nature, but also corrective discipline from their loving heavenly Father—not because their sin has quenched his love, but because he loves them too much to let them go endlessly wrong (*see* Hebrews 12:5–14).

Whatever differences we may have about the nature and nuances of holiness (the next chapter will explore that), I hope we shall all agree and remember that the Holy Spirit's first concern in his ministry to us is to lead us through faith in Christ as Saviour and Master into practical, personal holiness of life and that therefore it must be a priority concern on our part as Christians to make our own the prayer coined for us 150 years ago by Robert Murray McCheyne: "Lord, make me *as holy as it is possible for a saved sinner to be.*" Will you say "Amen" to that? Only so will it be worth your while and only so will your heart be in a fit state to read on.

4

Mapping the Spirit's Path:
Versions of Holiness

INTO BATTLE.   The idea of Christians at loggerheads about holiness sounds discreditable and self-condemned, just as news about a punch-up to promote pacifism would do. Are not meekness and forbearance aspects of holiness? Then must not controversy about the doctrine undermine the reality of holiness, both in the controversialists themselves and in their followers, whichever side they are on? Must not such controversy be both unspiritual and Spirit quenching? The answer is twofold. First, there is nothing unspiritual about controversy when the good of souls requires it, as it did in the controversies of (for instance) Christ and Paul, and when the good faith of one's opponents is respected. Second, the motive of those who make a virtue of avoiding controversy is likely to be nothing nobler than the self-protectiveness of folk who are at once conceited and thin-skinned and, perhaps, unaware of the value of truth. Controversy is sometimes a teacher's duty, even when holiness is his theme and few will applaud his polemics.

   This chapter will involve me in some controversy: The needs of those whom I aim to help require it. To keep the temperature down, I shall name as few names as I well can, and none of living exponents of the views I reject. Readers who find me denying what they themselves affirm will, I hope, see that I do it not for love of a fight (I do not enjoy fighting, though I cannot always avoid it), but for love of people like themselves. I know from my own experience and that of others that mistakes about holiness, however sincere, will lock one into unreality and strain in a way that destroys either the joy or the honesty of one's inner life, or perhaps both together, and I would save my readers from that if I can. If you reject what I say, please do at least remember why I said it.

Pastorally, the first battle is to convince Christians that holiness is necessary. I hope the last chapter said enough to bring conviction about that. But once Christians are committed to holiness as their goal, then a second battle begins, this time concerning the way to achieve holiness in daily life. The seven biblical parameters of holiness that the last chapter reviewed might seem to have circumscribed that topic fairly fully. Certainly, any differences that presuppose agreement on these seven principles can only be of secondary importance. Yet differences there are, both of idea and of emphasis, and my next step must be to sketch them out. Three main views need to be distinguished.

Augustinian Holiness

The first is the *Augustinian* approach, which was affirmed by Augustine against Pelagius and restated against medieval semi-Pelagianism by the Reformers and is still maintained by conservative Lutheran and Reformed teachers. Its root principle is that God out of grace (meaning, free, unmerited love to us sinners) and by grace (meaning, the Spirit active in our personal lives) must and does work in us all that we ever achieve of the faith, hope, love, worship, and obedience that he requires. In Augustine's own terms, God gives what he commands. This has to be so, because we are all naturally anti-God in heart and are never at any stage wholly free from sin's influence. We cannot respond to God at all without grace, and even when the Spirit of grace works in our lives, all our responses and all our righteousness are flawed by sin and thus, being less than perfect, merit rejection rather than anything else.

Augustinianism was consistently developed only in the Reformation churches (outside Protestantism, all professed upholders of Augustinian views apart from Gottschalk in the ninth century, Bradwardine and Wycliffe in the fourteenth, and the Jansenists in the seventeenth have modified to some extent its sovereign-grace thrust). In Protestantism the root principle as stated above was buttressed by two new emphases. The first was the Reformers' insistence that there is such a thing as full present acceptance with God (justification) and that Christ's righteousness imputed is its sole and sufficient ground. (Augustine retained notions of our being enabled by grace to merit our salvation, and in this historic Roman Catholicism has followed him.) The second was the Puritan and Pietist insistence on the decisiveness of regeneration (new birth), that irrevocable work of grace whereby through union with Christ one's heart is changed and faith is born, never to die. (Augustine doubted whether all whom God brings into the life of grace receive the gift of perseverance, and in this also historic Roman Catholicism followed him.) Within this happily amended framework the principle that in the Christian life God gives what he commands was spelled out with clarity and consistency by such men as Owen, Boston, Whitefield, Edwards, Spurgeon, Ryle, and Kuyper.

B. B. Warfield characterized Augustinianism as "miserable-sinner Christianity"[1]—a description that at first hearing sounds positively ghoulish to us in these self-applauding, resolutely healthy-minded days. But the chances are that we have missed its meaning. To start with, the language is old. The (very Augustinian) Anglican Prayer Book of 1549 contained an Ash Wednesday prayer in which worshipers confessed themselves "vile earth and miserable sinners," and the present-day Anglican practice of regularly saying together "There is no health in us . . . have mercy on us, miserable offenders" goes back to the same date. And the words do *not* imply that cultivated misery is a required state, nor should they be read as a hangover of late medieval morbidity or an expression of neurotic self-hatred and denial of personal worth (all of which interpretations, be it said, have actually found advocates in our time!). Behind *miserable* lies the Latin *miserandi*, expressing the thought that as sinners we always stand in need of God's mercy and pity, and this is not the sick unrealism of neurosis, but healthy Christian matter-of-factness. "Miserable-sinner Christianity" undoubtedly keeps our sinfulness in higher profile than other accounts of holiness do, but that is a mark of its clear-sighted realism, not of its barrenness or bankruptcy.

Augustinian Distinctives

Three stresses in particular shape the Augustinian view.

HUMILITY.   First comes its insistence that there is need for *the most deliberate humility*, self-distrustful and self-suspicious, in all our fellowship with God. Why? Because, whereas God is perfectly holy, pure, good, and unchangeably faithful in performing his promises, we are none of these things. We live in the second half of Romans 7, where "... I can will what is right, but I cannot do it" (Romans 7:18). We were born sinful in Adam, and sinful inclinations, dethroned but not yet destroyed, still remain in us now that we are in Christ. We are constantly beset by the seductions, deceptions, and drives of lawless pride and passion, of defiant self-assertion and self-indulgence (*superbia* and *concupiscentia*, "conceit" and "desire," are Augustine's words). So we need to get down very low before our Saviour God and to cultivate that sense of emptiness, impotence, and dependence that Jesus called poverty of spirit (Matthew 5:3); otherwise, pride will puff us up without our noticing it, and pride regularly goes before a fall (*see* 1 Corinthians 10:12). Augustinians are sure that Bunyan had the truth of the matter when he sang,

> He that is down need fear no fall,
>   He that is low, no pride;
> He that is humble ever shall
>   Have God to be his guide,

and they see it as part of the Spirit's work to induce in us a constantly expanding sense of the contrast between God's glorious holiness and our own inglorious sinfulness. Thus, as the work of sanctification goes on and we become more like God and more intimate with him, we grow more aware of the difference between us and him than we ever were before.

ACTIVITY. Next comes an equally emphatic insistence that there is need for *the most enterprising activity* by all God's servants in all walks and areas of life. Why? Because indwelling sin, which by nature is an instinctive reluctance to do the will of God, makes us apathetic and slothful and lazy with regard to "good works" and leads us to play games both with ourselves and with God to justify our slackness in that for which he saved us (*see* Ephesians 2:10; Titus 2:11–14).

Augustinianism is thus at the opposite extreme from the "stillness" of the evangelical quietists with whom John Wesley had to contend. They held that you cannot do anything that pleases God till, over and above the directives of Scripture and common sense and the calls to action issued by knowledge of your neighbors' needs, you have a specific inward urge from the Spirit to make a move. Without this, they said, you should never attempt anything of spiritual significance at all; not read Scripture, not pray, not go to church, not give to God's cause, not render service of any kind. Passive inaction is the only right course till the Spirit stirs you. John Wesley disagreed! "Do all the good you can" was a basic principle of the holiness that he taught, and he was a good Augustinian in encouraging initiative to this end.

To be sure, the Christian's enterprising activity should be neither random and zany nor self-confident and self-reliant. It must be guided by wisdom, which is the fruit of the clearest insight and best advice we can get, and it must be carried through in prayerful dependence on God and with humble willingness to change and improve one's plans as one goes along.

The activity Augustinian holiness teaching encourages is intense, as the careers of such prodigiously busy holy men as Augustine himself, Calvin, Whitefield, Spurgeon, and Kuyper show, but it is not in the least self-reliant in spirit. Instead, it follows this four-stage sequence. First, as one who

wants to do all the good you can, you observe what tasks, op-
portunities, and responsibilities face you. Second, you pray
for help in these, acknowledging that without Christ you can
do nothing—nothing fruitful, that is (John 15:5). Third, you
go to work with a good will and a high heart, expecting to be
helped as you asked to be. Fourth, you thank God for help
given, ask pardon for your own failures en route, and request
more help for the next task. Augustinian holiness is hard-
working holiness, based on endless repetitions of this sequence.

CHANGE.   Third comes a controlling insistence on *the reality
of spiritual change*—growth and advance, through what the Puritans called the vivifying of our graces and the mortifying of
our sins, toward an ever fuller Christlikeness. Augustinians
affirm without qualification the sovereign power of God's
love and accordingly are as optimistic about the transformation that the Holy Spirit can work in a believer's life as they
are pessimistic about the possibilities of unregenerate human
nature and realistic about the Christian's daily shortcomings
when judged by God's standard of perfection. Augustinians
see God's work of grace as first renewing the heart and then
progressively changing the whole person, from the inside
out, so to speak, into the image of Jesus in humility and love.
So they expect Christians to show forth increasingly the fruit
of the Spirit, however contrary these character qualities
might be to their natural temperament and inclination. They
also expect Christians to win victories over sudden, subtle,
and recurring temptations and by the Spirit's power to ". . .
put to death the deeds of the body . . ." (Romans 8:13; *see also*
Colossians 3:4), that is, actually to drain the life out of besetting sins, so that they beset no longer.
    The facts (1) that Augustinians do not claim to be any-
thing but sinners saved by grace, (2) that they deny anything
or anyone to be morally and spiritually perfect in this world,
(3) that they oppose perfectionist teaching in all its forms,
and (4) that they are very outspoken about their own shortcomings, have sometimes left a twofold impression: first, that

they think it important to "preach up sin," as George Fox put it—that is, to keep reminding Christians that sin is with them always—and, second, that their expectations of deliverance from sin's power in this life are scandalously low, adding up in practice to nil (zero!). But this is not so. John Owen, for instance, in his treatise on mortification, sets himself to tell the Christian what to do if he finds in himself "a powerful indwelling sin, leading him captive to the law of it, consuming his heart with trouble, perplexing his thoughts, weakening his soul as to duties of communion with God, disquieting him as to peace, and perhaps defiling his conscience, and exposing him to hardening." Owen ends by developing the following directive:

> Set faith at work on Christ for the *killing* of thy sin. His blood is the great sovereign remedy for sin-sick souls. Live in this, and thou wilt die a conqueror. Yea, thou wilt through the good providence of God live to see thy lust *dead at thy feet.*[2]

So much for the slander that Augustinians have no great expectations of deliverance from sin! They know, of course, that the mortifying of particular "deeds of the body" is not final deliverance from sin as such; anti-God energy remains in the Christian's spiritual system, ever seeking new outlets appropriate to one's age and disposition, and the battle against its manifold forms of expression is lifelong. But victories over sin and temptation are also expected to be lifelong as through the Spirit our great character change proceeds.

Romans 7:14-25

In any account of Christian holiness, Romans 7:14-25 will be a key passage, and in Augustinian teaching it has been prominent from the start. The typical exegesis is as follows.

In Romans 6:1-7:6, Paul announces his theology of liberation—that by virtue of their union with Christ, believers are freed from sin for righteousness, inasmuch as they are freed from bondage under the law for service in the Spirit (see 6:12-14, 22; 7:6). Then, in order both to vindicate the goodness of the law and yet to confirm that it cannot bring life to those whose consciences it educates and whose guilt it exposes (see 3:19, 20; 5:13, 20), Paul raises the question: How do the law and sin relate? He answers his own question by explaining that the law (1) teaches us what is required and what is forbidden, (2) hereby stirs up in our fallen natures the impulse to do what is forbidden, rather than what is required, and (3) while telling us the guilt of yielding to that impulse, (4) fails to give us any sort of power to resist it (7:7-25).

To make all these four points in the briefest and vividest way, Paul recounts his own experience, first in the past before his conversion (7-13) and then in the present, now that he is alive in Christ in the manner which 6:1-7:6 spells out. So verses 14-25 are what they appear to be: Paul's account of his experience with God's law at the time of writing. Alive in Christ, his heart delights in the law, and he wants to do what is good and right and thus keep it perfectly (7:15-23; see also 8:5-8). But he finds that he cannot achieve the total compliance at which he aims. Whenever he measures what he has done, he finds that he has fallen short (verse 23). From this he perceives that the anti-God urge called sin, though dethroned in his heart, still dwells in his own flawed nature ("flesh," see 18, 20, 23, 25). Thus the Christian's moral experience (for Paul would not be telling his own experience to make theological points, did he not think it typical) is that his reach persistently exceeds his grasp and that his desire for perfection is frustrated by the discomposing and distracting energies of indwelling sin.

Stating this sad fact about himself renews Paul's regular distress at it, and in the cry of verse 24, 25 he voices his grief at not being able to glorify God more: "Wretched man that I am! Who will deliver me from this body of death?" Then at once he answers his own question: "Thanks be to God through Jesus Christ our Lord! . . ." The question was asked in the future tense, so the verb to be supplied in the answer should be in the future tense too: "Thank God! He will deliver me through Jesus Christ!" Paul here proclaims that his present involuntary imperfection, summed up in the latter part of verse 25, will one day be made a thing of the past through the redemption of the body referred to in chapter 8:23 (7:24 was part of the "groan" mentioned there). For that future redemption we must long and wait, maintaining always the two-world, homeward-traveling, hoping-for-glory perspective that pervades the whole New Testament.

Romans 7 leads straight into the rhapsodic setting forth of the content of Christian assurance, expanding the themes of 5:1–11, which fills all thirty-nine verses of Romans 8. No condemnation, because no separation from God's love in Christ, and no trepidation, but rather expectations from God through Christ, are the themes giving this chapter its thrust. All of it is both theology and pastoral address; for Paul balances what the law has told Christians about themselves ("failed! weak! guilty!") with what the gospel tells them about themselves ("loved! saved! safe!"), and his purpose is to ensure that the gospel rather than the law has the last word in his readers' consciences and determines their final attitudes toward God, toward themselves, and toward life. Think of the Christian's personal life as a house with different aspects. Romans 7 depicts the cold, shadowed side that faces away from the sun, Romans 8 shows us the warm side where the sunshine is seen and felt. We only get out of Romans 7 into Romans 8 in the sense that, after letting the law speak to us about ourselves, we listen afresh to the gospel. But both aspects of experience—the pain of imperfection, and the joy of assurance, hope, and spiritual progress—should be ours constantly, consciously, and conjointly. We do and must live, so to speak, in both chapters together, every day of our lives. What Alexander Whyte meant on the occasion when he wagged his finger at his people and told them: "You'll never get out of the seventh of Romans while I'm your minister!" was that he would try to keep them mindful of this fact.

Strengths and Weaknesses

LACK OF COMPROMISE.   This tradition of holiness teaching has, I think, three special strengths. First, it is *uncompromising* about God's moral law. That law, which commands love to God and man, inwardly in desire as outwardly in deed, and which condemns all contrary attitudes and ways of acting, that law which Jesus both spelled out and lived out when he was on earth, is faced in its entirety. No blunting of its edge or diminishing of its thrust is permitted. Augustinianism follows John (1 John 3:4) in defining sin as lawlessness—"any want of conformity unto, or transgression of, the law of God," as answer 14 of the Westminster Shorter Catechism puts it—and insists that salvation from sin means freedom and ability for law keeping. Augustinianism thus embraces what Calvin called the third use of the law as the family code that by setting ideal standards, spurs God's children on to work as hard as they can at pleasing their Father. It is, accordingly, in its mainstream at any rate, as far from antinomianism (lawless living) as it well could be.

REALISM.   Second, Augustinianism is *realistic* about our own attainments. It insists that nothing is quite perfect yet and faces squarely the actual imperfections of believers in this life. For my part, I know that I have never framed a prayer, preached a sermon, written a book, shown love to my wife, cared for my children, supported my friends, in short, done anything at all, which I did not in retrospect realize could and should have been done better; nor have I ever lived a day without leaving undone some things that I ought to have done. I expect all readers of this book would have to say the same, and frankly I would have little respect for any who felt no need to do so. The story goes that a man once told Spurgeon that he had been sinless for two months, so the pastor, eager to test his quality, trod heavily on his toe; and at once his proud record (*proud* is surely the right word!) came to an inglorious end. Augustinians know that all human claims to sinlessness are delusive, and they never themselves pretend to be sinless. Instead, they praise God constantly for his patience and kindness toward Christians so imperfect as they are.

EXPECTANCY. Third, Augustinianism is *expectant* on a day-to-day basis. In addition to hoping and longing for perfection in heaven, Augustinians expect help from God in each day's trouble, strength from God for obedience in each day's tasks, and thereby progressive transformation of character through the Holy Spirit's engendering of holy habits. There is no room in their lives for apathy and inaction, even when for the moment they feel spiritually low. They expect great things from God and attempt great things for God, setting much store by patient, disciplined, determined persistence (what England calls "stickability," and North America "stick-to-itiveness") in the tasks of holiness. They find that the very strength of their expectations of being helped is used by the Spirit to give them energy to "keep on keeping on" in the humdrum routines of everyday; and they know that a great deal of our real holiness (as distinct from the phony posturings into which we are sometimes betrayed) consists precisely of this.

But are there not problems in this tradition, as well as strengths? Yes, there are. The basic problem is that right from the start, Augustinians, being confronted with ideas of self-generated merit—first in Pelagianism, then in Roman Catholicism, then in rationalistic Arminianism, which in effect makes faith a meritorious work—have couched their belief that no human action in this world is quite perfect in terms that sound ethically negative and pessimistic to the last degree. Thus, for instance, it is very daunting to read answer 149 in the Westminster Larger Catechism: "No man is able, either of himself, or by any grace received in this life, perfectly to keep the commandments of God, but doth daily break them in thought, word and deed." One could easily conclude from a statement like that it is not worth even trying to keep the law. More recently, Augustinians have reaffirmed the same negative perspective against the two main forms of Protestant perfectionism: the heart perfection of John Wesley and conservative Methodism and the act perfection of Keswick and associated movements, of which more shortly.

Questions and suspicions naturally arise from this negative way of speaking. The issues that critics have constantly raised are: Does this view not lead to expectations of deliverance from sin and of character change that are really too low? Does it not betray us into looking and asking for too little in the way of sanctifying grace, so that we actually receive and settle for too little? Does it not hereby quench the Spirit and limit God? Does it not miss much of the truth in Charles Wesley's triumphant line, "He *breaks the power* of cancelled sin"? Does it not oblige serious seekers after holiness to go elsewhere to learn about deliverance from sin's power? The answer is, no, not in its best exponents (Calvin, John Owen, and J. C. Ryle, for instance); but yes, in the case of some second-rank Augustinians who really do leave the impression that their interest is limited to orthodoxy and antiperfectionism and does not extend to holiness in any positive way. But all positions should be judged by their best exponents.

Wesleyan Perfectionism

The second position at which we should look is that which John Wesley developed in the mid-eighteenth century under the name of "Christian perfection." Its novelty was to affirm a second transforming work of grace, distinct from and ordinarily subsequent to the new birth (conversion). By this second work, so Wesley claimed, God roots all sinful motivation out of a Christian's heart, so that the whole of his mental and emotional energy is henceforth channeled into love for God and others: love that is Christlike and supernatural, strong and steady, purposeful and passionate, and free from any contrary or competing affection whatsoever.

This is a noble doctrine, which historically has been adorned by men of the caliber of Wesley's designated successor, the Anglican John Fletcher; William Booth and Samuel Logan Brengle among Salvationists; and the Baptist Oswald Chambers. The quest for the gift of holiness that it has sparked off has been the means of drawing thousands into transforming experiences of the love of God. Largely if not exclusively under its influence, Methodists of earlier days became loud singers and shouters in their praises, long agonizers in their prayers, and lion-hearted laborers for their Lord; it was as if their souls had been expanded to giant size. Though now almost extinct in the larger Methodist churches, Wesley's doctrine lives on in other circles, and godly men still profess to have had their lives transformed by entering into this "second blessing." That something momentous has happened to them is beyond doubt; the only question is whether Wesley's doctrine correctly describes it—whether, in short, Wesley's doctrine is God's truth. We shall try to form a judgment on this as we review his doctrine now.

The first thing to say is that Wesley's doctrine is Augustinianism augmented rather than abandoned. (I am referring when I say this only to the Augustinian tradition of holiness teaching; Wesley's Arminianism abandoned the essence of Augustine's doctrine of grace, but that is not my concern here.) John Wesley's heritage on both sides of his family was Puritan, so it should cause no surprise to learn that in his mature teaching on holiness he kept within our seven biblical parameters and reproduced the characteristic Augustinian emphases on God's law as binding Christians, on the insufficiency by absolute standards of every Christian's attainments, and on the reality of divine help for daily life. He did, indeed, lay great emphasis on Christian perfection as a Methodist distinctive; he thought of it as a Bible truth that he was the first clearly to have brought to light. Calvinists then and since have attacked him for holding that we can achieve the sinlessness Augustine denied to be attainable in this world. But that, as we shall see, is a misunderstanding (one for which Wesley himself, who declined to object to the phrase "sinless perfection," must bear some blame). It is in fact much more correct to understand his doctrine as reorchestrating elements in the Augustinian tradition than as breaking with it. Certainly, in disciplined, prayerful enterprise, in underlining our total dependence on God's sovereign love and power, and in high expectations of what God will do in human lives, Wesley was entirely Augustinian. Furthermore, the honest self-assessment that kept him from claiming perfection personally and led him to write in 1765, "I have told all the world I am not perfect . . . I have not attained to the character I draw,"[3] was as Augustinian as could be. To claim perfection has never been the Augustinian way!

Yet Wesley's doctrine of perfection, as he and his brother Charles set it forth in homiletic prose and ecstatic hymns respectively, gave the Wesleyan version of the Christian life a quality of ardor, exuberance, and joy—joy in knowing God's love, praising his grace, and resigning oneself into his hands—that went beyond anything we find in Calvin, the Puritans, and the earlier Pietists. In the Augustinian tradition, Augustine himself, Bernard, and Richard Baxter come closest to it, but the passionate reasonings and rhapsodies of the Wesley brothers seem to the present writer at any rate to excel them all in this respect.

The richness of Wesley's teaching on perfection reflects the range of sources from which he built it up. He regularly referred to it as *"scriptural* holiness," but his understanding of biblical teaching on holiness was drawn from many sources. An eclectic to his fingertips, he superimposed on the Augustinianism of the Anglican Prayer Book and the heaven-aspiring High Church moralism in which he was reared a concept of perfection (*teleiōsis,* the state of being *teleios,* to use the New Testament words) that he had learned from Greek patristic sources. "Macarius the Egyptian" (actually a fifth-century Syrian monk) and Ephraem Syrus were chief among these. Their idea of perfection was not of sinlessness, but of an ever-deepening process of all-round moral change. To this idea Wesley then added the lesson he had learned from those whom he called "the mystic writers" (a category including the Anglican William Law, the Roman Catholics Molinos, Fénélon, Gaston de Renty, Francis de Sales, and Madame Guyon, the Lutheran Pietist Francke, and the pre-Reformation *Theologia Germanica*). The lesson was that the heart of true godliness is a motivating spirit of love to God and man; without this, all religion is hollow and empty.

So much was clear to Wesley before his evangelical as-

surance dawned at Aldersgate Street in 1738. As he often insisted, his idea of perfection was formed long before he entered into what he called "the faith of a son." Once faith had
come, however, he took a final step, unique to himself, with
regard to the way that perfection is attained. He began to
claim that perfection, understood as a state of heart in which
love to God and man is all (a state to which in any case the
Holy Spirit will bring believers when they leave the body
at death), may be wrought instantaneously in us in this life
through our exercise of the same kind of insistent, expectant,
empty-handed, full-blooded, promise-claiming faith as was
previously the means of our justification. This second work
of grace, Wesley taught, will be signaled, just as the new
birth was, by the Spirit's direct, assuring witness in one's
heart to what has happened. Then one will continue to grow
spiritually within perfection, as previously one was growing
toward it.

Wesley's doctrine of perfection, then, had to do not with
sinlessness but with growth. Wesley understood perfection,
or "perfect love" as he often called it, not legally but teleo-
logically: Not, that is, as "Adamic" or "angelic" faultlessness,
but as advance into and then within, the state of concentrated, integrated, passionate, resolute godliness for which
mankind was both made and redeemed.

Perfection, then, is a state, but it is not static; it is a state of
wholeheartedly going on with God in obedient worship and
service that are fueled by love and love alone. It is, in essence,
a quality of inward life rather than of outward performance.
One who is perfect in Wesley's sense may still lack knowledge, err in judgment, and hence act foolishly. He may still
exhibit any, perhaps many, of "those inward or outward imperfections which are not of a moral nature . . . weakness or
slowness of understanding, dullness or confusedness of ap-
prehension, incoherency of thought, irregular quickness or
heaviness of imagination . . . the want of a ready or retentive
memory . . . slowness of speech, impropriety of language,
ungracefulness of pronunciation. . . ."[4] He will still be as-
sailed from time to time by temptations against which he will

have to fight in order to retain his integrity. His perfection, however, is not affected by these facts one way or the other, for perfection is simply a matter of love toward God and men being the constant driving force in his life.[5]

So perfection, according to Wesley, is a subjective condition, created and sustained by the Spirit of God, in which all the Christian's powers of mind and heart are consciously concentrated, first, on actually apprehending God's love to him as the Spirit witnesses to it, and second, on active, submissive, prayerful, joyful love toward his God and toward his neighbor for God's sake. This love expresses itself first and foremost in worship and praise, in glad resignation of ourselves into God's hands, and in readiness to do and suffer anything that God might appoint for us. It is a blessing to be desired, for it lifts one's whole life to a new level of power and delight. It should be sought, for Scripture contains both promises of it and testimonies to it, and if New Testament believers enjoyed it, so may believers today. This blessing God gives in sovereign wisdom when and as he sees fit and in particular cases (such as Wesley's own?) may deliberately withhold. But none will receive it unless they seek it and go on seeking it as long as may be necessary. Finally, it is a blessing that may be lost through carelessness and then perhaps restored when penitently sought again.[6]

Critique

Wesley's holiness teaching seems to merit both bouquets and brickbats. To start with the bouquets: his notion of holiness has great strengths.

It focuses on *motives* as the touchstone of holiness, as did Jesus himself when setting standards and detecting sins (*see* Matthew 5:21–30; 15:18–20). Thus it leaves behind all ethical externalism and mechanical piety, all Pharisaic formalism and living by numbers, and all ideas of religion as essentially routine performances.

Again it focuses on *love to God and men*, the fulfilling at motivational level of Christ's two great coɪ ˌmandments, as

the taproot of holiness and so leaves behind all negative notions of sanctity as mere abstinence from things thought defiling. "The words 'sanctify' and 'holy' . . . certainly carry the
idea of being purged from impurity but no hint of being robust in active goodness. 'Perfect love' reverses that. . . ."[7]

Finally, Wesley focuses on *faith*, the confident trust in
God of the self-despairing, as the means whereby holiness is
both sought and found. Effort and discipline there must be,
but with no self-reliance; our hope of becoming holy must be
in God, not in ourselves. All this is admirable—admirably
Augustinian, too!—as is Wesley's view of the holy life as one
of strenuous activity, his opposition to antinomianism,
quietism, emotionalism, and ethical passivity in all their
forms, and his refusal to set limits to the transforming power
of God's Spirit in us here and now.

THE PROBLEMS OF PERFECTION. But Wesley's doctrine of
perfection, the pure heart, or entire sanctification—the "second blessing," as Wesleyans, though not Wesley, came to
call it—whereby the Spirit of God in one single moment
roots out every motive from the Christian's heart except love,
raises problems. Had Wesley simply proclaimed that the Father and the Son do in fact from time to time make the loyal
disciple conscious of their presence in a vivid, heartwarming
way (*see* John 14:20–23) and that through these visitations one
may become immune for shorter or longer periods to previously besetting temptations and that all Christians should
constantly be asking their Lord to draw near and bless them
thus, no problem would exist, for he would then have been
speaking uncontroversially about undisputed realities of life
in the Spirit. But Wesley affirmed perfection as a doctrine—
that is, a normative account of a divine work that is as distinctive and characteristic (so Wesley held) as is the new
birth—and it was his claim that perfection as he described it
is a biblical doctrine that caused and causes the trouble.

Like the new birth, this subsequent work of grace was
conceived by Wesley as having both an objective and a subjective aspect. Objectively, the new birth was a dethroning of

sin and a transforming of personal attitudes into a new frame of humility and virtue; subjectively, it was the dawning of assured faith in God as having pardoned one's sins and adopted one into his family through Jesus Christ. Perfection, as Wesley saw it, had a comparable structure. Objectively, it was a final cleansing of the heart through the actual uprooting and destroying of "inbred sin" and the channeling of all a man's personal energies—intellectual, volitional, emotional, motivational—into the one sustained activity of loving God and others. Subjectively, it was the conscious realization, given directly by the Holy Spirit, that one has so been changed within that pure love is now one's only motive and that one is, in fact, praying, rejoicing, and giving thanks from an ardent heart all one's waking hours. So perfection was a doctrine about a specific work of the Holy Spirit in our inner being, which produces a characteristic mode of conscious experience. It was, as we saw, a much-loved novelty that Wesley's mind reached in two steps: first, by crystallizing in his early days a concept of perfection drawn mainly from the Greek fathers; second, by inferring after his Aldersgate Street experience that perfection, like justification, is not achieved gradually by works, but is bestowed instantaneously by grace only through faith only. And to non-Wesleyan Protestants this doctrine presents major problems.

What are these problems? Let me say first that I do not count among them the confusing and provocative way in which Wesley expressed his view—although this has in fact led to a great deal of misunderstanding and misdirected criticism over more than two centuries. It was indeed confusing for Wesley to give the name of *perfection* to a state which from many standpoints was one of continued imperfection. It was yet more confusing that he should define sin "properly so called," subjectively, as "voluntary transgression of a known law," rather than objectively, as failure, whether conscious or unconscious, voluntary or involuntary, to conform to God's revealed standards. It was supremely confusing when he let himself speak of sanctified persons as being without sin (because they were not consciously breaking any known law) while at the same time affirming that they need the blood of Christ every moment to cover their actual shortcomings. Wesley himself insisted that by the objective standard of God's "perfect law,"[8] every sanctified sinner needs pardon every day; that makes it seem perverse of him also to have insisted on stating his view of the higher Christian life in terms of being perfect and not sinning. Small wonder that those, now as then, who think that Christians' words about themselves should always proclaim their conscious lack of merit before God should find Wesley's way of speaking both muddleheaded and wrongheaded at the same time! He certainly could have said what he had to say without using the language of perfection and sinlessness at all, and the fact that he found this vocabulary in both Scripture and tradition cannot of itself excuse his willfulness or insensitiveness or truculence (it is hard to know which word best fits) in persisting with it when he saw what vast confusion it caused.

For my part, I propose from this point on to do what I think Wesley should have done and call his doctrine the *imparting of total love,* or *total love* for short. Thus I can leave behind the problems raised by his wording and be free to focus on the difficulties inherent in the notion itself. I see four of these.

First, the biblical proof is inconclusive. The texts to which Wesley appeals (see Note 5) are *either* promises of and calls to holiness, with expressions of confidence that God will one day deliver his people from sin, *or* New Testament declarations that for Christians some real deliverance from sin has now occurred. Wesley affirms that the promises find fulfillment in total and absolute terms in this life and appeals to the declarations, along with the prayers and commands, to buttress his conclusions. But it cannot be shown that the declarations express more than the relative deliverance wrought in the sinner's regeneration, whereby sin ceases to dominate his life. Nor, therefore, can it be shown that God's promises of deliverance require more for their fulfillment than the great change of regeneration, followed by progressive sanctification (which Wesley himself sees as coming before as well

as after the imparting of total love), followed by the final purifying of the heart that Wesley expected all saints who had
not already entered into total love to undergo at death. Nor
can God's calls to holiness and man's prayers for it be held to
prove more than that perfect holiness, and nothing less,
should always be our goal.

At the end of his sermon of 1765 "The Scripture Way of
Salvation," Wesley waxes eloquent as he calls on Christians
to seek total love, the positive aspect of full deliverance from
sin, as a gift from, through, and in Christ here and now.
"Look for it then every day, every hour, every moment! Why
not this hour, this moment? . . . If you seek it by faith, you
may expect it *as you are*, and if as you are, then expect it *now*
. . . Stay for nothing! Why should you? Christ is ready and
He is all you want. He is waiting for you! He is at the door!"[9]
The preacher makes it sound as if the gift is there for any and
every believer's asking. But biblically it would seem that the
right answer to Wesley's question "why not this hour?" is,
because God has promised it for heaven, and there is no
scriptural ground for confidence, let alone certainty, that he
will disburse it to any particular Christian in this life. At this
point, Wesley was making an error in his account of salvation corresponding to that which in modern discussions of
God's kingdom is called *realized eschatology*: He was failing to
distinguish correctly what is *now* from what is *not yet* in the
saving work of God.

Second, the theological rationale is unrealistic. Objectively, the
implanting or inducing of total love is defined as the uprooting or eradicating of sinful desire from the heart. Wesley
understood this change of moral nature as involving in some
mysterious way a change of physical nature also. This appears from his answer given in 1759 to the question, "If two
perfect Christians had children, how could they be born in
sin, since there was none in the parents?" Accepting the
question as it stands, he replied, somewhat oddly, as follows:

> It is a possible, but not a probable, case. I doubt whether
> it ever was or ever will be. [Why, for goodness' sake?] But

waiving this [!], I answer: Sin is entailed upon me not by my immediate but by my first parent [Adam] ... We have a remarkable illustration of this in gardening. Grafts on a crabstock bear excellent fruit. But sow the kernels of this fruit and what will be the event? They produce as mere crabs as ever were eaten.[10]

As E. H. Sugden observed, Wesley viewed "sin as a *thing* which has to be taken out of a man, like a cancer or rotten tooth."[11] So when he and brother Charles spoke of the root of sin being destroyed in the imparting of total love, they meant literally and psychophysically exactly what they said.

But in that case it ought to be impossible for a "perfect" or, in Wesleyan parlance, "sanctified" person to be "lured and enticed by his own desire" in temptation (James 1:13–15); for whence can come such desire—inordinate, unloving, self-serving, God flouting—when sin, according to the theory, has been rooted out of him? Temptation ought now to be as external to him, as little able to appeal to dispositional disorders and latent unloving inclinations in his personal makeup as it could do (presumably) in unfallen Adam and in the Lord Jesus Christ himself.

⨯Experience shows, however, that capacities for spontaneously reacting to people and circumstances in a way that is unloving, unethical, and sometimes violent remain with the holiest men all their days; indeed, much of their holiness consists in resisting and mortifying such reactions, which may be evoked at any time and may take a form of which the person did not know himself (or herself) capable till it actually happened. What the Puritans bluntly called *corruptions* (that is, self-worship and self-service in a myriad of shapes and disguises: sins of youth, of middle age, of old age, of overinvolvement and undue detachment, of oversensitiveness, and so forth) keep being triggered off in us by new stimuli, and humbling, shaming self-discoveries keep being made. Whether the person whose professed perfection Spurgeon shattered had in advance any idea how angrily he would react if his toe was stepped on, we do not know, but

F. B. Meyer, a saintly Baptist, put on record that he was shaken to the core when in late middle age he saw the crowds leaving him to listen to young G. Campbell Morgan and found himself eaten up with professional jealousy; for this was a form of ill-will to which he had always thought himself immune.[12]

So what should we think of any Christian whom we found supposing that because of a particular blessing in his past, such humbling experiences as Meyer's can never come his way anymore? Realism surely forces us to say that no Christian, however wholehearted at this moment, or at any future moment, in conscious love of God and neighbor, will ever be immune to shocks of this kind, in which new depths of his or her sinful nature are disclosed. Therefore Wesley's speculative notion that sin may be rooted out of believers in this life must be dismissed as untrue, and any Christian who supposes that this has actually happened to him must be regarded as self-deceived.

This leads straight on to our next difficulty with Wesley's doctrine.

Third, the practical implications are unedifying. Dilemmas arise, admitting of no satisfactory resolution. The prime dilemma is that just indicated: How are Christians who believe sin to have been rooted out of them to be realistic about their own continuing sinfulness? Wesley's teaching inevitably requires them not to be. Then a further dilemma arises: Should such Christians testify to their blessing? And if so, how? Not to testify would rob God of glory and men of help that the witness might bring them and would moreover be a cowardly evasion of possible trouble; but to testify in the terms Wesley envisages ("I feel no sin, but all love. I pray, rejoice, give thanks without ceasing. And I have as clear an inward witness that I am fully renewed as that I am justified"[13]) would seem to lock them unavoidably into smugness of a rather unlovely kind.

Wesley was a pastor of distinction, and his good pastoral sense is evident as he struggles with the question, "Should a 'fully renewed' Christian speak of the marvelous thing that has happened to him?"

"At first, perhaps" Wesley writes "he would scarce be able to refrain, the fire would be so hot within him; his desire to declare the loving kindness of the Lord carrying him away like a torrent. But afterwards he might; and then it would be advisable not to speak of it to them who know not God. . . . Nor to others without some particular reason, without some particular good in view. And then he should have especial care to avoid all appearance of boasting, to speak with the deepest humility and reverence, giving all the glory to God. Meantime, let him speak more convincingly by his life than he can do by his tongue."[14]

Good pastoral sense, undoubtedly, and yet not enough of it! Wesley appears here as the victim of his own misunderstanding of the experience that he theologized as the uprooting of sin. He did, in fact, regularly examine the supposedly perfect as to their experience and encourage them to testify to it in Methodist gatherings, expressing it in terms of their now being established in total love. How far he recognized the resultant risks of smugness and unreality is a moot point. R. Newton Flew wonders why Wesley never claimed for himself the perfection that he encouraged others to claim: ". . . was it some fastidiousness, some half-unconscious suspicion that avowal would be perilous to the health of his soul?"[15] The reason why, I suspect, was that Wesley knew himself well enough to be aware that for all his resolute devotion, joy in God's love, and good will to men, sin was alive in him still; therefore such a claim would have been dishonest. But we cannot thus applaud Wesley for not letting his cherished doctrine override his personal spiritual sensitivity without at the same time regretting the perfectionist pressure and propaganda by which, really, though unintentionally, he dulled that sensitivity in others and led them to embrace fundamental unreality at this point. For there is no doubt that the emphases and expectations of honored, masterful leaders like John Wesley do in fact have an enormous conditioning effect on the outlook of their more docile and suggestible followers.

Fourth, the counterthrust of Romans 7:14–25 is inescapable. Paul's shift from the past tense to the present in verse 14 has

no natural explanation save that he now moves on from talking about his experience with God's law in his pre-Christian
days to talking about his experience as it was at the time of
writing. Any other view represents him as an inept communicator who, by making a needless and pointless change of
tense, was asking to be misunderstood. The same representa-
tion follows from supposing that the *I* of verses 7–25 is not
Paul himself, but some imaginary figure. It surely is unplau-
sible to accuse Paul, who ordinarily communicates so clearly,
of being so stupid here. But if the words "I see in my members another law at war with the law of my mind and making
me captive to the law of sin which dwells in my members"
(verse 23) have a present reference, then clearly Paul's total
experience was not total love; sin still worked within him at
least at functional level, and he was not in Wesley's sense
perfect.

Wesley, with the Greek fathers and the Dutch Arminians,
read verses 7–25 as referring to pre-Christian experience
throughout. But this view cannot account for the change of
tense, nor for the ability to "will what is right" and the conscious delight in God's law that are affirmed in verses 18 and
22 (see what is said of the mind of persons who are "in the
flesh" in 8:7, 8!), nor for the way in which, *after* thanking God
for what on this view is presumably *present* deliverance from
sin's power, Paul sums up the situation by saying: ". . . So
then, I myself [not "of myself," as RSV, but "I the selfsame
person"] serve the law of God with my mind, but with my
flesh I serve the law of sin" (Romans 7:25). The only natural
meaning of this, on the Wesleyan hypothesis, is that the
needed deliverance has not yet, after all, been given, which
makes the two halves of the verse seem contradictory. (To
treat "I thank God through Jesus Christ our Lord" as an interjection not logically linked with the sentence that follows
it, as Wesley was obliged to do,[16] is very unnatural.) The
truth is that the only coherent exegesis of these verses is the
Augustinian, which was sketched out above. But the only
way that the Augustinian exegesis could be squared with
Wesley's doctrine of perfection would be to suppose that

Paul, like Wesley himself, had somehow missed this blessing and was having to speak out of his lack of it, which is surely not a view that anyone would seriously wish to defend.

I conclude, then, that Wesley's doctrine of present perfection wrought here and now by the Holy Spirit in response to faith cannot be found in the New Testament. Total love, wholly free from any admixture of sinful and self-seeking motivation, is heaven's promised life, but it is not attained here on earth, however far in love to God and men a believer is enabled to go. To teach Christians to infer from any present state of spiritual exaltation that all sinful desire is now permanently gone from them is a damaging mistake; the inference is false, and those who draw it thereby sentence themselves to some degree of moral and spiritual unreality. The radiant holiness that marked the Wesleyan saints was achieved despite their belief about the eradicating of sin, not because of it.

Yet the nobility of Wesley's ideal of the Christian temper—all joy, thanksgiving, and love—stands as an abiding rebuke to anyone tempted to settle for anything less. And when Wesley's doctrine of total love is heard simply as a witness to what Thomas Chalmers was later to call "the expulsive power of a new affection"—that is, as telling us how love to the Father and Jesus, called forth by the divine love that redeemed us, drives out meanness, bitterness, and pride—it exposes all shallow, self-absorbed and self-indulgent elements in our devotion with devastating force.

Keswick Teaching: A Halfway House

By "Keswick teaching" I mean that modified version of the Wesleyan view developed a little over a century ago to parry criticism of the claim that God's second decisive work of grace eradicates sin from the Christian's heart. It has also gone by the name of "victorious-life teaching"; under that name it is still met today. Its architects, as I noted earlier were American Presbyterians like Robert Pearsall Smith, husband of the Quaker Hannah Whitall Smith, and English Anglicans like Evan Hopkins and Bishop H. C. G. Moule, and it was called "Keswick teaching" because it was regularly given at the Convention for the Deepening of the Spiritual Life held annually at Keswick, in England's Lake District, since 1875. Indeed, the Keswick Convention was founded for this purpose, though "Keswick teaching" has little or no place in the instruction given at the convention nowadays.

Keswick teaching in all its many modes and forms takes its rise from what Paul says in Romans 6:1–14. There the apostle declares that Christians are ". . . dead to sin and alive to God in Christ Jesus" (verse 11); "our old self was crucified with him so that the sinful body might be destroyed, and we might no longer be enslaved to sin" (verse 6); therefore "yield yourselves to God as men who have been brought from death to life, and your members to God as instruments of righteousness" (verse 13). From this teachers like Robert Pearsall Smith deduced a formula for entry upon a "higher life," "life on the highest plane," a life in which, though one's sinful heart remained as it was before, the down drag of wrong desire and moral weakness is effectively nullified. Apparently it was common in the mid-nineteenth century to understand "dead to sin and alive to God" as a metaphor for Christian repentance and resolve (*see* Galatians 5:24) rather than as a declaration of what God has done in making one a new creature in Christ, and it seems to have come as something of a revelation to Smith and others to realize what Paul is really saying here, namely that the Christian has *already* been changed and renewed at the root of his being in such a way that now he cannot be dominated by sin as a ruling power in the way that he was before. We should be glad that they got the message!

But the way they applied this truth was, to say the least, peculiar. Instead of making it the basis of a call to expectant endeavor in the practice of righteousness, as Paul does in verses 13, 14, they made it the basis of a call to faith in a special sense of that word, according to which faith entails a deliberate nonexertion ("resting," as they called it), for which *passivity* is the only natural name. Faith, thus understood, they said, is the grand secret of holiness. What they meant by faith here was, first, believing consciously and persistently that one is indeed dead to sin and alive to God; second, relying consciously and persistently on Christ through the Holy Spirit to defeat sin and prompt righteousness in one's life on a moment-by-moment basis; and third, making specific use of the Spirit's power in every temptation to evil by specifically asking Christ to raise one and keep one raised above that temptation. Without this faith, they said, freedom from sin's dominion will never be a fact of one's experience. One will try to do what is right by self-effort, relying on one's own natural resources, but one will fail, and deservedly so, since one's state of mind is in reality one of pride and self-ignorance and of unbelief in the power of one's indwelling Saviour.

So the teachers sang of "Holiness by faith in Jesus, Not by effort of our own"; they denounced the churches for teaching, or at least letting it be believed, that while justification is by faith, sanctification is by works; they censured all conscious exertion toward obedience as expressing self-reliance and all laboring to do right as "the energy of the flesh" (a phrase that soon gained shibboleth status in their teaching); and they insisted that the way of faith is consciously to let Christ do things in and through you rather than try to do them yourself.

By this teaching they made the outworking of holiness a matter of mental and spiritual technique. If when sinful urges come, you set yourself to resist them directly (they said), you will be beaten by them, but if you hand them over to Christ to defeat, he will do so for you, and you will go on unscathed. From the inner passivity of looking to Christ to do everything will issue a perfection of performance. (How could it be otherwise, when it is Christ alone who acts?) One will in this way be saved from all actual sinning, though not from the turbulence of sin in one's heart. One's sinful heart (said the teachers with emphasis) will not be changed at all in this world. Yet one's inner sinful cravings, however strong, will be completely counteracted by the Spirit's power in one's outward conduct (*counteraction* was a technical term in Keswick teaching), once one has learned in conscious weakness every moment to ask Christ to take over.

Thus, while rejecting the claim to sinlessness of heart as perfectionist heresy, Keswick teachers proclaimed sinlessness of acts in the sense of conscious deliverance from all known wrong. Though they broke with Wesley's belief that God gives perfect love in this life, they held to his concept of "sin properly so called (that is, a voluntary transgression of a known law),"[17] and in terms of it depicted the Christian life as potentially one of total and endless victory over every form of temptation and moral weakness. To cease striving and struggling to be holy and to embrace the habit of confessing impotence and trusting Jesus, they said, is to enter upon the "higher life" in which living is consistently "victorious, happy, and glorious" in a sense beyond anything that the British national anthem envisages for the sovereign. Victory over sin, happiness in Jesus, and a life full of God is, said the teachers, the richest heritage imaginable, and it is promised in the gospel through the Holy Spirit's ministry to all who are Christ's and have learned the secret of living by faith.[18]

Keswick's Strengths

Some words of appreciation ought to be spoken before we go any further.

KESWICK TEACHING FOCUSES ON A REAL PERPLEXITY. How do you do what you know is good and therefore want to do and avoid doing what you know is bad yet still want to do? Socrates held that virtue is knowledge in the sense that those who know what is right do it automatically, but all experience combines to prove him wrong. Ovid was a pagan Roman poet, but when he said that while knowing and approving what was better, he actually pursued what was worse, he formulated the problem of the weak human will in a way that strikes agonized echoes in the heart of every

Christian who is the least bit self-aware. How Paul experienced this perplexity, both before and after becoming a Christian, we have already seen. Every pastor knows that the problem of the divided heart and the double pull is as widespread as the common cold and that inability to get a handle on it remains a huge stumbling block in many well-intentioned lives. For highlighting this problem and addressing it directly, Keswick teaching should be commended, however little we may agree with the solution that it offers.

ALSO, KESWICK TEACHING FOCUSES ON A REAL PITFALL. Rightly it warns against prayerless self-reliance. In diagnosing self-confident efforts after righteousness and usefulness as the energy of the flesh and in insisting that such efforts may be expected to prove abortive and barren, Keswick teaching was on target, and for this, too, it should be commended.

FURTHER, KESWICK TEACHING FOCUSES ON A REAL PRIVILEGE. The believer's union with Christ in death and resurrection and the change of heart thereby produced, are indeed the source both of freedom from sin for righteousness (Romans 6:14, 17, 18, 20–22) and of the grateful love to God that motivates Christian obedience (Romans 12:1). As against the natural man's Pelagian idea of holiness as ordinary human morality, Keswick teaching rightly stressed that sanctification is what Walter Marshall the Puritan called a "gospel mystery"[19] (that is, a supernatural work of grace) and that holiness of life is not achieved apart from the Holy Spirit's inward ministry. This emphasis also calls for commendation.

FINALLY, KESWICK TEACHING MINISTERS TO REAL PEOPLE. It is a fact today, just as it was a century ago, that many Christians for whatever reason do not make repentance (turning from sin to God) the foundation-principle of their daily living and hence are weak, dry, and sluggish spiritually and need more than anything else to be searched and humbled and challenged to that total consecration of themselves to God that would be repentance in full expression. Keswick teachers always stressed that decisive total consecration is the precondition of experiencing holiness by faith, since only the fully consecrated are filled with the Spirit and only in Spirit-filled saints will the Spirit's power flow effectively for the flooring of each temptation and the fulfilling of all righteousness.

To be sure, Keswick language—language, be it said, of pulpit speech rather than of theological reflection—has often made it sound as if what is involved here is like the water supply in British homes, where the feed is by gravity and the taps (British for *faucets*) will only run when turned on if the tank upstairs is full. Teachers of Keswick type have regularly spoken of being "filled with the Spirit" (a phrase used homiletically in Ephesians 5:18 and descriptively in Luke 1:41, 67; Acts 2:4; 4:8, 31; 9:17; 13:9) as if in biblical theology this is as precise and ultimate a category of relationship to God as being justified, or dead and risen with Christ, which is obviously very doubtful. But the summons to consecration that Keswick teachers have issued to slack Christians has always been strong and searching, and there is no question that in thus calling for full commitment they have ministered effectively to many double-minded, halfhearted, world-dominated, sin-indulging believers ("carnal" folk, "men of the flesh . . . babes in Christ" as Paul calls them in 1 Corinthians 3:1) at the precise point of their spiritual blockage. Here is a fourth feature of Keswick teaching to commend.

There is, however, a debit side.

Problems of Keswick Teaching

Keswick teaching, as I said above, is in essence Wesleyan perfectionism modified to exclude the unrealistic claim that sin is uprooted from the sanctified Christian heart. Accordingly, its distinctive mark in all its many forms was and is the characteristic insistence of the Wesleyanism from which it withdrew: namely, that justification and sanctification, new birth and holiness, are distinct blessings which both become ours by the same means. That means is an exercise of faith that in both cases consists of calling a halt to self-reliant activity ("works") in order to receive from Christ as a free gift that for which one had been working—acceptance with God in the one case, the achieving of obedience in the other.

With a clearheaded, clear-cut man centeredness that would have shocked John Wesley (though it was only the natural development of the Arminianism that he so pertinaciously professed), nineteenth-century Wesleyans parceled out God's salvation into two distinct gift packages, each consisting of a separate work of grace—Christ's work as justifier being the first and his work as sanctifier being the second. Through the "holiness revival" of the middle and late nineteenth century, to which "Keswick teaching" gave wings, this idea of salvation as two separable salvations, one from sin's guilt and the other from sin's power, became standard in all evangelical thinking save that of confessional Lutherans and Calvinists, and in some quarters it still survives.

Its last gasp (at least, its latest gasp; I for one hope it is the last) is the assertion I sometimes hear that choosing to be a "carnal Christian"—that is, one who receives Christ as Saviour but not as Sanctifier—is an open option, though not a very good one. This putting asunder of what God has joined in his Son's mediatorial office—namely, the role of priest with that of prophet (teacher) and king—is evidently a latter-day fruit (a bitter fruit, be it said) of the two-package way of thinking.

To its credit, the original Keswick teaching did not lapse in this way. Though it distinguished the two packages, it did not suggest that the Christian is free to opt for the first without the second (faith without repentance, salvation without sanctity). Instead it made the authority of God's call to holiness axiomatic and moved straight to the question "How ought this call to be answered?" But it brought the Wesleyan conceptual grid with it, and this raised problems.

KESWICK ON ROMANS 6. The Keswick way of reading and applying Romans 6:1–14—indeed, 6:1–8:13, which was read as a single unit of instruction on living without sinning—was the result of forcing the passage through this grid, in other

words, of seeing justification and sanctification as separate
blessings separately received by parallel acts of faith. Paul in
Romans 6 is answering the double-barreled question as to
whether and why justified persons should practice righteousness. Read through the Wesleyan grid, however, the chapter
became Paul's answer to the question "How may righteousness be sought successfully?" That answer, as Keswick teachers preached it, came out as follows. To achieve holiness in
outward life, you must first receive the blessing of sanctification in your inward life—that is, you must enter upon the life
that wins, the life of continual victory over sin through a
constant exercise of faith. You plug in to this life by totally
consecrating yourself to God (which it is assumed you have
never before done). Having plugged in, you live this life by
remembering that you are dead and risen with Christ and he
by his Spirit lives in you, and on this basis you ask and allow
him to defeat sin in you every time you find it raising its
head. To maintain consecration and exercise faith in this way
is your part; do it, and your faithful Lord will certainly do his.
In this way you will experience that nonsubjection to sin that
is the birthright of all who are under grace, and living in this
new experience (new to you, anyway), you will know peace,
joy, spiritual growth, and usefulness to others as never before. This was the "crisis followed by a process" on which
Keswick teaching dwelt, the secret of sanctity that Paul was
thought to be unveiling in Romans 6 (verses 1–14, especially
11–14 along with 12:1–2, showing the crisis; verses 15–23, the
process). Such was "scriptural holiness" (note the borrowing
of Wesley's phrase!) according to the Keswick view.

Whether Keswick teaching should be blamed for the pietistic elitism that grew up around it both sides of the Atlantic—the sense of superiority that comes of thinking one
knows esoteric spiritual secrets; the inward-looking, anti-
intellectual prickliness; the smug complacency that uses
peace, joy, rest, and *blessing* as its buzzwords—can be disputed.
Maybe the doctrine attracted people who were already lean-
ing in this direction for temperamental reasons, in which case
the worst that can be said of it as a nurturing diet for them is

that it has never seemed able to correct these particular forms of immaturity and spiritual pride. But what cannot, I think, be disputed is that Keswick teaching is open to biblical and theological criticism on several grounds, over and above what has been said so far.

A LIMITED VIEW OF HOLINESS.   As an account of holiness, setting forth the Christian moral ideal, Keswick teaching falls badly short. It grasps neither the Augustinian vision of a life that glorifies God by praise, obedience, service, and the pursuit of value, nor the Wesleyan goal of ardent, endless love toward God and man. Instead, it centers upon the essentially negative ideal of a life free from the tensions of moral reach (aspiration) exceeding moral grasp (achievement) and from the censures of conscience for not having done all one should. Unbroken joy and tranquillity are the goals set, and these prove to be linked not so much with achieving righteousness as with avoiding the sense of moral failure. But surely it is plain that this ideal is self-centered rather than God or neighbor centered and that it makes against, rather than for, growth in moral and spiritual sensitivity. To make present happiness one's present purpose is not the path of biblical godliness. A quiet, sunny, tidy life without agony, free from distress at the quality of one's walk with God and one's work for others, is not what Scripture tells us to aim at or expect, and Scripture will not justify us if we do. But this Christian version of the secular middle-class dream was the siren song of classic Keswick teaching. No wonder that historically the Keswick movement has been a bourgeois, well-heeled affair, white-collar and socially complacent. Why are so many modern Evangelicals slower than other Christians to respond to their neighbors' needs and to weep at the way God is dishonored in today's world? Part of the reason may be that three generations of projecting at each other the Keswick ideal of life have desensitized us at these points.

TOO MUCH AND TOO LITTLE.   As an account of the Holy Spirit's work in sanctification, Keswick teaching falls short again, for it seems to affirm both too much and too little at the same time. I say "seems" because its architects were laymen and pastors whose agenda was to dissociate themselves from Wesleyan perfectionism while retaining the Wesleyan second-blessing frame, and it may be that the wider theological implications of the concepts they formed as means to this end escaped them. However, if we take their words at face value, the judgment expressed above is inescapable. They really did affirm a perfection of acts, and they really did deny that after conversion God further changes our hearts, and both claims are wrong.

To start with: The Keswick promise of complete victory over all known sin goes beyond anything that the New Testament permits us to expect in this world (*see* 1 John 1:8–10; Galatians 5:17; Romans 7:14–25, about which I have already spoken and will say more shortly). The Christian's present righteousness is relative; nothing he does is sinlessly perfect yet. Behind his best performances lies a heart too little fervent and motives too mixed, and as Jesus' judgments on the Pharisees show, it is morally unreal to evaluate an agent's acts without regard for his motives and purposes (*see* Matthew 6:1–6; 16–18; 23:25–28). Moreover, as has already been pointed out, the Christian never does anything so well that he does not see ways in which he could have done it better. In his attempts to fulfill God's commands, he is like a musician interpreting the score or an actor the script; even when he does well enough to enjoy his own performance, he can always see room for improvement, and his own integrity as an interpreter will make him his own severest critic. Only the very insensitive and the mentally unbalanced will ever be able to imagine that anything they have done is sinlessly perfect. If the Christian is at all alert toward God and in touch with himself, he knows these things, thinks of them often, and is humbled. To be sure, the New Testament anticipates an increasing degree of deliverance from known sins as the Christian life goes on, but to promise total victory over them all here and now is biblically unwarranted and spiritually unrealistic.

Keswick teaching, however, makes this promise, and highlights the wonder of it by simultaneously affirming that we must expect our sinful hearts to remain unchanged from the time of our new birth to the end of our earthly lives. But this is a second mistake, for it ignores the fact that believers are being ". . . changed into his [Christ's] likeness from one degree of glory to another . . . ," and ". . . transformed by the renewal of . . . [their] mind" (2 Corinthians 3:18; Romans 12:2). There is a progressive strengthening of spiritual desires and discernments and with it an observable weakening of particular sinful cravings and habits as the Holy Spirit works in their lives. They will be conscious of the ongoing change to some extent and will be able to testify to it. As I said earlier, any Christian who had no such testimony would be giving cause for concern about his spiritual welfare and would indeed make one wonder if he was regenerate at all.

Here, then, are two respects in which classic Keswick teaching lost touch with the realities of the Christian moral life. I should like to believe, as I said above, that those who developed these features of the teaching had not thought out the implications of what their anti-Wesleyan zeal led them to say and did not really mean it, but whether that would be fair to them I do not know.

LIMITED BY PASSIVITY. As an account of the Christian's relationship to God the Holy Spirit, Keswick teaching fails yet a third time. A strong quietist element went into its making,[20] and quietism prescribes passivity. Quietism, we saw, holds that all initiatives on our part, of any sort, are the energy of the flesh; that God will move us, if at all, by inner promptings and constraints that are recognizably not thoughts and impulses of our own; and that we should always be seeking the annihilation of our selfhood so that divine life may flow freely through our physical frames. We have already seen how the idea of inner passivity was worked into the Keswick formula for holy action. How far members of this school of thought have gone in teaching the annihilation of selfhood and what tangles they have got into over the question whether, when I go passive, I am switching God on ("using" him) or he is switching me on, are fascinating inquiries that we cannot pursue here; nor is this the place to dwell on the incoherent Arminianism that is involved in the notion of "using" the Holy Spirit in and by your passivity, as you "use" the car that you drive or the washing machine that you program and start. What must be said now is that by biblical standards this passivity frame of reference is altogether wrong, for the Holy Spirit's ordinary way of working in us is through the working of our own minds and wills. He moves us to act by causing us to see reasons for moving ourselves to act. Thus our conscious, rational selfhood, so far from being annihilated, is strengthened, and in reverent, resolute obedience we work out our salvation, knowing that God is at work in us to make us ". . . both . . . will and . . . work for his good pleasure" (Philippians 2:13). This is holiness, and in the process of perfecting it there is, properly speaking, no passivity at all.

Passivity means conscious inaction—in this case, inner inaction. A call to passivity—conscientious, consecrated passivity—has sometimes been read into certain biblical texts, but it cannot be read out of any of them. Thus, for instance, to "yield" or "present" oneself to God (Romans 6:13; 12:1), or as it is sometimes put, to "surrender" or "give ourselves up" to him, is not passivity. Paul's meaning is not that having handed ourselves over to our Master, we should then lapse into inaction, waiting for Christ to move us instead of moving ourselves, but rather that we should report for duty, saying as Paul himself said on the Damascus road, "What shall I do, Lord? . . ." (Acts 22:10) and setting no limits to what Christ by his Spirit through his Word may direct us to do. This is activity! Again, being "led by the Spirit of God" (Romans 8:14; Galatians 5:18) is not passivity. Paul's meaning is not that we should do nothing till celestial promptings pop into our minds, but that we should resolutely labor by prayer and effort to obey the law of Christ and mortify sin (see Galatians 5:13–6:10; and Romans 8:5–13, to which verse 14 looks back). This too is activity!

Surely we need not go further. The point is plain. Passivity, which quietists think liberates the Spirit, actually resists and quenches him. Souls that cultivate passivity do not thrive, but waste away. The Christian's motto should not be "Let go and let God" but "Trust God and get going!" So if, for instance, you are fighting a bad habit, work out before God a strategy for ensuring that you will not fall victim to it again, ask him to bless your plan, and go out in his strength, ready to say no next time the temptation comes. Or if you are seeking to form a good habit, work out a strategy in the same way, ask God's help, and then try your hardest. But passivity is never the way, and the overtones of passivity in Keswick teaching ("don't struggle with it yourself, just hand it over to the Lord") are unbiblical in themselves and hostile to Christian maturity.

POOR PASTORAL ADVICE. As pastoral advice, Keswick teaching is disastrous. This fourth failure is the most pathetic of all, particularly in light of the fact that the teaching was developed to bring pastoral help. The unreality of its passivity program and its announced expectations, plus its insistence that any failure to find complete victory is entirely your fault, makes it very destructive. I know this; I have been at the receiving end of it. The quickest way, I think, to make my point here is to share that experience, so let me quote some paragraphs in which I once described (in the third person) my struggles as a new Christian in Oxford in 1945 and 1946.

His perplexity was this: he had heard and read his teachers describing a state of sustained victory over sin. It was pictured as a condition of peace and power in which the Christian, filled and borne along by the Holy Spirit, was kept from falling and was moved and enabled to do things for God which were otherwise beyond him. To yield, surrender and consecrate oneself to God was the prescribed way in. . . . But the student's experience as he tried to follow instructions was like that of the poor drug addict whom he found years later trying with desperate concentration to walk through a brick wall. His attempts at total consecration left him where he was—an immature and churned-up young man, painfully aware of himself, battling his daily way, as adolescents do, through manifold urges and surges of discontent and frustration . . . it all seemed a long way from the victorious, power-packed life which those Christians were supposed to enjoy, who by consecration had emptied themselves of themselves.

But what should he do? According to the teaching, all that ever kept Christians from this happy life was unwillingness to pay the entry fee—in other words, failure to yield themselves fully to God. So all he could do was repeatedly reconsecrate himself, scraping the inside of his psyche till it was bruised and sore in order to track down still unyielded things by which the blessing was perhaps being blocked. His sense of continually missing the bus, plus his perplexity as to the reason why he was missing it, became painful to live with, like a verruca or a stone in your shoe that makes you wince with every step you take.

However, he happened to be something of a bookworm, and in due course he stumbled across some reading which became a lifeline, showing him how to deal with himself as he was and enabling him to see the thing he had been seeking as the will-o'-the-wisp that it is. . . . A burned child, however, dreads the fire, and hatred of the cruel and tormenting unrealities of overheated holiness teaching remains in his heart to this day.

Now I was that student, and the books I read were volumes 6 and 7 of the works of the Puritan John Owen (Goold's edition) and J. C. Ryle's *Holiness*. . . .[21]

The question arises: How, then, is it that many thousands over more than a century have been able to testify to lives transformed by Keswick teaching? The answer, I believe, lies in two facts. Fact one is that this teaching extols Jesus Christ and faith in him and his power in human lives, and many have heard in it no more than that. They have not perceived or bothered about the theological implications of Keswick's key concepts; like British Columbians with their salmon and Englishmen with their kippers, they have felt free to eat the fish and leave the bones. Fact two is that, as was said at the beginning of this book, God is very gracious and truly gives himself to all who truly seek him (*see* Jeremiah 29:13; Acts 10:34, 35), never mind whether their theology is good or not so good. The modern bureaucrat conscientiously withholds benefits till the application forms have been completely and correctly filled up, but our God is not like that! And we should be very glad that he is not. Keswick teaching has moved many to seek him with increased devotion and a quickened desire for his help against their sins, and they have found what they sought. Hallelujah!

But does any of this justify the inaccuracies of Keswick teaching? No. It is not much of a recommendation when all you can say is that this teaching may help you if you do not take its details too seriously. It is utterly damning to have to say, as in this case I think we must, that if you do take its details seriously, it will tend not to help you but to destroy you. Manufacturers publicly recall cars that have been built with faulty parts, because defective parts spell danger. One wishes that teachers and institutions that have in the past spread Keswick teaching would recognize the pastoral danger inherent in its defective parts and recall it in the same explicit way.

THE WITNESS OF ROMANS 6–8.   Fifth (and this for me is the climactic criticism): As an explication and application of the teaching of Romans 6–8 about the life of the justified believer, Keswick teaching is, quite simply, impossible. For as was noted earlier, Romans 6 is not answering the question "How may a justified believer live a holy life?" but explaining why he must. The explanation continues to 7:6. In 7:7 a new question is raised: Can the Law be exonerated from the charge of being sinful and evil, since through it sinful passions come to birth, as 7:5 informed us? Paul is resolving this new question till the end of the chapter. Then, following the dictates of pastoral logic ("therefore" in 8:1 seems to mean "now the next thing you need to hear me say is . . ."), Paul launches, as we saw earlier, into a theological rhapsody on the certainties and realities of the new life in Christ: the life of "no condemnation" for sin (verse 1), no separation from Christ's love (verses 38, 39), and no trepidation in the present moment (verses 15, 26–30, *see also* verses 32–36). At no point, however, in these chapters is he addressing himself to the question "What is the method whereby a believer may experience full deliverance from all known sin?" And there is no warrant for reading anything they contain as an attempt on Paul's part to answer that question.

Also, no summons to any sort of inner passivity may be read out of the command to "yield yourselves to God" in 6:13; for in the first place, there will be no passivity involved if you "yield your members to sin" (same verse, same verb), and in the second place this "yielding" to God is explicitly defined for us in verses 17, 18 as a matter of being ". . . obedient from the heart to the standard of teaching to which you were committed . . ." and so becoming a slave of righteousness. This command to yield (verse 13) is simply a theological inference, the practical corollary of the revealed truth that in Christ believers are ". . . dead to sin and alive to God" (verse 11). It is not a summons to a personal crisis that will change the whole quality of one's spiritual experience; it is just a plain, decisive statement of what Christians ought to do. Paul's paragraph, 6:11–14, is his direct answer to the question of verse 1: ". . . Are we to continue in sin [going on with all the wicked and ungodly things that we did before we believed] that grace may abound?" It is a two-part answer. Verses 11–13 say in effect "You shouldn't"; verse 14 ("sin will have no dominion over you, since you are not under law but under grace") says in effect, "Anyway, you couldn't." You shouldn't, because you have been raised with Christ to walk in newness of life (verse 13); you couldn't, because your old sin-loving, sin-serving self—the dispositional you that was—has been crucified with Christ and is already dead (verse 6), in other words, is a thing of the past (being "under grace" involves that). But nothing about inner passivity is said here or anywhere in these chapters.

Finally the belief that full deliverance from all known sin is enjoyed by consecrated, Spirit-filled Christians using the faith technique makes it impossible to read Romans 7:14-25 in the natural way. What has been said about this passage already has, I think shown that it is best seen as a frank and representative acknowledgment by a lively, healthy Christian (Paul) that sin, stirred up in him by the very law that forbids and condemns it, still controls him to an extent that is grievous to contemplate and that the law, though holy, just, good, and spiritual, gives him no power at all against it, being "weakened by the flesh" (8:3). Keswick teachers developed a new exegesis of this passage. They read it as the testimony of a Christian spiritually out of sorts through trying to fight sin in his own strength, and they claimed that when one learns the secret of holiness through consecration and faith and lets Christ, through the Holy Spirit, do his work at the point of temptation, one travels "out of Romans 7 into Romans 8," Romans 8 being then read as testimony specifically to the victorious life. H. C. G. Moule, in his volume on Romans in the *Expositor's Bible* (1894), gave this view its most scholarly statement—changing his mind, incidentally, for in his earlier treatment of Romans in the *Cambridge Bible* series (1879) he had taken the Augustinian line. But the Keswick exegesis cannot be made to stick.

It is, to start with, gratuitous. Paul's aim in Romans 7:7-25 is not to teach any lesson about Christian experience, but to exonerate the law from the suspicion of being sinful and evil, and he cites experience simply to make his theological point about the relation between the law in the mind and sin in the heart and life. Why should he introduce here, without explanation or comment, a description of a spiritual state in which, according to Keswick theory, no Christian ever ought to be? The point he is making throughout this section is that sin is distinct from and opposed to the holy law through which it works. If verses 14-25 are showing that in Christian experience *as such* this remains obtrusively true, they have much more weight in the argument than if they are only showing this to be true in *substandard* Christian experience.

Putting it the other way round, for Paul to write here only about substandard Christian experience and not universal Christian experience would be introducing an irrelevant distinction that made his argument not stronger, but weaker. The Keswick exegesis thus reflects badly on Paul's brains!

Moreover, Paul gives his analysis from verse 14 on in the first person singular, present tense. Of course he means it to be representative and universal and expects every Christian reader or hearer of the letter to say in his heart, *Yes, that's where I live, too.* But that very fact gives all the more force to the question "Why did he write the analysis this way, if it was not an account of his own actual state of self-awareness at the time of dictating Romans?" Should we suppose that Paul really was spiritually out of sorts up to the moment of dictating 7:14-25, but that he rose to a higher and healthier condition before starting Romans 8? If not, how on the Keswick view can we account for that first person singular, present tense?

Again, no text in 7:14-25 requires, suggests, or even fits well with the Keswick exegesis;[22] why then read that exegesis into these verses, when it cannot be read out of them? Keswick expositors did it in order to save the theory that the feeling that one's worship and service is less than perfect, due to the distracting, diverting, and deadening operations of sin still active in one's spiritual system, is no part of healthy Christian consciousness. But we have already seen reason not to accept this theory, which in any case Galatians 5:17 contradicts. The truth is that there is no objective justification for importing the Keswick exegesis at all.

Moreover the Keswick exegesis when imported is disruptive. Leaving other awkwardnesses aside, it renders verse 25 as incoherent as the Wesleyan view did. It turns Paul's "Thanks be to God" into a celebration of deliverance here and now from the condition depicted from verse 14. It affirms that the verb to be supplied is in the present or past tense ("he *does deliver* me" or "he *has delivered* me"), and that Romans 8:1-13 is telling us how the deliverance has come— namely, through the gift of the Spirit, bringer of victory to

Christians who exercise faith. But what then is the link between the two halves of verse 25? How can Paul *follow* thanksgiving for *present* deliverance by saying "*So then,* I myself in my mind am a slave to God's law, but in the sinful nature a slave to the law of sin" (NIV)? The only possible answer (which some commentaries offer) is: by becoming logically incoherent under the pressure of his own strong feelings, so that he wrote at the end of verse 25 the sentence he should have written at the end of verse 23 and before verse 24. But to posit such a lapse by so strong and clear a thinker in a letter so carefully composed (and for Paul so diplomatically important) as Romans is not in the least plausible. The only appropriate course is to revert to the Augustinian exegesis, which removes the problem.[23]

CONCLUSIONS.   The foregoing pages suggest three conclusions, one historical, one theological, and one devotional.

The historical conclusion is that Wesleyan and Keswick teachings about holiness have been influential mainly because they offer what all Christians long for: fuller deliverance from sin and closer fellowship with Christ than any yet experienced. In situations where Reformed Augustinianism was stressing the Christian's continuing sinfulness, as part of its testimony against justification by works, a vacuum was felt to exist in relation to hopes of holiness, and these doctrines stepped in to fill it. They were heard, valued, and followed because of what they offered to the heart rather than because they had any special cogency for the mind.

The theological conclusion is that Scripture supports Augustinianism against the other two positions, where they diverge from the Augustinian path, but censures many Augustinians for making too much of our continuing sinfulness and too little by comparison of the scriptural expectation of ongoing moral change into Christ's image through the Holy Spirit.

The devotional conclusion is that when Christians ask God to make them more like Jesus, through the Spirit's power, he will do it, never mind what shortcomings appear in their theology. He is a most gracious and generous God, as was said before.

Christ at the Center

This book began as a quest for a better theology of the Holy Spirit than some Christians today seem to have. One main task of his ministry is producing holiness in believers. In the last chapter we tried to crystallize from Scripture a framework of thought adequate to what the sanctifying Spirit actually does. In this chapter we have reviewed the three main evangelical views about the Spirit's gift of holiness, in order both to savor their strengths and to get rid of some ideas about the Spirit that could prove Spirit quenching. To be sure, the discussion has been far from complete. I have not touched on the social aspect of holiness, the sanctifying of relationships; I have said nothing about the training of conscience to discern the will of God; I have not attempted to deal with the life of prayer; and these are enormous gaps, which for the present I shall have to leave yawning. Moreover, I have not yet related my analysis to our guiding principle that the Holy Spirit's new covenant ministry in all its distinctive aspects is essentially to glorify Christ to us and in us and through us and to cause us consciously to live in and from our relationship to him as our Saviour, Lord, and God. Perhaps the best way to pull together the threads of this and the previous chapter will be to state three simple scriptural points about holiness to which that guiding principle leads us and which the facts already reviewed will serve to illustrate. Here they are.

1. HOLINESS MEANS CHRIST CENTEREDNESS AS ONE'S WAY OF LIFE. Holiness is a matter of being Jesus' disciple, of listening to his word and obeying his commands, of loving and adoring him as one's Redeemer, of seeking to please him and honor him as one's Master, and so of making ready for the day when we shall see him and be with him forever. Augustinians have always known this, though they have sometimes been too preoccupied with their battles against Pelagianism

and Arminianism to let it show. The Wesleys knew it, and Charles Wesley's hymns in particular celebrate it with matchless vividness. Keswick folk always knew it, and the constant stress in their teaching on "looking to Jesus the pioneer and perfecter of our faith . . ." (Hebrews 12:2) has in practice kept them from the bad effects that some of their theological formulations might have been expected to produce. Straightforward, Christ-loving Christians, who may have felt defeated by the complexities of my discussion in these chapters, know it too; like John the Baptist, they are happy to decrease so that their Master may increase, and they would say of themselves what the evangelist George Whitefield said of himself: "Let the name of Whitefield perish, but Christ be glorified!" This Jesus centeredness is the basic form of Christian holiness, and it is to this that the Spirit leads us all in his sanctifying work. The holiest Christians are not those most concerned about holiness as such, but those whose minds and hearts and goals and purposes and love and hope are most fully focused on our Lord Jesus Christ. On this, surely, we can and should agree.

2. HOLINESS MEANS LAW KEEPING AS ONE'S WAY OF LOVE.   Holiness springs from knowing the love of one's holy God in Christ. The holy person, gazing at Calvary's cross, knows that he has been loved mightily and loves his God and his neighbor mightily in response. Of the three traditions we examined, the Wesleyan voiced this most vigorously; Augustinians like Augustine, Bernard, and Whitefield fully displayed it in their lives, though it cannot be said that Augustinianism has always been so clearheaded and warmhearted about it as the Wesleys were; Keswick teaching, with its constant tincture of religious egoism, made less of the point than did either of the other two views. However, no evangelical Christian can ever have been wholly unaware that the heart of holiness is love.

How then is love to God and men to find expression? The answer is by keeping God's commands and holding to his revealed ideals for human life—in other words, by keeping his law, as interpreted for Christians in the New Testament. Law keeping out of love is the true path of holiness. But this is something biblical Christians have not always managed to grasp well. There have always been those on the one hand who have claimed that if the Spirit indwells you and the motive of love is strong within you, you do not need to study God's law in Scripture in order to learn his will, for you will always be made immediately aware in every situation what it is that he wants. On the other hand there have always been those whose zeal for law keeping has so dried up their love that they ended up more like Pharisees than Christians. Of our three traditions, the Augustinian, with its vivid sense of the difference between the ways of the kingdoms of this world and life in the kingdom of God, along with its passion for Christianizing all life, has done most to make God's will and standards clear from Scripture, while holding tenaciously to love, joined with the praise of God, as the authentic Christian motive. Wesley's ethic of devotion and philanthropy was highly individualistic, but within its range it was biblical and thoroughly worked out. Keswick teaching tended always to assume that you knew God's requirements and your only question was how to find power to observe them, and since Keswick's vision of the good life was (speaking generally) pietistic and world denying, not to say world ignoring, it was not to be expected that very much homework on God's law would be done in its sphere of influence. Yet there is here no difference of basic principle: All three traditions have always known that the way to show that you love God and men is to keep God's law.

Perhaps, however, none of them has laid enough stress on the fact that Jesus Christ himself is, so to speak, the law incarnate and is also the Christian's Lawgiver through the teaching he began on earth and completed from his throne, via the apostles. Yet it is so, and a fundamental part of the Holy Spirit's work is to lead Christians to acknowledge and honor Jesus in both capacities as they obey his teaching and follow his example. As Evangelicals a century ago backed off from the theme of God's fatherhood because the liberals made much of it, so for centuries they seem to have backed off from the theme of the imitation of Christ because Roman Catholics have made much of it. But "let's be different" is a principle of reaction, and reaction rarely works righteousness. The truth seems to be that the imitation of Christ is a theme the Spirit is calling us all to explore more diligently, inasmuch as Jesuslikeness of character and attitudes is the truest holiness for us all. On this also, surely, we can and should agree.

3. HOLINESS MEANS EXPERIENCING THE BAPTISMAL PATTERN AS ONE'S LIFE OF FAITH. Christian baptism, whether administered by immersion, pouring, or sprinkling is passing under water, which signifies death, and then coming "out from under," which signifies resurrection. The death and resurrection signified are both physical (future) and spiritual (present). And the spiritual death and resurrection that is in view is not just the once-for-all event of becoming a Christian, but the continuing experience of "always carrying in the body the death of Jesus, that the life of Jesus may also be manifested in our bodies" (2 Corinthians 4:10). For this is to be the pattern of our whole lives. Through the self-negations of love and obedience and the tribulations of pain and loss for Jesus' sake, we enter into a thousand little deaths day by day, and through the ministry of the Spirit, we rise out of those little deaths into constantly recurring experiences of risen life with Christ.

> Jesus, my all in all thou art:
>   My rest in toil, my ease in pain,
> The medicine of my broken heart,
>   In war my peace, in loss my gain,
> My smile beneath the tyrant's frown,
> In shame my glory and my crown:
>
> In want my plentiful supply,
>   In weakness my almighty pow'r,
> In bonds my perfect liberty,
>   My light in Satan's darkest hour,
> In grief my joy unspeakable,
> My life in death, heaven in hell.

Thus Charles Wesley verbalized this category of experience, and it could hardly be put better. The life of holiness is supernatural, not only because of the Spirit's secret work in our hearts, but also because help from Christ is constantly known in it. In this sense it is a life of constant, conscious, expectant faith. The Spirit stirs us to look to Christ for the moral strength we need—gentleness, compassion, willingness to share and forgive; patience, tenacity, consistency; courage, fairmindedness, forbearance, the capacity to keep sweet, and so forth. And as, having prayed and praying still, we seek to practice these virtues, we find that we are enabled to do so. All three traditions have always proclaimed this (though Keswick teaching obscured itself by introducing the passivity motif), and if there is one thing more than another that the church needs today, it is to learn afresh the reality of Christ's supernatural sanctifying power, by which alone holiness can be achieved in our era of ethical relativism and moral collapse. So the call to all Christians is to prove and proclaim this power, and make as much of it as we can! On that, too, surely, we can all agree.

I give the final word to Charles Wesley, the supreme poet of Christian experience. Here he expresses to perfection the prayerful state of mind of those in whom the Spirit is working holiness; and if it strikes us that one or two of his phrases suggest doctrinal misconceptions, we should tell ourselves that just as there is a time for making an issue of such things, so also there is a time for letting them pass. Listen to him, and learn to identify.

> Jesus, my strength, my hope,
> On thee I cast my care,
> With humble confidence look up,
> And know thou hear'st my prayer.
> Give me on thee to wait,
> Till I can all things do,
> On thee, almighty to create,
> Almighty to renew.

I want a godly fear,
A quick discerning eye
That looks to thee when sin is near,
And sees the tempter fly;
A spirit still prepared,
And armed with jealous care,
Forever standing on its guard,
And watching unto prayer.

I want a true regard,
A single, steady aim,
Unmoved by threatening or reward,
To thee and thy great name;
A jealous, just concern
For thine, immortal praise;
A pure desire that all may learn
And glorify thy grace.

I rest upon thy word:
The promise is for me;
My succour and salvation, Lord,
Shall surely come from thee:
But let me still abide,
Nor from my hope remove,
Till thou my patient spirit guide
Into thy perfect love.

5

Mapping the Spirit's Path: The Charismatic Life

A NEW SPIRITUAL FORCE.   In our study of what keeping in step with the Holy Spirit involves for us today, we must next take a long, hard look at the charismatic movement. For this movement claims to be a major channel, perhaps *the* major channel, of the Holy Spirit's work in and through the church at this present time. Not yet a quarter of a century old, it boasts more than 20 million adherents and has significantly touched the entire world church—Roman Catholic, Orthodox, Anglican and nonepiscopal Protestant—at all levels of life and personnel and across a wide theological spectrum. Sometimes it is called Neo-Pentecostalism because, like the older Pentecostalism that spread round the world at the start of this century, it affirms Spirit baptism as a distinct post-conversion, post-water-baptism experience, universally needed and universally available to those who seek it. The movement has grown, however, independently of the Pentecostal denominations, whose suspicions of its nonseparatist inclusiveness have been (and in some quarters remain) deep, and *charismatic renewal* is its own preferred name for itself today. For it sees itself as a revitalizing reentry into a long-lost world of gifts and ministries of the Holy Spirit, a reentry that immeasurably deepens individual spiritual lives and through which all Christendom may in due course find quickening. Charismatic folk everywhere stand on tiptoe, as it were, in excited expectation of great things in store for the church as the movement increasingly takes hold.

Already its spokesmen claim for it major ecumenical significance. "This movement is the most unifying in Christendom today," writes Michael Harper. "Only in this movement are all streams uniting, and all ministries being accepted and practised."[1] The claim is true. It is a common complaint that ecumenical energy of the conventional sort is waning; but transdenominational charismatic fellowship, with its international leadership and attendant linking organizations, goes from strength to strength.

Ecumenically its technique is distinctive: It seeks first and foremost to realize oneness in Christ experientially, in celebration and ministry, confident that theological convergence will follow. "This open stance," writes Richard Quebedeaux, "whereby the Holy Spirit is seen to lead people to theological truth *following* (rather than prerequisite to) a common experience, is clearly ascendant throughout Neo-Pentecostalism; it is one reason why [in it] evangelicals, liberals and Roman Catholics have been joined together (spiritually, at least) for the first time."[2] Though in each main-line denomination charismatics are a relatively small minority, the movement's cumulative impact has been considerable and is likely to be greater rather than less as the future unfolds.

Writing in 1953, before the charismatic renewal began, Lesslie Newbigin typecast the Protestant and Catholic views of the church as "the congregation of the faithful" and "the body of Christ" respectively and went on to describe the Christianity of the Pentecostal churches as an authentic third stream of Christian awareness, embodying a view of the church as "the community of the Holy Spirit." This, he said, is now needed to fertilize and irrigate the other two views. He put his point as a question: "May it not be that the great churches of the Catholic and Protestant traditions will have to be humble enough to receive [a new understanding of the Holy Spirit] in fellowship with their brethren in the various groups of the Pentecostal type with whom at present they have scarcely any fellowship at all?"[3] Newbigin's question still looms, and with an extended application, as we survey the pervasive phenomenon of charismatic renewal a quarter of a century later.

Tensions

The two constituencies in which charismatic renewal has made most impact are the Roman Catholic and the evangelical. The former, after some initial gulping and spluttering, has accepted the charismatic emphasis as prompted by God and is currently digesting it without too much trouble. In the latter it has led to major tensions that in some quarters are still acute. One of the top ten questions among Evangelicals today is whether one is for or against the charismatics. It is a bad, polarizing, party-minded, Corinthian sort of question; I regularly parry it by saying that I am for the Holy Spirit. But why is it asked so often and so anxiously? The answer is that the charismatic movement, stepchild of Pentecostalism, which itself sprang at the start of this century out of the older Wesleyan heritage, is so much like historic evangelicalism that differences from that evangelicalism are at once felt as a threat and a challenge. Only those who have basic convictions in common can clash directly.

DIFFERENCES AND SIMILARITIES.   To be specific: The evangelical movement, which plays a minority role in most Protestant denominations today, centers upon a loyalty to God's revealed truth and a longing to see that truth reform and renew those denominations, and with them the whole Christian world. The charismatic movement celebrates the ministry of the Holy Spirit in Christian experience—an authentic evangelical theme, as we have seen—but fights no battle for purity of doctrine, trusting instead in the unitive power of shared feelings and expression. The evangelical movement calls for conversion to Jesus Christ and seeks to ground believers is a rational, disciplined piety. The charismatic movement summons them to open their lives to the Holy Spirit and to expect nonrational and suprarational elements to appear in their subsequent communion with God. Evangelical theology is precise and sharp honed as a result of centuries of controversy reflecting the conviction that where truth fails, life will fail, too. Charismatic theology by comparison looks loose, erratic, and naive, and the movement's tolerance of variations, particularly when these are backed by "prophecies" received through prayer, suggests a commitment to given truth in Scripture that is altogether too fragile.

Yet Evangelicals and charismatics are plainly at one in relation to such supposedly evangelical distinctives as faith and repentance; love to the Lord Jesus Christ, who forgives and saves; lives changed by the Spirit's power; learning about God from God through Scripture; bold, expectant, intimate free-form prayer; small-group ministry; and a delight in swinging singing. The two movements, evangelical and charismatic, in reality are overlapping circles. Many Evangelicals will define themselves as charismatics; many charismatics will define themselves as Evangelicals. Historically and in its current style, notwithstanding its embrace of people with some nonevangelical beliefs, the charismatic movement appears as evangelicalism's half-sister, which helps to explain why self-conscious evangelical reactions to the phenomena of charismatic renewal sometimes seem to smack of sibling rivalry!

That, however, is not the whole story. Genuine theological differences exist, and the debating of them can be sharp. Thus, some Evangelicals think the quest for postconversion Spirit baptism and experience of those sign gifts that accompanied the ministry of the apostles—tongues, interpretation of tongues, healing gifts, faith to effect miracles, and the receiving of direct communications from God through visions, dreams, and inward impressions to be relayed as prophecy—is categorically negated by Scripture, and they suppose that what charismatics find when they seek these things is given them by Satan to their damage, rather than by God for their good. Other Evangelicals regard charismatic experience, theologized in conventional charismatic terms, as at least an authentic mutation of biblical godliness, still valid for some if not required of all. Other Evangelicals value the worshipful, informal, ardent, warmhearted charismatic ethos, while rejecting the distinctives of charismatic theology and ascribing the phenomena of Spirit baptism and the supposed sign gifts to the psychological power of group expectations and pressures. Of these evangelical interpreters, some minimize, some maximize, the reality of God's grace in charismatic experience. Charismatics, for their part, see need to insist on the renewal today of the sign gifts and the necessity of Spirit baptism and to arraign the noncharismatic community for having quenched the Spirit by not seeking what they themselves have been privileged to find. Though living in peace is an ideal that most charismatics would claim to have embraced, it is sometimes honored in the breach as well as in the observance.

Also there have been bad experiences. The charismatic movement has often invaded churches in the form of a reaction (sometimes justified) against formalism, intellectualism, and institutionalism and in favor of a freewheeling experientialism. Such a swing of the pendulum is bound both to win converts and to produce division; frustration-fed reactions always do. Many churches have split because charismatics have either hived off or, in effect, have driven others out—in both cases with an apparently good conscience. Other churches contain charismatic cliques who keep a low profile but constantly scheme to move things their way, hoping in due course to take over. Exuberant folk who keep saying that every Christian who is really alive will speak in tongues, that only charismatics achieve anything for God these days, that noncharismatic believers are substandard, and that the only reason why any Christians lack charismatic experience is that through ignorance or unwillingness they have failed to seek it are not easy to integrate into ordinary congregations. It is no wonder if pastors who have tried end up feeling bruised and are cool toward the movement that spawned these ideas.

If, however, we are to evaluate the charismatic renewal

fairly and see clearly what the Spirit of God is doing in it, we must try to distance ourselves from the memory of our own experiences, whether bad or good; otherwise we shall tend to generalize from those experiences alone, and that will be far too small a sample of evidence. When I published an article on the charismatic renewal some years ago, I had letters from a man who had known two cases of charismatic clergymen leaving their wives and running off with their choir directors; he wanted me to subscribe the generalization that this is how all charismatic clergy behave and was clearly pained to find that I could not do so. But one swallow does not make a summer, and two rascal clergymen do not make a behavior pattern. My own experiences in fellowship with charismatics have been almost all good, but I shall not generalize from these either. In seeking to understand the charismatic phenomenon, I shall cast my net as wide as I can.[4]

Charismatic Distinctives Reviewed

What are the distinctive convictions of this transdenominational, cross-traditional movement?

The first thing to point out is that, in relation to the creeds and confessions of their own churches, charismatics have nothing distinctive to say at all. They appear as theological primitives, recalling their churches not only to apostolic Christian experience, but also to the "old paths" of supernaturalist belief. They are "sound" (though sometimes superficial) on the Trinity, the Incarnation, the objective significance of the Atonement and the divine authority of the Bible, and they see Christianity conventionally in terms of the three traditional r's: ruin, redemption and regeneration. But theological reflection does not turn them on; they know that this is not what their movement is really about. Their biblical exposition is simple to the point of naiveté, and few of them seem to know or care that in their own ranks different theologies of charismatic experience are promoted. In their own denominations, their concern is not so much to rethink inherited traditions, doctrinal and devotional, as to reanimate them; so Roman Catholics pray the Mass, invoke the Virgin (whom they view as a pioneer charismatic), and run through the rosary with renewed ardor, while Anglicans rejoice to find that Cranmer's liturgy is now marvelously alive for them. ("Every word of it glows," a middle-aged charismatic said to me.)

Generally speaking, and ignoring the centrifugal lunatic fringe that the renewal, like every other lively movement in this fallen world, was bound to produce sooner or later, charismatics are loyal denominationalists who take as their starting point what their church professes and devote their thoughts, prayers, and efforts to revitalizing its practice. And it is in connection with the revitalizing of practice through the renewing of experience that the charismatic distinctives are voiced. They are five in number, and though each of the five is affirmed with a wide variety of emphasis, sophistication, and flexibility and fitted into various theological schemes according to who is speaking, they stand together as in broad terms the ideological masthead of charismatic renewal all the world over. They are as follows:

1. A MAJOR POSTCONVERSION ENRICHING OF PERSONAL CHRISTIAN EXPERIENCE. It is claimed that usually, if not invariably, a momentous divine work takes place in each Christian's life some time after he has begun actively to respond to God. This work differs in idea from both conversion as understood by evangelical Protestants and baptismal incorporation into Christ as traditionally understood by Catholic sacramentalists, Roman, Orthodox, and Anglican. Usually (so the claim runs) this blessing needs to be specifically sought from God, and perhaps sought at length (though this belief characterizes the old Pentecostalism rather than the new, which more often stresses the immediate availability of the Spirit's fullness). The name usually given to it, commonly though not invariably on the basis that the New Testament phraseology echoed does in fact refer to this second work of grace, is baptism in, or with, or by, the Holy Spirit.

Spirit baptism is ordinarily expounded as a vast intensifying of the Christian's consciousness of four things:

1. The sovereign love to him of the God who through redemption and adoption has become his heavenly Father and his own consequent privilege as an heir of glory and in a real sense already a possessor and inhabitant of heaven
2. The closeness and adequacy of Jesus Christ the Lord as his living, loving Saviour, Master, and Friend
3. The indwelling, enabling, and supportive power of the Holy Spirit in all dimensions and depths of his personal life
4. The reality of the demonic (personal evil) and of spiritual conflict with "... the world rulers of this present darkness ..." (Ephesians 6:12) as a basic element in Christian life and service

2. SPEAKING IN TONGUES. Glossolalia (uttering sounds unintelligible to oneself) is claimed to be the usual accompaniment and sign of baptism in the Holy Spirit. It is seen as a God-given capacity for prayer and praise, valuable because, as experience shows, it enables worshipers to sustain and indeed heighten moods of adoration, penitence, petition, and intercession in a way they could not do otherwise. The gift is regarded as mainly, though not entirely, for private devotional use. Subjectively, it is a matter of letting one's vocal chords run free as one lifts one's heart to God, and as with learning to swim, confidence in entrusting oneself to the medium (the water in the one case, babbling utterance in the other) has much to do with one's measure of success and enjoyment.

Glossolalia is not, as is often thought (and as the NEB mistranslations in 1 Corinthians 14 suggest[5]), an ecstatic thing. "Christian speaking in tongues is done as objectively as any other speaking, while the person is in full possession and control of his wits and volition, and in no strange state of mind whatever"[6] and once the novelty has worn off, "at times the glossolalic feels a singular *lack* of emotion while speaking in tongues."[7] Usually, though not invariably, glossolalia persists in the experience of those who have once begun it, as a mode of prayer that seems real and right for them, into which they can slip at will; and though they allow it to be a lesser gift, according to Paul's estimate in 1 Corinthians 14:1-19, yet they prize it because of the devotional help it brings them. Whether one's first entry into it was spontaneous and involuntary or by learning a vocal technique for it (both happen) does not affect its devotional value once one can manage it.

3. SPIRITUAL GIFTS.   Understanding gifts as capacities to express and communicate the knowledge and power of Christ for the edifying of the church (which, as we saw, seems to be Paul's concept of a *charisma*), charismatics usually claim that all the "sign gifts" of the New Testament period are now once more being received, after centuries of almost total abeyance. That the more ordinary gifts of teaching, rule, management, giving, and supporting (*see* Romans 12:4-8; 1 Corinthians 12:28-30) have been constantly bestowed down the Christian centuries and are being given still is not denied. Nonetheless, the renewal of sign gifts is seen as, so to speak, icing on the church's cake, showing that at this point unbelief and apathy—the result of mistakenly assuming that these gifts were permanently withdrawn when the apostolic age closed—have now given place to eager and expectant faith that God honors according to the dominical formula ". . . according to your faith be it done to you" (Matthew 9:29).

Persons baptized in the Holy Spirit, so it is urged, ordinarily receive several gifts, and no Christian is entirely giftless. Therefore, every-member ministry, achieved by discerning and harnessing each Christian's gifts, should become standard practice throughout the body of Christ on earth, and congregational behavior patterns must be sufficiently decentralized, flexible, and leisurely to permit and not inhibit this. All gifts are for building up the body and must be regulated in exercise for the furthering of that purpose, according to Paul's "body model" of diverse functions expressing mutual care (*see* 1 Corinthians 12:4–26).

In the first days of the charismatic renewal, there was some reason to fear that interest was limited to forming clusters of quickened individuals apart from the churches, in the manner of the now deceased Oxford Group; but charismatic leaders and their followers have consistently made it clear that the revitalizing of the church as such is central in their prayers and purposes and that unity in the Spirit, not division, is their goal. If there are cantankerous and disruptive charismatics, it is enough to say that this is despite the teaching they are given, not because of it, and to point out that in any case the charismatic community has no monopoly of this particular character type.

4. WORSHIP IN THE SPIRIT. Worshiping God should be a personal realizing of fellowship with the Father and the Son through the Spirit and thereby a realizing of spiritual community with the rest of God's assembled family. As Jesus Christ must be central in all worship as the Mediator and Redeemer, who with the Father and the Spirit is loved and adored, so worshipers must constantly seek to grasp and explore their God-given identity in the family where they are all God's children and Jesus Christ is their elder brother. So when the congregation meets, the liturgical structure of worship must be loose enough to allow for spontaneous contributions and ad libs and sufficiently relaxed, informal, and slow moving to let all bask in the sense of togetherness with God and each other.

Different charismatic communities work for this in different ways, but the goal is common. In both its slow pace and its way of highlighting points by repetition, slightly varied but not much, charismatic worship is to, say, historic Anglican and Roman Catholic liturgical forms as Bruckner is to Haydn or Wagner to Mozart. Perhaps it would not be wholly misleading to call charismatic worship romantic, concentrating on the expression of responsive attitudes and feelings, whereas the older liturgical style is classical, exalting God and uplifting worshipers by its majestic excellence of form. This is certainly true in hymnology, where the repetitive, slow moving, sometimes incoherent style of charismatic hymns and choruses contrasts strikingly with the more theologically and poetically accomplished words, and brisker tunes, of earlier days. At all events, charismatic worship aims above all to achieve genuine openness to God at the deepest level of our personal being, so that each worshiper will move beyond the mere churning over of notions in the mind to find God himself and to celebrate and enjoy the realities of life in him. For this, so charismatics insist, time is needed and time must be taken. And it is, I think, not peculiar to me to find that a two- or three-hour session of worship in the charismatic style, so far from leaving one exhausted, can be deeply cleansing and invigorating at the motivational and emotional level.

5. GOD'S STRATEGY OF RENEWAL. Charismatics as a body are sure that, however much or little there may have been of charismatic manifestations and ministry between the first and twentieth centuries, charismatic renewal is certainly central at present in God's purpose of revitalizing his church. Those who identify with the movement thus feel themselves not merely free but obliged to think and talk big, sometimes in ways that strike other Christians as naive, concerning the significance of this particular way of knowing God of which they find themselves trustees. The form in which this conviction that charismatic renewal is the key to the church's health today is expressed varies from spokesman to spokesman, but on the conviction itself there is substantial agreement.

Such are the characteristic charismatic certainties. Historically, they all find their origin in the Pentecostal wave that broke over world Protestantism in the first years of this century. Doctrinally, apart from the claim that Spirit baptism is instantly available (which older Pentecostals did not say), and the fashionable emphasis on "body life" as mutual ministry, most charismatics have simply taken over, at least in broad outline, the older Pentecostal theology. This theology, as we can now see, was a relatively traditional evangelical pietism of Wesleyan descent, with an emphasis on Spirit baptism as a postconversion necessity, on tongues as a sign of it, and (a matter I have not stressed so far) on supernatural divine healing. In their spirituality, the charismatics' goal of realizing the life of God in the Christian soul emotionally, existentially, and evidentially, as well as cerebrally, also corresponds to that of the older Pentecostalism.

Charismatic Theologies: Restoration or Realization?

But now we must note that the charismatic movement is theologically diverse. While most Protestant and lay Roman Catholic charismatics seem to have bought into some form of the Wesleyan-Pentecostal teaching that I have described, those with their roots in Catholic theology (Roman, Orthodox, Anglican) follow a different path at crucial points, as do also some Reformed thinkers who are involved. Richard Quebedeaux is correct when he writes:

> Protestants and Catholics, conservatives and liberals, do not automatically discard their own theological and ecclesiastical differences when they come together in the movement. Nor do the movement's leaders themselves agree on the precise definition of the Baptism of the Holy Spirit. Protestant Neo-Pentecostals, for instance, often view the Baptism of the Holy Spirit as a "second work of grace" after conversion ... Roman Catholics ... look at the Baptism of the Holy Spirit as an interior experience (usually with outward manifestations) of the Spirit's filling and transforming power in the life of a believer who has received the Holy Spirit through the sacrament of water baptism. The exact nature of the *charismata* (such as tongue speaking and divine healing) and their operation as outlined in 1 Corinthians 12–14 are also debated. ...[8]

Broadly speaking, the position is this. Most Protestant charismatics theologize their experience in terms of *restora-*

tion, claiming that in response to faith God is reproducing today all that he did at Pentecost and later in Samaria, Caesarea, and Ephesus (Acts 2, 8, 10, 19), and also in Corinth (1 Corinthians 12-14). Catholic thinkers, however, usually theologize charismatic experience in terms of *realization* of what was latent before, namely the indwelling of God's Spirit to further man's recovery of God and of wholeness in him by whatever means help each individual. In this they are joined by some Protestants who wish to repudiate the idea that all receiving and using spiritual gifts depends on first undergoing Spirit baptism as a second work of grace or that in the experience of Spirit baptism the Spirit himself is actually received either for the first time or in fuller measure and greater strength than was the case before.

The ways part again, of course, as soon as explanations of the Spirit's prior indwelling are given, for the Catholics see it as the direct effect of water baptism while most if not all of these Protestants of whom I speak link it with the new birth (regeneration-conversion-faith-repentance) that water baptism signifies. But in theologizing charismatic experience as *realization* of the power of the Spirit who already indwells and in preferring to talk of the *release* rather than of the *reception* of the Spirit in connection with the start of that experience, these Protestants are at one with the Catholics against the theology that emerges from the Pentecostal stable.

Linked with this theological cleavage within the charismatic community is another. Being generically Arminian to an extent that John Wesley himself was not, the Pentecostal theology regularly assumes that what God can do for his people is determined by whether or how far they "believe for the blessing," whether the blessing be Spirit baptism, deliverance from some sin, healing, or some other divine gift. On this basis it becomes very easy—some would say, fatally easy—to conclude that God always wishes to do among his people all that he did in New Testament times, but will be unable to do so if his people neglect to seek from him each particular gift when and as they need it. The assumption here is that this seeking, so far from being itself God's work, the fruit of his prevenient grace in our hearts, is our independent contribution to the total situation and one without which his hands are tied. Accordingly, Protestant charismatics under Pentecostal influence tend to read all the details of New Testament charismatic experience as paradigms and, in effect, promises of what God *will* do for all who ask, while thoughtful Catholics plus the Protestant charismatic minority of whom I spoke above read them rather as demonstrating what God *can* do as spiritual need requires.

The two notions are not, of course, completely exclusive of each other. The restoration is attributed partly, at least, to a realization of the indwelling Spirit's power (for no sober Protestant or Catholic when challenged will seriously deny that the Spirit in some sense indwells Christians prior to their Spirit baptism), and the realization is seen as resulting partly, at least, in a restoration of lost dimensions of Christian experience (for no sober Catholic or Protestant when challenged will seriously deny that God can reproduce all the phenomena of the New Testament at any time, if he so wills). The two approaches, however, lead to different attitudes toward charismatic phenomena and lack of them. For most Protestants, and some Catholics, it becomes virtually mandatory to insist that all New Testament manifestations of the Spirit are available and intended for all churches everywhere and that Christians and churches that fail to seek them and therefore to find them are thereby shown to be at least in this respect second-rate. Most Catholics, however, and some Protestants, go no further than to claim that current charismatic phenomena are analogous to those mentioned in the New Testament and that God now gives them in freedom when and as he sees that they will be beneficial.

Let me say at once that this latter position seems to me sounder, partly because current charismatic phenomena do not fully correspond to those of 1 Corinthians 12–14, as we shall shortly see, partly because the assumption that what God did in first-century Jerusalem and Corinth he will want to reproduce everywhere in every age is more than I can defend, and partly because I do not believe that if he wishes to reproduce these phenomena today, the fact of not being explicitly asked to do so will at all tie his hands. But the only point I am making at present is that there is more than one charismatic theology, and our reflections must take account of that fact.

Tests of Faith and Life

The most radical question that gets asked about the charismatic movement is whether it is inspired by the Spirit of God at any point at all. It claims to be a manifestation of spiritual renewal, but some, convinced that the sign gifts were for the apostolic age only and/or discerning no biblical basis for the norm of two-stage entry into full Christian experience, have been inclined to dismiss it as eccentric, neurotic, or even demonic. But this is too hasty. Scripture yields other principles for judging whether movements are God inspired or not—principles about God's work, will, and ways that the Apostles themselves apply in letters like Galatians, Colossians, 2 Peter, and 1 John to various supposedly superspiritual versions of the faith. Two basic tests emerge: one credal, one moral.

The credal test may be formulated from two passages, 1 John 4:2–3 and 1 Corinthians 12:3. The first passage says that any spirit—that is, evidently, anyone claiming to be Spirit inspired—who fails to confess the Incarnation is not of God. The thrust of this fully appears only as we recall that for John the incarnation of God's Son led on to his sacrificial death for our sins (1:1–2:2; 3:16; 4:8–10), so that denying the former involved denying the latter, too. The second passage affirms that the Spirit of God leads no one to say "cursed [anathema] be Jesus," but leads men rather to call him Lord (kyrios), which otherwise they could never sincerely do (see 1 Corinthians 2:14). Both passages illustrate the truth that is central to this present book, namely, that the Spirit's constant task is to make men discern and acknowledge the glory of Jesus Christ. So the credal test, for charismatics as for all other professed Christians, is the degree of honor paid by confession, attitude, and action to the Son whom God the Father has made Lord.

The moral test is given by statements such as those of John, that he who truly knows and loves God will show it by keeping his commandments, avoiding all sin and loving his brethren in Christ (*see* 1 John 2:4; 3:9, 10, 17, 24; 4:7–13, 20, 21; 5:1–3).

When we apply these tests to the charismatic movement, it becomes plain at once that God is in it. For whatever threats and perhaps instances of occult and counterfeit spirituality we may think we detect round its periphery (and what movement of revival has ever lacked these things round its periphery?), its main effect everywhere is to promote robust Trinitarian faith, personal fellowship with the divine Saviour and Lord whom we meet in the New Testament, repentance, obedience, and love to fellow Christians, expressed in ministry of all sorts towards them—plus a zeal for evangelistic outreach that puts the staider sort of churchmen to shame.

It will put the charismatic renewal in better perspective if we now draw up a credit and debit balance sheet. First, we ask what particular features of it call for unambiguous approval when biblically assessed. At once a dozen suggest themselves.

Positive Aspects

1. CHRIST CENTEREDNESS. Faith in, devotion to, and personal fellowship with the living Christ of Scripture are at the movement's heart. Charismatic books and songs show that whatever may be true of this or that individual, the mainstream of the renewal is robustly Trinitarian, and the stress on the Holy Spirit's ministry does not displace the Lord Jesus from his rightful place as Head of the body, Lord and Saviour of each human limb in it, and the constant focus of affection and adoration in the worship of his and our Father. On the contrary, the Spirit's floodlight ministry in relation to the Lord Jesus is well understood, vigorously affirmed, and

by all accounts richly enjoyed wherever the renewal takes
hold.

2. SPIRIT-EMPOWERED LIVING.   Emphasis is laid on the need
to be filled with the Spirit and to be living a life that one way
or another displays the Spirit's power. With the New Testament, charismatics stress that the Christian's life is truly supernatural, in the sense that Christ through the Spirit enables
believers to do what by nature they could never have done.
This emphasis shames the formalism and self-reliant complacency in moral matters that disfigures so many Christian
groups.

3. EMOTION FINDING EXPRESSION.   There is an emotional
element in the makeup of each human individual, which calls
to be expressed in any genuine appreciation and welcoming
of another's love, whether it be the love of a friend or a
spouse or the love of God in Christ. Charismatics understand
this, and their provision for exuberance of sight, sound, and
movement in corporate worship caters to it. In the interests
of decency and order and perhaps of social respectability,
too, dead-pan physical restraint has long been the conventional way to express reverence in worship, at least in the
English-speaking world, and any breach of this norm becomes at once suspect. What makes charismatics more de-
monstrative, however, is not lack of reverence for God, but
fullness of happy love for Jesus Christ and Christian people;
anyone who has shared in the holy hugging of charismatic
congregations or seen charismatic bishops dancing in church,
as I have, knows that. Granted, charismatic forms of emotional expression can easily become an exhibitionist routine,
but then cool bodily stillness, with solemn fixity of face, can
equally easily be the expression of a frigid, heartless formalism. Between these two you may make your choice, but by
scriptural standards there is no doubt that a disorderly liveliness, the overflow of love and joy in God, is preferable to a
tidy deadness that lacks both. A living dog, after all, really is
better than a dead lion (*see* Ecclesiastes 9:4).

4. PRAYERFULNESS. Charismatics stress the need to cultivate an ardent, constant, wholehearted habit of prayer. They know that "prayer is the Christian's vital breath, the Christian's native air," as the hymn puts it, and they labor to pray accordingly. This, as we saw earlier, is where their glossolalia usually comes in—not as the declaring of revelations from God in an auditory code for those with the gift of interpretation to crack, but as a personal prayer language for voicing those petitions, praises, and thanksgivings that are already in their hearts, which is what Paul seems to say that tongues in church in his day were (*see* 1 Corinthians 14:2, 13–17). Many who pray in tongues pray much and for long periods of time; it is doubtful whether those who do not pray so much have any right to criticize what they are doing.

5. JOYFULNESS. Charismatics stress the need to cherish and express Christian joy in speech and song. At the risk of seeming naive, Pollyannaish, and smug, they insist that Christians should rejoice and praise God at all times and in all places, and their commitment to joy is often writ large on their faces, just as it shines bright in their behavior. Joy is an uncomplicated, unsophisticated state of mind, and the charismatic way of cultivating it mirrors very clearly the longing for simplicity in knowing and loving God, which lies at the movement's heart. Sociologically, the charismatic movement is for the most part middle-class, and its pursuit of warmhearted, relaxed delight in God as a basic mood for living might seem at first to be just a counterpart to the secular euphoria at which the middle classes always tend to aim; but there is more to it than this. Certainly, their pursuit of simple joy sets charismatics apart from the grimmer and more judgmental sort of believers, but not, it seems, from the teaching of the New Testament (*see* Romans 14:17; Philippians 3:1; 4:4; Ephesians 5:18–20; Colossians 3:15–17; 1 Thessalonians 5:16–18). In truth, their stress on joy is right on target.

6. EVERY-HEART INVOLVEMENT IN THE WORSHIP OF GOD. Charismatics, as we have seen, insist that all Christians must

be personally active in the church's worship, not necessarily by speaking in the assembly (though that kind of participation, when done in an orderly and helpful way, surely merits approval), but primarily by opening their hearts to God and seeking to realize for themselves the divine realities about which the church sings, prays, and learns from Scripture. The concept of worship as a spectator sport, in which a few players (minister and singers) are watched with more or less approval by the crowd in the stands (in this case, the pews), is anathema to charismatics, as indeed it should be to all believers. There can surely be no dispute that in congregational worship everyone, leaders and led together, should be actively lifting up their hearts and minds to God, and if bodily movements such as raising eyes and hands heavenward help people to do that, they ought not be objected to.

7. EVERY-MEMBER MINISTRY IN THE BODY OF CHRIST.   Paul's vision of church growth, as we have noticed already, has to do with Christians expressing Christ to each other in all sorts of mutual service, support, and help, as love dictates. "Speaking the truth in love," he says, "we are to grow up in every way into him who is the head, into Christ, from whom the whole body, joined and knit together by every joint with which it is supplied, when each part is working properly, makes bodily growth and upbuilds itself in love" (Ephesians 4:15, 16). Charismatics take this vision seriously. They insist that active service on the part of each believer is the only regimen under which any church can mature; they deny that preaching alone can mature a church, if it is detached from meaningful mutual ministry; and they urge constantly that all Christians must find and use their powers of service to others, whatever these prove to be—loving speech, loving action, loving care, loving prayer, as the case may be. They see lay passivity as the church's wasting disease and make it a top priority to do all they can to cure it, risking the pitfalls and tackling the problems of decentralized ministry as they arise.

8. MISSIONARY ZEAL.   Charismatics' concern to share Christ, their readiness to testify to their own experience of him, and

their unwillingness to be discouraged when their witness is coolly received are exemplary. No evangelical advocate of lay witness could ask for more. The boldness of Acts 4:13 and 31 is much in evidence in charismatic circles.

9. SMALL-GROUP MINISTRY.   Like John Wesley, who organized the Methodist Societies round the weekly class meeting of twelve members under their class leader, charismatics know the potential of groups. Charles Hummel, with his eyes on the United States, writes of "the hundreds of interdenominational fellowship meetings in homes throughout the country. They convene weekly for worship and praise, Bible study, mutual encouragement and exercise of gifts, as the Holy Spirit manifests them. These groups supplement the regular services of churches in which the members are usually active."[9] The same is true in England and elsewhere. It is not only charismatics who have in the second half of the twentieth century discovered or rediscovered the value of small groups for prayer and ministry; certainly, however, the charismatics have made as much of this discovery as any other folk have done, if not indeed more. In any case, the witness of history is that such groups emerge spontaneously when the Spirit stirs the church and that they are always needed if a large community is to maintain spiritual vitality over any length of time.

10. ATTITUDE TOWARD CHURCH STRUCTURES.   Charismatics are clear that the church's structures, local and denominational (using *structures* as sociologists do, to mean patterns of organized association), must always function as means for expressing the life of the Holy Spirit and for realizing every-member ministry. Structures that prevent these things from happening must be judged Spirit quenching and amended accordingly. The charismatic attitude toward traditional structures (rubrics and forms for worship, patterns of weekly meetings for different groups within the congregation, and so on) is thus neither blindly *conservative* (change nothing!) nor blindly *revolutionary* (change everything!), but in the true sense of the word *radical* (see to the root of the problem and

change as much as needs to be changed in order to resolve it).

Few churches are untouched by the dead hand of tradition in the matter of structures; some are firmly entrenched against any changes in their accustomed way of doing things, and to these charismatic radicalism will inevitably appear as a threat. But in seeing present structures as always negotiable, so as to make room for the full use of God-given spiritual gifts, rather than assuming that God's first purpose in giving gifts is to maintain present structures, charismatics are surely in line with the New Testament. Traditional ways of proceeding, familiar routines of office, and memories of past blessing on long-standing behavior patterns doubtless give a sense of security and may well sustain morale at the human level; nonetheless, the charismatics are right to insist that if traditional procedures quench the Spirit by bottling up gifts that were given to be used in the fellowship, then these procedures must be modified or augmented accordingly, so that God may build up the body of Christ in his own appointed way.

11. COMMUNAL LIVING.   Charismatics have pioneered some bold experiments in community life, in particular the establishing of extended families composed of nuclear families who unite to fulfill ministries of shelter and support that no nuclear family on its own could manage. Some of these communities, to be sure, have come to grief, but there is no doubt that others have seen a forging of relationships, a maturing of personalities, and a strengthening of outreach to needy individuals that would not otherwise have taken place at all. One can only admire and applaud.

12. GENEROUS GIVING.   When the gospel touches people's pockets, one knows that the Spirit is at work in their lives, and while statistics are hard to come by, there is no question that sacrificial giving is a reality among charismatic Christians in a way that is rarely matched elsewhere. An inner-city, working-class charismatic church known to me in England hoisted its missionary giving from £187 in 1965, to

£2,929 in 1970; £21,100 in 1975; and £47,000 in 1980 (double the figures for approximate dollar equivalents). During that period its congregation grew from under 40 to some 250 regulars. Thus an average of £7 per head rose to an average of £188 per head over fifteen years for world church causes, with equivalent amounts being given annually to meet the church's domestic budget. This, I think, is typical. The charismatic ethos of childlike openness, spontaneity, warmth, and expectancy in relationships with God and men produces readiness to give till it hurts and to count the experience a privilege. In this, too, charismatics put most other Christians in the shade.

So much and doubtless more belongs on the credit side, but now we must raise a balancing question. What charismatic characteristics might impede that corporate advance toward Christlikeness at which New Testament teaching aims? Ten defects of charismatic qualities—defects sometimes observed, at least on the movement's fringes, and always threatening—seem to call for mention here. Any of them would suffice to keep a group which fell victim to it in a state of immaturity matching that which Paul faced at Corinth.

Negative Aspects

1. ELITISM.   In any movement in which significant-seeming things go on, the sense of being a spiritual aristocracy, the feeling that "we are the people who really count," always threatens at gut level, and verbal disclaimers of this syndrome do not always suffice to keep it at bay. In this case, elitist tendencies get reinforced by the restorationist theology that sees charismatic experience as the New Testament norm for all time and is inevitably judgmental towards noncharismatic Christianity. When you have gone out on a limb, as many have, in order to seek and find something that you now think everyone should be seeking, though many are not, it is hard not to feel superior.

2. SECTARIANISM. The absorbing intensity of charismatic fellowship, countrywide and worldwide, can produce a damaging insularity whereby charismatics limit themselves to reading charismatic books, hearing charismatic speakers, fellowshiping with other charismatics, and backing charismatic causes; and this is the thin end of the sectarian wedge in practice, however firm one's profession of aiming at catholic unity.

3. EMOTIONALISM. Only a fine line divides healthy emotion from unhealthy emotionalism, and any appealing to or playing on emotion crosses that line every time. Though the white-collar charismatic movement of today is (for cultural rather than theological reasons, it seems) generally calmer than original blue-collar Pentecostalism ever was, its preoccupation with expressing feelings of joy and love makes it vulnerable here. Its warmth and liveliness attract highly emotional and disturbed people to its ranks, and many others find in its ritual emotionalism some relief from strains and pressures in other areas of their lives (marriage, work, finance, and so forth). But such sharing in group emotion is a self-indulgent escapist "trip" that must debilitate in the long run. Generally the movement seems to teeter on the edge of emotional self-indulgence in a decidedly dangerous way.

4. ANTI-INTELLECTUALISM. Charismatic preoccupation with experience observably inhibits the long, hard theological and ethical reflection for which the New Testament letters so plainly call. The result often is naiveté and imbalance in handling the biblical revelation; some themes—gifts and ministry in the body of Christ, for instance—are run to death, while others, such as eschatology, get neglected. Looking for a prophecy (supposedly, a direct word from God) when difficult issues arise, rather than embracing the hard grind of prayerful study and analysis, is a tendency that sometimes obtrudes; so at other times does a doctrinaire insistence that for Spirit-filled, Bible-reading Christians all problems of faith and conduct will prove to be simple. The charismatic

movement has been called "an experience seeking a theology"; *lacking* and *needing* would fit, but whether *seeking* is warranted is sometimes open to doubt.

5. ILLUMINISM.   Sincere but deluded claims to direct divine revelation have been made in the church since the days of the Colossian heretic(s) and the Gnosticizers whose defection called forth 1 John, and since Satan keeps pace with God, they will no doubt recur till the Lord returns. At this point the charismatic movement, with its stress on the Spirit's personal leading and the revival of revelations via prophecy, is clearly vulnerable. The person with unhealthy ambitions to be a religious leader, dominating a group by giving them the sense that he is closer to God than they are, can easily climb on the charismatic bandwagon and find there good-hearted, emotionally dependent folk waiting to be impressed by him. So, too, the opinionated eccentric can easily invoke the Spirit's direction when he refuses to let his pastor stop him from disrupting the congregation with his odd ideas. Living as it does on the edge of illuminism, the movement cannot but have problems here.

6. "CHARISMANIA."   This is Edward D. O'Connor's word for the habit of mind that measures spiritual health, growth, and maturity by the number and impressiveness of people's gifts and spiritual power by public charismatic manifestations.[10] The habit is bad, for the principle of judgment is false; and where it operates, real growth and maturity are likely to be retarded.

7. "SUPER-SUPERNATURALISM."   This is my word for that way of affirming the supernatural which exaggerates its discontinuity with the natural. Reacting against flat-tire versions of Christianity, which play down the supernatural and so do not expect to see God at work, the super-supernaturalist constantly expects miracles of all sorts—striking demonstrations of God's presence and power—and he is happiest when he thinks he sees God acting contrary to the nature of things,

so confounding common sense.[11] For God to proceed slowly and by natural means is to him a disappointment, almost a betrayal. But his undervaluing of the natural, regular, and ordinary shows him to be romantically immature and weak in his grasp of the realities of creation and providence as basic to God's work of grace. Charismatic thinking tends to treat glossolalia, in which mind and tongue are deliberately and systematically disassociated, as the paradigm case of spiritual activity and to expect all God's work in and around his children to involve similar discontinuity with the ordinary regularities of the created world. This almost inevitably makes for super-supernaturalism.

8. EUDAEMONISM.   I use this word for the belief that God means us to spend our time in this fallen world feeling well and in a state of euphoria based on that fact. Charismatics might deprecate so stark a statement, but the regular and expected projection of euphoria from their platforms and pulpits, plus their standard theology of healing, show that the assumption is there, reflecting and intensifying the "now I am happy all the day, and you can be so too" ethos of so much evangelical evangelism since D. L. Moody. Charismatics, picking up the healing emphasis of original restorationist Pentecostalism—an emphasis already strong in "holiness" circles in North America before Pentecostalism arrived—regularly assume that physical disorder and discomfort are not ordinarily God's beneficent will for his children. On this basis, with paradigmatic appeal to the healings of Jesus and the apostles, plus the claim, founded on Isaiah 53:3–6, 10 as interpreted in Matthew 8:16, 17 and 1 Peter 2:24, that there is healing in the atonement,[12] plus reference to Paul's phrase *"charismata of healings"* ("gifts of healings," AV; "healers," RSV) in 1 Corinthians 12:28, they make supernatural divine healing (which includes, according to testimony, lengthening of legs, straightening of spines and, in South America, filling of teeth) a matter of constant expectation[13] and look for healing gifts in their leaders almost as a matter of course.

But the texts quoted will not bear the weight put upon

them, and the New Testament references to unhealed sickness among Christian leaders[14] make it plain that good health at all times is not God's will for all believers. Also, the charismatic supposition loses sight of the good that can come in the form of wisdom, patience, and acceptance of reality without bitterness when Christians are exposed to the discipline of pain and of remaining unhealed.[15] Moreover, the charismatic supposition creates appalling possibilities of distress when on the basis of it a person seeks healing, fails to find it, and then perhaps is told that the reason lies not in God's unwillingness or inability to heal, but in his own lack of faith. Without doubting that God can and sometimes does heal supernaturally today and that healings of various kinds do in fact cluster round some people's ministries, I judge this expression of the eudaemonist streak in charismatic thought to be a major mistake and one that works against Christian maturity in a quite radical way.

The same must be said of the crass insistence by some charismatics (and others, too, be it said) that if you honor God, he will prosper your business, and you will make money and enjoy comfort. In practice it often does not work so. A long line of bankrupt believers proclaims this, and while some may have brought trouble on themselves by supposing that because they were Christians they were somehow exempt from the rigors of proper business management and coping with economic change, that is not the case with them all. In Scripture Christians are given no general promises of wealth, only of testing and tribulation. Directions are certainly given for handling wealth if in God's providence it comes your way, but it is evident that universal wealth is not expected.

In theology, what is being affirmed here is another form of the eudaemonist error: God (so it is being implied) does not mean his children ever to suffer the pains of poverty. The claim may sound plausible when made by a wealthy speaker in a luxurious hotel ballroom, but one has only to imagine it being voiced to Christian villagers in India or Bangladesh or some drought-ridden part of Africa to see how empty it is.

God does indeed sometimes bless the business life of his children in a striking way (first, however, by giving them commercial wisdom, which they use to good effect), but when folk are told that he will do this for all his children, eudaemonism is once more taking over and false hopes are being raised, which could bring on total breakdown of faith when events dash them down. And even if they are not dashed, but fulfilled, their very presence in a man's heart will have encouraged him in unreality and kept him from maturity.

9. DEMON OBSESSION.   In recovering a sense of the supernaturalness of God, charismatics have grown vividly aware of the reality of supernatural personal evil, and there is no doubt that their development of "deliverance" ministry and the impulse they have given to the renewal of exorcism[16] have been salutary for many. But if all life is seen as a battle with demons in such a way that Satan and his hosts get blamed for bad health, bad thoughts, and bad behavior, without reference to physical, psychological, and relational factors in the situation, a very unhealthy demonic counterpart of super-supernaturalism is being developed. There is no doubt that this sometimes happens and that it is a major obstacle to moral and spiritual maturity when it does.

10. CONFORMISM.   Group pressure is tyrannical at the best of times and never more so than when the group in question believes itself to be superspiritual and finds the evidence of its members' spirituality in their power to perform along approved lines. Inevitably, peer pressure to perform (hands raised, hands outstretched, glossolalia, prophecy) is strong in charismatic circles; inevitably, too, the moment one starts living to the group and its expectations rather than to the Lord, one is enmeshed in a new legalistic bondage, whereby from yet another angle Christian maturity is threatened.

Yet, having said all this, it is well to remind ourselves that those who live in glass houses should not throw stones. No type of Christian spirituality is free from dangers, weaknesses, and threats to maturity arising from its very strengths, and it is not as if Christian maturity (which includes all-round liveliness of response to God, as well as sobriety of judgment) were overwhelmingly visible in noncharismatic circles today. In matters of this kind it is the easiest thing in the world to dilate on specks in my brother's eye and to ignore logs in my own, so we had better move quietly on.

Is Charismatic Experience Unique?

An important question to ask at this point is: How far are the distinctives of charismatic experience confined to professed charismatics? I suspect that something of an optical illusion takes place here; from the strangeness to them of charismatics' outward gestures, other Christians infer that charismatics' inward experiences must be very different from their own. But I doubt whether this is so.

Take Spirit baptism. The experience that charismatics and Pentecostals describe under this name was analyzed above in terms of assurance of God's love and preparation for the conflict with evil. Because speaking in tongues is regularly said to be part of the experience, many jump to the conclusion that charismatic Spirit baptism differs entirely from anything known to nonglossolalics. But if we leave the tongues on one side for a moment and focus on the analysis itself, we realize that this is not so. Substantially identical with Spirit baptism, as described, is the experience of "the sealing of the Spirit" spelled out by Thomas Goodwin, the seventeenth-century Puritan, in his sermons on Ephesians 1:13.[17] Similar also are many of testimonies to the moment of entry upon "perfect love" among Wesley's followers in the eighteenth and nineteenth centuries.[18] The same correspondence of content appears in the experience of baptism in the Holy Spirit, understood as an enduing of the Christian with power for service, which such last-century leaders as Charles Finney, D. L. Moody, A. B. Simpson and R. A. Torrey set forth in their teaching, and by which each claimed to have been personally transformed in his ministry.[19] The so-called "Keswick experience" of being "filled with the Holy Spirit," as described for instance by the Baptist F. B. Meyer, also corresponds,[20] and so do many of the spiritual intimacies recorded by exponents of the Christian mystical tradition, both Catholic and Protestant.

Nor is it only to mystics and Evangelicals that such experiences come. The Anglican Bishop Moorhouse was a reticent and unmystical High Churchman. He wrote, however, for posthumous publication a testimony to the night when, in the year before his ordination, after anxious prayer for closer fellowship with God, he "awoke filled with the most marvelous happiness, in such a state of exultation that I felt as though a barrier had fallen, as though a door had suddenly been opened, and a flood of golden light poured in on me, transfiguring me completely. I have never felt anything in the least like it. . . ."[21] It is only natural to suppose that these experiences, all of which have assurance of God's love at their core, are the result of characteristically similar action by the Holy Spirit in each case. It is certainly impossible to treat any one of them as wholly different from any of the others.

Or take glossolalia itself. One man voices the ardor of his praise or the agony of his prayer in tongues, another in his native speech; but is the exercise of heart essentially different? Richard Baer affirms a "fundamental functional similarity between speaking in tongues and two other widespread and generally accepted religious practices, namely, Quaker silent worship and the liturgical worship of the Catholic and Episcopal churches," arguing that in all three the analytical reason rests to allow deeper dimensions of the person to be touched by God.[22] Is this idea obviously wrong?

Or take the Spirit-wrought awareness of how the God of the Bible sees us and how his word in Scripture applies to our life situations. If one man objectifies it by calling it prophecy and announcing it in oracle form, while another expresses it as his personal certainty of what God is saying to him and to others, does that argue any essential difference in the inward work of God in the heart in the two cases?

Is it only charismatics who seek or who find bodily healing through prayer or who practice successful exorcism by prayer in Jesus' name?

Is it only charismatics who minister in love to each other, however little others may have been instructed in the developed doctrine of spiritual gifts?

I suggest that, in reality, charismatic and noncharismatic spiritualities differ more in vocabulary, self-image, groups associated with, and books and journals read, than in the actual ingredients of their communion with the Father and the Son through the Spirit. Charismatic experience is less distinctive than is sometimes made out.

Mapping the Spirit's Path: Interpreting the Charismatic Life

THE NEED TO RETHEOLOGIZE.   We move now to the main question, to which we have thus far been clearing the way. In what terms should we theologize—that is, explain in terms of God—the characteristic charismatic experience? What should we take the Holy Spirit to be doing in the lives of charismatics at the point where they profess a spiritual experience transcending that of other Christians? This is in fact the major question the movement raises; by concluding from its central convictional and ethical fruits that God is in it and by finding closer correspondence between "charismatic" and "noncharismatic" spirituality than is sometimes noticed, I have made it a more difficult question than it would be otherwise. If the typical spiritual experience in charismatic communities was Christless, loveless, and prideful, our question would not arise, for there would be no reason to ascribe such experience to the Holy Spirit at all; but as it is, the question presses acutely and cannot be evaded. For the fact we must now face is that the theology most commonly professed within the movement to account for its own claimed distinctives is deeply unbiblical.

The problem this fact creates for a movement that sees itself as a force for the renewing of true Christian experience is surely obvious. *Experience* is a slippery word, and *experiences* (that is, specific states of thought and feeling) coming to imperfectly sanctified sinners cannot but have dross mixed with their gold. No *experience* just by happening can authenticate itself as sent by God to further his work of grace. The mere fact that a Christian has an experience does not make it a Christian experience. The sign that an experience is a gift of God's grace is that when tested by Scripture, it proves to have at its heart an intensified awareness of some revealed truth concerning God and our relationship to him as creatures, sinners, beneficiaries, believers, adopted sons, pledged servants, or whatever. We have measured charismatic experience by this criterion and not found it wanting. But when that experience is pointed to—and it often is—as evidence for beliefs that appear to be biblically mistaken, we are left with only two options: either to reject the experiences as delusive and possibly demonic in origin, after all, or to retheologize them in a way which shows that the truth which they actually evidence and confirm is something different from what the charismatics themselves suppose. This is the choice we now have to make with regard to at least the main stream of charismatic testimony.

Some, noting the mistakes charismatic experience is said to verify, have taken the first course and written off the movement as delusive and dangerous. Nor can one altogether blame them when one thinks of the euphoric conceit with which the mistaken assertions are sometimes (not always) made, the naive mishandling of Scripture that often goes with them, and, most distressing of all, the seeming unconcern of so many charismatic spokesmen about questions of truth. I confess myself to be one among the many whom these features of the movement bother. Nonetheless, I think I see God's touch in charismatic experience, and therefore I venture upon the second course—that of retheologizing. The reader must judge how I get on.

First we glance at the traditional Pentecostal account of charismatic experience, which most Protestant charismatics outside Germany embrace. This, the *restorationist* view as I have called it, makes the essence of the disciples' experience on Pentecost day, as described in Acts 2, and of the Corinthian experience, as described in 1 Corinthians 12–14, into norms, ideals, and goals for Christians now. The view centers on a conception of Spirit baptism as "an experience distinct from and usually subsequent to conversion in which a person receives the totality of the Spirit into his life and is thereby fully empowered for witness and service."[1] Until Spirit baptism takes place, the Christian is thought to lack essential resources that God has in store for him; therefore he is charged to seek this experience till he finds it.[2] When it comes thus to upgrade him, glossolalia usually (some say invariably) occurs as the outward sign of what has happened. Since only hereby does he receive "the totality of the Spirit" (however that odd phrase be construed), his experience as thus theologized may properly be viewed as completing his initiation into Christ, just as in Anglo-Catholic theory among Episcopalians, receiving the Spirit in confirmation has been seen as completing the initiation that water baptism began.[3]

Recent thorough examinations of this view by James D. G. Dunn, F. D. Bruner, J. R. W. Stott and A. A. Hoekema[4] make it needless for us to weigh it in detail here. Suffice it to say, first, that if accepted, it compels an evaluation of non-charismatic Christianity—that is, Christianity that neither knows nor seeks postconversion Spirit baptism—as low-road, second-class, and lacking something vital; but, second, that it cannot be established from Scripture, for this view has no coherent answer to biblical counterquestions like the three following.

The Theology of Spirit Baptism

Can it be convincingly denied that 1 Corinthians 12:13 (NIV), *". . . We were all baptized by one Spirit into one body—whether Jews or Greeks, slave or free—and we were all given the one Spirit to drink," refers to one aspect of what we may call the "conversion-initiation complex" with which the Christian life starts, so that according to Paul every Christian as such is Spirit baptized?* Surely not.

The only alternative to this conclusion would be to hold, as the late R. A. Torrey influentially did, that Paul here speaks of a "second blessing," not mentioned in his letters elsewhere, which he knew that he and all the Corinthians had received, though some Christians today have not.[5] But (1) this hardly squares with Paul's earlier description of the Corinthians as, despite all their gifts, unspiritual babes in Christ, unable as yet to take solid food (1 Corinthians 3:1–3). (2) It forces one *either* to deny that Christians who lack the "second blessing" belong to the one body of Christ *or* to disregard the natural meaning of "into one body" and render "into" (Greek, *eis*) nonnaturally, as meaning "for the sake of" or "with a view to benefiting," which the Greek can hardly stand. (3) If the latter line is taken, as on occasion it has been, it constitutes a vote of censure on Paul for a needlessly and almost mischievously misleading use of words.[6] Commentators who dismiss natural meanings in favor of nonnatural ones always in effect insult the author they are expounding for being an unclear and confusing communicator, and that is certainly the case here. What Paul is saying in context (*see* 1 Corinthians 12:12–27) is that Christ's gift of the Spirit has made us all into one Spirit-sustained body and that we must learn to live accordingly. The natural reference of verse 12 is to what is involved in receiving the Spirit at conversion (*see* Romans 8:9). Reference to a second blessing has to be read into the text; it cannot be read out of it.

Some, accepting that this is so, have urged that this initiatory baptism *by* the Spirit in 1 Corinthians 12:13 is distinct from Christ's subsequent baptism *with* or *in* the Spirit, referred to in Mark 1:8; Matthew 3:11; Luke 3:16; John 1:33; Acts 1:5, 11:16. But in all seven passages the same preposition (*en*) is used, making the Spirit the "element" in which Christ baptizes, so that the distinction is linguistically baseless.[7]

Doubtless some believers have benefited and others would benefit from a postconversion experience of inner enlargement, but this is not Spirit baptism in Paul's sense.

Can it be convincingly denied that the narratives of Acts, from Pentecost on, assume that faith-repentance (*Luke alternates these words when specifying response to the gospel*) *and the gift of the Spirit*

in the fullness of his new covenant ministry come together? Surely
not.

Paul's words at the close of the first Christian evangelistic
sermon, "Repent, and be baptized every one of you in the
name of Jesus Christ for the forgiveness of your sins; and you
shall receive the gift of the Holy Spirit" (Acts 2:38) are unam-
biguously clear on this point. So, as Luke narrates it, is the
abnormal character of the "two stage" Samaritan experience
(8:14-17)—the only such abnormality, be it said, in the whole
book, for the Ephesian "disciples" who had not received the
Spirit (see 19:2-6), were, as it seems, not yet Christians when
Paul met them, any more than Cornelius was a Christian before hearing Peter (see 11:13). That Peter and John saw the absence of Pentecostal manifestations among the believers at
Samaria as anomalous is evident from Luke's story. The case
of Cornelius, who received the Pentecostal gift while faith-
fully drinking in Peter's gospel, confirms the conjunction between faith-repentance and bestowal of the Spirit, which
Peter affirmed in Acts 2:38, and further shows (as Peter's
words in 2:38 did not) that it is the outgoing of the heart to
God, rather than the water baptism that from the human side
expresses it, which occasions God's gift.[8]

With regard to the Samaritan experience, the guess (it
cannot be more) that God withheld the manifestation of the
Spirit (in Luke's language, "the Holy Spirit" simply) till
apostles might be its channel, so as to stop the Samaritan-
Jewish schism being carried into the church, seems rational
and reverent. The gift showed that Samaritans and Jews were
being equally blessed through Christ; the mode of its giving
showed that all Christians, Samaritan and Jewish equally,
must recognize the divinely established leadership and authority of Christ's Jewish apostles. Hebrews 2:4 mentions
charismata as authenticating the apostles' witness, and all such
manifestations that the New Testament notices were connected with their personal ministry; though that, of course, is
no proof that there never were any that were not so connected or that there are none now.

Can it be convincingly denied that, as Luke presents the matter, *the sole reason why Jesus' first disciples had a "two stage" experience, believing first and being Spirit baptized after, was dispensational, inasmuch as nine o'clock on Pentecost morning was the moment when the Spirit's new covenant ministry among men began; so that their "two stage" experience must be judged unique and not a norm for us at all?* Surely this, too, is certain.

The common Pentecostal-charismatic handling of Acts 2, like that of the holiness teachers (Torrey and others) from whom it came, misses this point; yet it is really inescapable. Luke's theology of the Pentecostal event as fulfilling Jesus' promise and Joel's prediction (1:4, 5; 2:17–21) and the thrust of Acts as a whole combine to put it beyond doubt. It is evident that Luke wrote his second volume to tell how the age of the Spirit dawned following Jesus' ascension and how in the Spirit's power the gospel ran from Jerusalem to the capital of the empire. He recorded particular experiences—Pentecost itself; the conversions of the Ethiopian eunuch, Paul, Cornelius, Lydia, and the jailer; Ananias's and Sapphira's heart failure when their duplicity was exposed; the humbling of simoniacal Simon and the blinding of Elymas; the visions of Stephen, Cornelius, Peter, and Paul—as so many milestones on the gospel's road to Rome, not as models or paradigms of how God always acts. I guess Luke would have been both startled and distressed had he foreseen how some of his latter-day readers would misconstrue him in these matters. For insofar as his story is paradigmatic in purpose, it is "an object lesson in the nature of the church and its mission"[9] rather than in the stages of universal Christian experience.

Against the Pentecostal-charismatic thesis that the reception of the Spirit by the apostles at Pentecost after prayer, with glossolalia, as a second stage of their Christian experience, is presented in Acts as a revealed norm for all subsequent believers, it must therefore be said: (1) This is nowhere stated or implied in Acts itself. (2) It is inconsistent: If speaking in tongues is part of the universal pattern, why not hearing a roaring wind? (3) In the other recorded instances of the Spirit and tongues being bestowed together (Samaritans probably, 8:18; Cornelius's group and the Ephesians definitely, 10:46; 19:6) these gifts came through apostles to folk not seeking, praying, or "tarrying" for them. (4) In all four cases the manifestation of the Spirit came to whole groups, not just to seeking individuals within those groups, to the exclusion of nonseekers. (5) Acts 4:8, 31; 6:3, 5; 7:55; 9:17; 11:24; 13:9, 52 speaks of persons being filled with, or full of, the Spirit, with no reference, explicit or implicit, to tongues. But if being Spirit-filled without glossolalia was the lot of some, then, it may be God's path for some now. (6) From the way he tells the story, Luke seems to have understood his four cases of "Pentecostal" manifestations as God's testimony to having accepted on equal footing in the new society four classes of folk whose coequality here might otherwise have been doubted—Jews, Samaritans, Gentiles, and disciples of John. Whether any more such manifestations took place in the apostolic age we do not know, but it would be gratuitous to assume without evidence that they did in any situations where the lesson of coequality in Christ was already understood.

Clearly much that cannot be read out of the book of Acts has to be read into it to make the Pentecostal case.

Two more counterquestions about tongues now arise.

Can it be convincingly denied that when Paul wrote, "Do all speak in tongues?" (1 Corinthians 12:30), he expected the answer, "No"? Again, surely not.

Older Pentecostals distinguished between glossolalia as a universal, involuntary manifestation attesting Spirit baptism and as a continuing, non-ecstatic, controllable gift that not all have. This is the point of the otherwise enigmatic sentence in the eighth paragraph of the Statement of Fundamental Truths of the Assemblies of God: *"The Evidence of the Baptism in the Holy Ghost. . . .* The speaking in tongues in this instance is the same in essence as the gift of tongues (1 Corinthians 12:4–10, 28), but different in purpose and use." Most charismatics, it seems, agree with most Pentecostals that glossolalia is the universal sign of Spirit baptism and seem to go beyond them both in valuing it as a devotional aid and in expecting that all Spirit-baptized Christians will practice it regularly.

Glossolalia is certainly the movement's badge in the eyes of the Christian public, and it is clear that charismatics as a body are happy to have it so. But in expecting tongues to be the rule among Spirit-filled persons, their restorationism, unlike that of the Pentecostal churches, plainly goes beyond anything said by Paul, which gives point to the next question.

Can charismatic glossolalia, which is frequently a learned skill and technique, which lacks language structure, and which its own practitioners regard as mainly for private use, be convincingly equated with the tongues of 1 Corinthians 12–14, which were for public use, which were a "sign" to unbelievers ("a negative sign towards their judgment," as Stendahl explains it[10]), and which Paul "thought about as a language," conveying meaning and therefore capable of being interpreted?[11] Can the identity of these two glossolalic phenomena be convincingly affirmed? Surely not. The negative resemblance of unfruitful understanding (1 Corinthians 14:14) may be there,[12] but the extent of the correspondence overall is quite uncertain.

On the nature, worth, provenance, and cessation of New Testament tongues, much is obscure and must remain so. Various interpretations on key points are viable, and perhaps the worst error in handling the relevant passages is to claim or insinuate that perfect clarity or certainty marks one's own view. The texts (Acts 2:4–11; 10:46; 11:17; 19:6; 1 Corinthians 12–14) are too problematical for that.

Some exegetes, with Charles Hodge, regard both the Pentecostal and the Corinthian tongues as a gift of languages (xenolalia, xenoglossia).[13] Others, with Abraham Kuyper, regard both as the uttering of unintelligible sounds (which Kuyper guesses may have been the language we shall all speak in heaven), so that the Pentecostal miracle (". . . we hear them telling in our own tongues the mighty works of God" [Acts 2:11]) was one of miraculous hearing rather than miraculous speaking (unless Kuyper's guess about heaven is right, in which case it was both).[14] Of a piece with Kuyper's guess is the view, often met, that Paul saw Christian glossolalia as "tongues of angels" (1 Corinthians 13:1), angelic as distinct from human language. But while this, like so much else that is proposed in the discussion of 1 Corinthians 12–14, is not absolutely impossible, Paul's words in 13:1 are sufficiently explained as a rhetorical hyperbole meaning simply "no matter how wonderful a performance my glossolalia may be." Most, with Calvin, think the Pentecostal tongues were languages and the Corinthian tongues were not, but there is no unanimity. Each case is arguable, and Hoekema is right when he says, "It seems difficult, if not impossible, to make a final judgement on this matter."[15]

Then, too, opinions vary on (1) how far Paul's *thelō* in 1 Corinthians 14:5 expresses positive desire rather than concessive willingness, courteously phrased, for the Corinthians to speak in tongues and (2) why he thankfully records that he speaks in tongues more than all of them (14:18)—whether because he wanted to testify that tongues enriched his ministry or his devotions or simply because he wanted leverage for making his point about necessary restraint in the next verse. Again different viewpoints are defensible.

Views vary also as to what Paul meant by "the perfect" (*to teleion*) at whose coming tongues will cease (13:10)—whether it is maturity in love,[16] or the complete New Testament canon and the fully equipped state of the church that has it,[17] or (the majority view) the life of heaven upon which Christians will enter when the Lord comes. The second view entails that the gift of tongues was withdrawn before the first century closed; the first and third leave that question open, just as the question whether sign gifts were ever given apart from the apostles' personal ministry must finally be left open.

⸱ But one thing is clear: *prima facie*, Paul is discussing *public* use of tongues throughout 1 Corinthians 13, 14, and it is neither necessary nor natural to refer any of his statements to glossolalia as a private exercise. Charismatics often explain 14:4 ("he who speaks in a tongue edifies himself . . .") and 18 (". . . I speak in tongues more than you all") in terms of private glossolalic prayer, but exegetically this is a guess that is not only unprovable but not in fact very plausible. It involves a gratuitous modeling of first-century experience on the charismatics' own ("Paul and the Corinthians must have been like us"); furthermore, it is hard to believe that in verse 4 Paul can mean that glossolalists *who do not know what they are saying* will yet edify themselves, when in verse 5 he denies that the listening church can be edified unless it knows what they are saying.[18] But if in verse 4 Paul has in view tongues speakers who understand their tongues, today's charismatics cannot regard his words as giving them any encouragement, for they confessedly do not understand their own glossolalia. And the supposition that these verses relate to private glossolalia cannot in any case be supported from Paul's flow of thought, to which private glossolalia is irrelevant. This supposition can be read into the text, as so much else can in these chapters, but not read out of it.

As for the tongues spoken for two generations in Pentecostal churches[19] and nowadays by millions of charismatics also, linguists, sociologists, doctors, psychologists, and pastors have studied them firsthand with some thoroughness.[20] The study has its hazards, for the phenomenon is widespread among all sorts of people, and the risk of generalizing from untypical cases is high. Also, it is clear that some students find glossolalic piety unsettling, indeed unnerving, so that strong defensive prejudices arise to cloud their judgment.[21] However, there seems to be, if not unanimity, at least a growing agreement among present-day investigators on the following points.

(1) Whatever glossolalists may believe to the contrary, glossolalia is not language in the ordinary sense, though it is both self-expression and communication; and whatever Freudian theorists may have suspected or feared, it is not a product of the kind of disassociation of mind and bodily function that argues stress, repression, or mental sickness. It is, rather, a willed and welcomed vocal event in which, in a context of attention to religious realities, the tongue operates within one's mood but apart from one's mind in a way comparable to the fantasy languages of children, the scat singing of the late Louis Armstrong,[22] yodeling in the Alps, and warbling under the shower or in the bath. Dennis Bennett, who

was a pioneer of charismatic renewal in the Episcopal Church, actually identifies childish pseudolanguages with the glossolalic gift and on this basis claims that "it is not unusual to find a person who has been speaking in tongues ever since childhood but who did not know the significance of what he or she was doing." How this squares with Bennett's conviction that glossolalia is a Spirit-given consequence of conversion is not clear, but it shows most helpfully what sort of thing Bennett takes glossolalia to be in himself and in those to whom he ministers.[23] It is not the prerogative of one psychological type rather than another, nor is it the product of any particular set of external circumstances or pressures.

(2) Though sometimes starting spontaneously in a person's life, with or without attendant emotional excitement, glossolalia is regularly taught (loosen jaw and tongue, speak nonsense syllables, utter as praise to God the first sounds that come, and so forth) and through such teaching it is in fact *learned*. It is not something hard to do if one wants to.

(3) Contrary to the somber ideas of earlier investigators, who saw it as a neurotic, psychotic, hysterical or hypnotic symptom, psychopathological or compensatory, a product of emotional starvation, repression or frustration, glossolalia argues no unbalance, mental disturbance or prior physical trauma.[24] It can and does occur in folk so affected, for whom it is often, in effect, a support mechanism,[25] but many, if not most, glossolalics are persons of at least average psychological health, who have found that glossolalia is for them a kind of exalted fun before the Lord.

(4) Glossolalia is sought and used as part of a quest for closer communion with God and regularly proves beneficial at conscious level, bringing relief of tension, a certain inner exhilaration, and a strengthening sense of God's presence and blessing.

J. V. Taylor testifies to it as sharpening Christian alertness all round: "Almost all who have described to me their experience of this gift put their emphasis on the far more vivid awareness it has brought them of God and of Jesus Christ, of the world around, and especially of what other people are feeling, saying and needing."[26]

(5) Glossolalia represents, focuses, and intensifies such awareness of divine reality as is brought to it; thus it becomes a natural means of voicing the mood of adoration, and it is not surprising that charismatics should call it their "prayer language." As a voice of the heart, though not in the form of conceptual language, glossolalia, in Christianity as elsewhere, always "says" something—namely, that one is consciously involved with and directly responding to what Rudolf Otto called the "holy" or "numinous," which sociologists and anthropologists now generally call "the sacred."

(6) Usually glossolalia is sought, found, and used by folk who see the tongues-speaking community as spiritually "special" and who want to be fully involved in its total group experience.

All this argues that for some people, at any rate, glossolalia is a good gift of God, just as for all of us power to express thought in language is a good gift of God. But since glossolalists see their tongues as mainly if not wholly for private use and do not claim to know what they are saying, while Paul speaks only of tongues that are for utterance and interpretation in public and perhaps thinks that the speaker will always have some idea of his own meaning, it is not possible to be as sure of the identity of the two phenomena as restorationism requires.

Interpretation

Uncertainty peaks, as it seems to me, in connection with the interpretation of tongues. By *interpretation* I mean the announcing of the message content that (so it is claimed) a glossolalic utterance has expressed. Restorationism invites us to equate both tongues and interpretation with the *charismata* at Corinth. Paul's word for "interpret" is *diermeneuō* (1 Corinthians 12:30; 14:5, 13, 27), which can mean explaining anything not understood (so in Luke 24:27) and in connection with language naturally implies translating the sense that is "there" in the words (as in Acts 9:36). Paul certainly speaks as if the Corinthian sounds carried translatable meaning (14:9-13), and present-day interpreters assume the same about present-day tongues, offering their interpretations as translation, in effect.

But then their performances perplex. Interpretations prove to be as stereotyped, vague, and uninformative as they are spontaneous, fluent, and confident. Weird mistakes are made. Kildahl tells how the Lord's Prayer in an African dialect was interpreted as a word on the Second Coming.[27] An Ethiopian priest whom I tutored went to a glossolalic gathering which he took to be an informal multilingual praise service and made his contribution by standing and reciting Psalm 23 in Ge'ez, the archaic tongue of his native Coptic worship; at once it was publicly interpreted, but as he said to me next day in sad bewilderment, "It was all wrong." Kildahl also reports that of two interpreters who heard the same tape-recorded glossolalia, one took it as a prayer for "guidance about a new job offer" and the other as "thanksgiving for one's recent return to health after a serious illness." Told that there was a clash here, "without hesitation or defensiveness, the interpreter said that God gave to one interpreter one interpretation, and gave to another interpreter another interpretation."[28] The interpreter's experience is that "interpretations" come to mind immediately; in other words, such thoughts as impress themselves on the mind straight after the tongues have been heard are taken as being interpretations of them. The claim is that God gives the interpretations directly; and as with charismatic prophecy, for which a similar claim is made, so long as what is said is biblically legitimate, it stands irreformable because it is uncheckable. One can see how empathy with a glossolalic speaker as a person, or with his or her tone of voice, or with the atmosphere of a meeting, could produce "interpretations" that would be relevant and would edify, particularly if the interpreter's mind was well stocked with Scripture truth to start with. But how such interpretations could directly express the meaning of sounds just heard, so as to be in effect translations from an unknown language into a known one, is harder to understand.

Without venturing to dismiss all interpretation as delusive on the basis of a few slips that showed, and while agree-ing with Samarin that the sense of group rapport which the glossolalia-plus-interpretation ritual creates may be valuable in itself,[29] I think it would be hazardous to assume that here we have a restoring of the gift of interpretation of which Paul wrote. The evidence is just too uncertain.

Hoekema suggests that when tongue speaking brings blessing, its source is "not the glossolalia as such but the state of mind of which it is said to be the evidence, or ... the seeking for a greater fulness of the Spirit which preceded it."[30] This suggestion seems solider than any version of the claim that current glossolalia, in which the mind is in abey-ance, is edifying in and of itself. So, too, interpretations may bring blessing by ministering scriptural encouragement, without necessarily being God-given renderings of God-given languages, as some think they are, and as interpreta-tions at Corinth perhaps were.

Now some counterquestions must be asked about healing and prophecy.

Gifts of Healing

Can charismatic healing ministries be convincingly equated with the healing gifts mentioned in 1 Corinthians 12:28, 30? Surely not.

The model for healing gifts in the apostolic churches can only have been the apostles' own healing gifts, for which in turn Jesus' own healing ministry was the model. But Jesus and the apostles healed directly with their word (Matthew 8:5–13; 9:6, 7; John 4:46–53; Acts 9:34) or their touch (Mark 1:41; 5:25–34; Acts 28:8). Healing was then instant (Matthew 8:13; Mark 5:29; Luke 6:10; 17:14; John 5:9; Acts 3:7; once in two stages, each of which was instant, Mark 7:32–35). Organic defects (such as wasted and crippled limbs) were healed, as well as functional, symptomatic, and psychosomatic diseases (Acts 3:2–10; Luke 6:8–10; John 9). On occasion they raised individuals who had been dead for days (Luke 7:11–15; 8:49–55; John 11:1–44; Acts 9:36–41). They healed very large numbers (Luke 4:40; 7:21; Matthew 4:23, 24; Acts 5:12–16;

28:19), and there is no record that they ever attempted to heal without success (save in the one case where the disciples failed to pray and Jesus had to take over [Mark 9:17–29]). Moreover, their healings lasted; there is no hint of folk whom they healed relapsing soon after. Now whatever else can be said of the ministry of Pentecostal and charismatic healers of our time and of those whose praying for the sick has been a matter, as it seems, of specific divine calling, none of them has a track record like this.

We may not therefore assume, as is sometimes done, that what charismatics have now in the way of healing resources must be what Paul was talking about in 1 Corinthians 12:28. In apostolic times the gift of healing was much more than charismatics appear to have now. The most we can say of charismatic healers is that at some moments and in some respects they are enabled to perform like the gifted healers of New Testament times, and every such occasion confirms that God's touch still has its ancient power. But that is much less than saying that in the ministry of these folk the New Testament gift of healing reappears.[31]

Can charismatic prophecy be convincingly viewed as the restoring of a New Testament sign gift? Surely not.

By *prophecy* I mean the receiving and relaying of what purports to be a divine message. Prophecy is a regular feature of charismatic fellowship. The usual beliefs about it are (1) that it is a direct revelation from God of thoughts in his mind, which otherwise would not be known; (2) that it frequently includes specific directions by God, concerning his plans for the future; (3) that its proper verbal form is that of Old Testament oracles, in which the *I* who speaks is regularly God himself; and (4) that it was a sign gift in the apostolic church, which, with the other sign gifts, was in abeyance in the church from the mid-patristic era till the twentieth century. But all of this is doubtful.

First, Joel's prediction, quoted by Peter at Pentecost, was of universal prophecy as one mark of the age of the Spirit (Acts 2:17–21). Prophesying was thus an activity in which all believers were able and perhaps expected to share (*see* Acts

19:6; 1 Corinthians 14:1, 23–25); though it also appears that not all believers could properly be called prophets (1 Corinthians 12:29), presumably because their sharing in prophetic ministry was too intermittent. Since, however, prophesying is in principle a universal Christian activity, so far from expecting to find it confined to the apostolic age, we should not expect to find it absent in any age, and therefore we should be somewhat suspicious of theories that assume that it has been absent for most of the church's life.

In the second place, though individual prophets both before and after Christ were on occasion inspired to tell the future (*see* Matthew 24:15; Acts 11:28; 21:10, 11; 1 Peter 1:10–12; Revelation 1:3; 22:18), the essence of the prophetic ministry was forthtelling God's present word to his people, and this regularly meant application of revealed truth rather than augmentation of it. As Old Testament prophets preached the law and recalled Israel to face God's covenant claim on their obedience, with promise of blessing if they complied and cursing if not, so it appears that New Testament prophets preached the gospel and the life of faith for conversion, edification, and encouragement (*see* 1 Corinthians 14:3, 24, 25; Acts 15:32). Paul wishes all the Corinthian church without exception to share in this ministry (1 Corinthians 14:1, 5). So it is natural to suppose that ordinarily, and certainly sometimes if not every time, a prophetic "revelation" (1 Corinthians 14:26, 30) was a God-prompted application of truth that in general terms had been revealed already, rather than a disclosure of divine thoughts and intentions not previously known and not otherwise knowable. By parity of reasoning, therefore, any verbal enforcement of biblical teaching as it applies to one's present hearers may properly be called prophecy today, for that in truth is what it is.

Third, Paul's directive that when Christian prophets speak in the assembly, others must ". . . weigh what is said" (1 Corinthians 14:29) shows that the potentially universal prophecy of the New Testament was less than infallible and irreformable and might need to be qualified, if not indeed corrected. There is no indication that any New Testament

prophets gave their messages in a verbal form that person-
ated the Father or the Son, and David Atkinson is surely right
when he says, "the common use of the first person singular
in charismatic congregational prophecy today . . . would not
seem to be of the essence of prophecy, but rather to be a be-
havioural habit developed within the subculture . . . the authority of the prophetic message is not [in] its form, but its
content, and to use a form like that makes the weighing of
the content that much harder."[32] It is just because adequate
expression and consistently proper thoughts are not guaran-
teed that noncanonical prophetic utterances need to be
tested, that is, heard with discrimination. The idea that the
direct-speech-of-God verbal form in which the canonical
prophecies were given ought to be reproduced in the deriva-
tive, noninfallible, noncanonical prophecy that continues in
the church thus appears as a confusion and a mistake.

Finally, when (as sometimes happens) charismatic prophets make predictions of the future, couching them perhaps in
the first person singular as if they were direct divine declarations, it would certainly be a mistake to infer their authenticity simply from their verbal form or from the fact of their
being made at all. The biblical rule, given in the Old Testament but permanently applicable, is that as all putative
prophecy must be tested for its doctrinal content (see Deuteronomy 13:1–3), so the authenticity of predictions must be
tested by watching to see if they are fulfilled (Deuteronomy
18:22). The only effect such predictions should ever have on
anyone's conduct is to induce preparedness of mind for the
possibility that they will be fulfilled, alongside of preparedness for the possibility that they will not. The rule of action,
however, must always be God's revealed word and the wisdom that orders life by it (see Deuteronomy 29:29; Proverbs
1–9); we are not to be led by the possibly deluded predictions
of self-styled prophets. (I think in this connection of the certainly sincere charismatic prophet who told me in 1979 that
God had not brought me to Vancouver to write books, as I
supposed, but to lead Christian people through a time of
great internal division in the city churches. Well, the

churches seem much as they were in 1979, and here I sit writing this book.)

The proper conclusion surely is that, rather than supposing prophecy to be a long-gone first-century charisma now revived and therefore to be dressed up in verbal clothes that will set it apart from all other forms of Christian communication over the past eighteen or nineteen centuries, we should realize that it has actually been exhibited in every sermon or informal "message" that has had a heart-searching, "homecoming" application to its hearers, ever since the church began. Prophecy has been and remains a reality whenever and wherever Bible truth is genuinely *preached*—that is, spelled out and applied, whether from a pulpit or more informally. Preaching is teaching God's revealed truth with application; such teaching with application is prophecy, always was, and always will be and is no more so among charismatics today than at any other time in any other Christian company, past, present, or future. Undoubtedly, declaring without premeditation and in the first person singular, as from God grammatically, applications of Bible truth to situations and persons, with celebration of things that have happened and anticipations of what will happen in the future, is a practice God has blessed to many in our time, both speakers and hearers. But to see it as essentially different from the historic and familiar practice of Christian encouragement and admonition, both formal and informal, and therefore to identify it as a New Testament sign gift, now restored, is incorrect.[33]

Verdict on "Restorationist" Theology

The operative word in all my seven questions has been *convincingly*. That all these ventures of assertion and denial have been tried is not in question. My point is that no arguments to date have been cogent enough to make them stick, and it seems clear enough that none ever will be. Certainly there have been providences and manifestations among charismatics (others, too) corresponding in certain respects to the

miracles, healing, tongues, and (more doubtfully) interpretations of tongues that authenticated the Apostles and the
Christ whom they preached (see 2 Corinthians 12:12; Romans
15:15-19; Hebrews 2:3, 4; and the Acts narratives). Certainly,
too, both in and beyond charismatic circles, there have been
all down church history "second blessings" and anointings
of the Spirit corresponding in certain respects to Pentecost.[34]
But it cannot be convincingly concluded from any of this
evidence that the archetypal New Testament realities have
now, after long abeyance, been given back to the church just
as they were.

We need not deny that some Christians' experience of
spiritual deepening in all traditions since the end of the first
century may have felt like the Apostles' Pentecostal experience; all we need do is note that New Testament theology
forbids us to interpret it in Pentecostal terms or to interpret
any experience apart from conversion itself as receiving the
Spirit of Christ in the fullness of his new covenant ministry.
Nor need we express a view on the perhaps unanswerable
question as to whether God's withdrawing of the so-called
sign gifts after the Apostles' ministry was over meant that he
would never under any circumstances restore them as they
were. We need only observe that they have not actually been
restored as they were, though some charismatics claim the
contrary. In short, it seems plain that restorationism as a theology of charismatic experience will not do, and if we want to
discern what God is doing in this movement, we must think
about it in other terms.

One further remark is in order here. In evaluating charismatic phenomena, it needs to be remembered that group beliefs shape group expectations, and group expectations shape
individual experiences. A group with its own teachers and literature can mold the thoughts and experiences of its members to a startling degree. Specifically, when it is believed that
an enhanced sense of God and his love to you in Christ and
his enabling power (the Spirit's anointing), accompanied
by tongues, on the model of the Apostles' experience in Acts
2, is the norm, this experience will certainly be both sought

and found. Nor will it necessarily be a delusive, Spiritless, self-generated experience just because certain incorrect notions are attached to it; God, as we keep seeing, is very merciful and blesses those who seek him even when their notions are not all true. But such an experience will then have to be tested as an expectation-shaped experience, and the expectations that shaped it will have to be tested separately, to see if they can be justified in terms of God's revealed truth. So, too, if stylized relaying of messages from God is expected, it will certainly be forthcoming, whether or not the Bible justifies the idea of a revival of prophecy of canonical type; and then testing the content of the message in each case will have to be carried through as something quite distinct from passing a verdict on the expectation by which the relaying process was shaped.

Let me repeat: I do not for one moment suggest that there is no spiritual substance to these expectation-shaped experiences. All that I have been seeking to show is that the restorationist claims on which the expectations themselves have been based will not stand examination and that a different theological account of the Spirit's work is needed. This, I think, has now been fully proved. Therefore I move on.

An Alternative Theology

I offer now an alternative proposal for theologizing charismatic experience—sketchy and tentative, indeed, but in line, I think, with the Bible doctrine of man, of salvation, and of the Spirit. It is in line, too, with the largely positive evaluation of charismatic spirituality that I reached earlier, an evaluation that is not affected by the inadequacy of the theology that often goes with it. I introduce my proposal by pinpointing some facts which by now are surely clear.

The charismatic movement, like other movements in the church, is something of a chameleon, taking theological and devotional color from what surrounds it and is brought to it and capable of changing color as these factors change. Everywhere it, or the older Pentecostalism out of which it grew,

began with some form of restorationism resting on the axiom
that the disciples' baptism in the Spirit in Acts 2 is a model
for ours. But it has not everywhere stayed with that theology
and it is deeply interesting to see what differences have
emerged, and why.

In the United States, where holiness-Pentecostal traditions remain strong in denominations, books, and teaching
institutions, Protestant charismatics are mostly restorationists still (at least, their literature suggests that). But in Britain,
where Reformed soteriology, which stresses the unity of salvation in Christ, has had more impact than Wesleyan
anthropocentrism, which parcels out salvation into a set of
separate "blessings," charismatic leaders have in many cases
dropped the doctrine of baptism in the Holy Spirit as a necessary second work of grace and substituted for it the
thought that our entry into a fuller experience of the Spirit
(sometimes called the *release* of the Spirit) is simply the subjective realization of what initiation into Christ involves.
Their German Protestant counterparts, most of whom are Lutheran, mostly follow this path also. English-speaking Roman
Catholic charismatics, too, have come to say very much the
same, in opposition to Pentecostal Spirit-baptism teaching.
They stress the objective gift of the Spirit in water baptism in
a way that Evangelicals are bound to challenge, but avoid the
Arminian idea that faith, or "openness to God," is a trigger
activating God in his character as a deliverer of goods—a
model that Protestant charismatics have not always managed
to avoid. Charismatic experience, as I said earlier, comes
today with more than one theology. Now we must observe
that, as the last paragraph indicates, where the original charismatic teaching has been revised, the thrust of the revision
has been to assimilate it to accepted "home church" doctrine,
whatever that happens to be. Charismatics, while maintaining spiritual solidarity with other charismatics, are more and
more seeking theological solidarity with their own parent
segment of Christendom.

Moreover, the earlier theology of the *charismata*, which
maximized their supposed discontinuity with the natural and

thus their significance as proof of God's presence and power in one's life, is being replaced by "naturalizing" accounts of them, which reflect unwillingness to oppose the supernatural to the natural as the first restorationists did. (It was this super-supernaturalist view of the life of grace as characteristically discontinuous with nature that at bottom divided pioneer Pentecostalism from the rest of the evangelical world and made it so unpopular; super-supernaturalism frightens people—and no wonder.) But now among charismatics (not so much among Pentecostal church members, who are tied to the older tradition) spiritual gifts are increasingly viewed as sanctified natural abilities. Bennett, as we saw, would have us know that some folk speak in tongues from childhood without realizing it. So, too, divine healing is increasingly domesticated by being expounded as a natural element in the church's regular ministry to the whole man, rather than being highlighted, as formerly, as the fruit of a special supernatural gift that some Spirit-baptized individuals have from God.[35] These emphases also have the effect of moving charismatic thought into line with the mainstream Christian tradition, which sees grace not as overriding or destroying nature, but rather as restoring and perfecting it, eliminating our radical sinfulness but not our rational humanity.

It seems clear that all along the line charismatics today are cultivating, in place of the sense of being different from other Christians, which marked them a decade ago, a sense of solidarity with their own churches. Formerly there was in the movement an undercurrent of sectarian judgmentalism with regard to Christians and congregations of noncharismatic spirituality, but that has now mostly gone. At leadership level, the charismatic way of life with God is recommended as vital and fruitful without censuring other forms of devotion; and if some new converts are less tolerant, the leaders know that the pendulum-swing of converts' reaction against what hurt and disillusioned them before they left it is a universal human problem that only time can resolve. Any continuing censoriousness and divisiveness among recent converts to the charismatic way, therefore, should be seen as a local and temporary problem and not be allowed to blind us to the fact that charismatics today as a body, some millions strong, are seeking to deepen their churchly identity at all points. *

So it should not jar when I offer for testing a hypothesis that assumes that what God is doing in the lives and through the experience of "card carrying" charismatics is essentially what he is doing in the lives of all believing, regenerate people everywhere—namely, working to renew Christ's image in each, so that trust, love, hope, patience, commitment, loyalty, self-denial and self-giving, obedience and joy, may increasingly be seen in us as we see these qualities in him. Earlier I listed twelve points where the characteristic charismatic emphases were biblical, healthful, and needed; these support my hypothesis very clearly. I have also argued that at each point where restorationism strikes out on its own, affirming God's renewal of New Testament distinctives as norms for our time (Spirit-baptism as at Pentecost, with gifts of tongues, interpretation, healing, prophecy), it is wrong; therefore, charismatic experience, being shaped in part by eccentric expectations arising from eccentric beliefs, has in it elements of oddity and distortion also. My line of thought will be found to recognize that, though I believe it affirms the central and essential elements of charismatic experience in a positive way. I now proceed to expound my hypothesis. Let it be tested by the facts of that experience on the one hand and by the Bible on the other. Only if it fits the facts will it merit attention, and only if it squares with Scripture will it deserve acceptance. My readers shall be the judges, as I said before.

Assuming, now, that the categories of New Testament theology, being God taught, have ontological status, that is, express the truth and reality of things as God sees and knows it, and assuming further that Christlike wholeness is God's purpose for charismatics as for other Christians, I reason thus.

God in redemption finds us all more or less disintegrated personalities. Disintegration and loss of rational control are aspects of our sinful and fallen state. Trying to play God to ourselves, we are largely out of control of ourselves and also out of touch with ourselves, or at least with a great deal of ourselves, including most of what is central to our real selves. But God's gracious purpose is to bring us into a reconciled relationship with himself, through Christ, and through the outworking of that relationship to reintegrate us and make us whole beings again.

The relationship itself is restored once for all through what Luther called the "wonderful exchange" whereby Christ was made sin for us and we in consequence are made the righteousness of God in him (2 Corinthians 5:21). Justified and adopted into God's family through faith in Christ, Christians are immediately and eternally secure; nothing can sever them from the love of the Father and the Son (Romans 8:32–39). But the work of recreating us as psychophysical beings on whom Christ's image is to be stamped, the work of sanctification as older evangelical theology called it, is not the work of a moment. Rather, it is a lifelong process of growth and transformation (2 Corinthians 3:18; Romans 12:2; Ephesians 4:14–16, 23, 24; Colossians 3:10; 1 Peter 2:2; 2 Peter 3:18). Indeed, it extends beyond this life, for the basic disintegration, that between psychic (conscious personal) life and physical life, will not be finally healed till "the redemption of our bodies" (Romans 8:23; *see also* 1 Corinthians 15:35–57; 2 Corinthians 5:1–10; Philippians 3:20, 21). Not till then (we may suppose) shall we know all that is now shrouded in the mysterious reality of the "unconscious," the deep Loch Ness of the self where the monsters of repression and fear, and below them the id and the archetypes, live, and in which Freud and Jung and their colleagues have fished so diligently (*see* 1 Corinthians 13:12). Nor, certainly, till we leave this mortal body shall we know the end of the split-self dimension of Christian experience, analyzed in Romans 7:14–25 and Galatians 5:16–26, whereby those whose hearts delight in God's Law nonetheless find in themselves allergically negative reactions and responses to it—reactions and responses that, as we saw earlier, Paul diagnoses as the continuing energy of "sin which dwells within me," dethroned but not destroyed, doomed to die but not dead yet. Still, however, the indwelling Holy Spirit, whose presence and ministry are the first installment of the life of heaven (Romans 8:23; 2 Corinthians 1:22; Ephesians 1:13, 14; Hebrews 6:4, 5) and who is sovereign in communicating to us the touch and taste of fellowship with the Father and the Son (John 1:3; 3:24; 14:15–23), abides and works in us to lead us toward the appointed goal, and he deals with each one's broken and distorted humanity as he finds it.

TONGUES.   So what about glossolalia? We saw that present-day tongues speaking, in which the mood is maintained but the mind is on vacation, cannot be confidently equated from any point of view with New Testament tongues. Against the background of this perception, it is often urged that since God's goal is full integration of the individual under fully self-conscious, rational control, the overall pattern of ongoing sanctification must involve steady recovery of such control as we move deeper into what Scripture calls sincerity, simplicity, and single mindedness, whereby in all my many doings ". . . *one* thing I do . . ." (Philippians 3:13; *see also* 2 Corinthians 11:3; James 1:7, 8). In that case (so the argument runs) there can be no place for glossolalia, in which rational control of the vocal chords is given up. But a double reply may be in order.

First, since the charismatic deliberately chooses glossolalia as a means of expressing adoration and petition on themes he has in mind, but on which he wants to say more to God than he can find words for, it is not quite true to allege that rational control is wholly absent.

Second, it does not seem inconceivable that the Spirit might prompt this relaxation of rational control at surface level in order to strengthen control at a deeper level. Wordless singing, loud perhaps, as we lie in the bath can help restore a sense of rational well-being to the frantic, and glossolalia might be the spiritual equivalent of that; it would be a Godsend if it were. Also, if its effect really is to intensify and sustain moods of praise and prayer that otherwise one could not sustain because of wandering thoughts, it could be a positive character builder and lead into what exponents of mystical prayer term *contemplation.* This might be specially beneficial to folk who, as victims of the bustle, superficiality, and unauthentic brittleness of modern living, are not in touch with themselves at a deep level and whose Christianity is in consequence more formal, notional, conventional, stereotyped, imitative and secondhand than it should be. (The charismatic movement is, after all, a mainly urban phenomenon, and it is in towns that these pressures operate most directly.)

In this way glossolalia could be a good gift of God for some people at least, on the basis that anything that helps you to concentrate on God, practice his presence, and open yourself to his influence is a good gift. (For others, however, with different problems, whom God already enables to pray from their heart with understanding, glossolalia would be the unspiritual and trivial irrelevance that some now think it to be wherever it appears. It would be a case of one man's meat being another man's poison.)

SPIRIT BAPTISM.   What, then, about Spirit baptism? We have seen that right at the heart of this "second blessing," as conceived by charismatic teachers and testified to by charismatic believers, is joyful assurance, knowing God's fatherly love in Christ and so tasting heaven. I have already pointed out that in this it links up with just about every "second blessing" experience, Protestant or Catholic, to which witness has ever been borne. I now suggest that the right way to theologize and explain these experiences is as in essence deepened awarenesses of the Spirit of adoption bearing witness to the Father's love in Christ (*see* Romans 8:15–17) and of the coming of the Father and the Son, through the Spirit, to make themselves known to the obedient saint (*see* John 14:15–23). The witnessing of the Spirit and the revelatory coming of the Father and the Son are constant divine actions, but there are times when the Christian finds himself more than ordinarily conscious of them and of the love and mercy expressed in them and communicated by them, and these are the moments of experience to which testimonies to Spirit baptism refer.

These experiences are a fulfilling of Paul's prayer for believers "... to be strengthened with might through his [God's] Spirit in the inner man, and that Christ may dwell in your hearts through faith; that you, being rooted and grounded in love, may have power to comprehend with all the saints what is the breadth and length and depth and height, and to know the love of Christ which surpasses knowledge, that you may be filled with all the fulness of God" (Ephesians 3:16–19). They produce the state of heart described by Peter, in which, loving the Christ in whom we believe, we "rejoice with unutterable and exalted [literally, glorified] joy" (1 Peter 1:8). They are not strictly experiences of receiving the Spirit, though they leave one newly conscious of the Spirit's presence within; nor are they strictly experiences of sanctification, though their effect is sanctifying; nor are they strictly experiences of empowering, though they do empower. They are in essence experiences of assurance, that is, the subjective realization of what it means to be one with Christ.

No such experience as this is really isolated from, and discontinuous with, the rest of one's conscious life, although in narrating it the temptation will always be to make it sound isolated and discontinuous, particularly if a "second blessing" theology of Wesleyan or Keswick type lies in one's mind already. But experience of this kind is in fact no more, just as it is no less, than an intensifying of the sense of acceptance, adoption, and fellowship with God, which the Spirit imparts to every Christian and sustains in him more or less clearly from conversion on (see Galatians 4:6; 3:2).

Why should there be this intensifying—which, so far from being a once-for-all thing, a "second [and last!] blessing," does (thank God!) recur from time to time? We cannot always give reasons for God's choice of times and seasons for drawing near to his children and bringing home to them in this vivid and transporting way, as he does, the reality of his love.[36] After it has happened, we may sometimes be able to see that it was preparation for pain, perplexity, loss, or for some specially demanding or discouraging piece of ministry, but in other cases we may only ever be able to say: "God chose to show his child his love simply because he loves his child." But there are also times when it seems clear that God draws near to men because they draw near to him (*see* James 4:8; Jeremiah 29:13, 14; Luke 11:9–13, where "give the Holy Spirit" means "give experience of the ministry, influence, and blessings of the Holy Spirit"); and that is the situation with which we are dealing here.

Different concerns drive Christians to renew their vows of consecration to God and seek his face—that is, to cry in sustained prayer for his attention, favor, and help in present need, as is done for instance in Psalms 27:7–14. The occasion may be guilt, fear, a sense of impotence or failure, discouragement, nervous exhaustion and depression, assaults of temptation and battles with indwelling sin, ominous illness, experiences of rejection or betrayal, longing for God (all these are instanced in the Psalms); it may be other things, too. When God reveals his love to the hearts of such seekers, putting into them, along with joy, new moral and spiritual strength to cope with what weighed them down, the specific meaning of the experience *for them* will relate to the needs that it met. No wonder, then, that some have theologized it as an enduement for holiness, and others as an empowering for service, and that charismatics, conceiving it as deeper entry into the life of the Spirit, have explained it as embracing both. However, the biblical reality to which they are all testifying, each in a partly perceptive and partly misleading way, is God's work of renewing and deepening assurance.

Let Pentecostal and charismatic testimonies to Spirit baptism be weighed in the light of this hypothesis. Let the correspondence between the teaching and expectations that preceded the blessing and the testimony subsequently given to it be measured. Let the variable physical adjuncts of the blessing—shouting, glossolalia, physical jerks, electric currents in the limbs, trance phenomena and other hysterical symptoms—be discounted, for the view being tested sees all these things as reflecting our own more or less idiosyncratic temperament and psychology, rather than any difference between God's work of deepening one as distinct from another man's assurance and sense of communion with his Redeemer. Do these things, and I think it will be found that the theology I here propose fits the facts.[37]

Conclusions

Some conclusions are now in order. Here are nine.

1. SPIRIT BAPTISM.   The common charismatic theology of Spirit baptism (common, at least, in the worldwide movement as a whole, if not in particular segments of it in Britain and Germany) is the Pentecostal development of the two-level, two-stage view of the Christian life, which goes back through the last-century holiness movements (Keswick, Higher Life, Victorious Life), and the power-for-service accounts of Spirit baptism that intertwined with them, to John Wesley's doctrine of Christian perfection, otherwise called perfect love, entire sanctification, the clean heart, or simply the second blessing. This charismatic theology sees the Apostles' experience at Pentecost as the normative pattern of transition from the first and lower level to the higher, Spirit-filled level. But this idea seems to lack both biblical and experiential justification, while the corollary that all Christians who are strangers to a Pentecostal transition experience are lower-level folk, not Spirit filled, is, to say the least, unconvincing. Yet the honest, penitent, expectant quest for more of God (out of which has come for so many the precious experience miscalled Spirit baptism) is always the taproot of spiritual renewal, whether impeccably theologized or not; and so it has been in this case.

2. SIGN GIFTS.   The restorationist theory of sign gifts, which the charismatic movement also inherited from older Pente-

costalism, is inapplicable; nobody can be sure, nor does it seem likely, that the New Testament gifts of tongues, interpretation, healing, and miracles have been restored, while Spirit-given prophecy, which in essence is not new revelation (though in biblical times this was often part of it), but rather power to apply to people truth already revealed, is not specially related to the charismatic milieu; it has in fact been in the church all along. Yet the movement's accompanying emphasis on every-member ministry in the body of Christ, using ordinary spiritual gifts, of which all have some, is wholly right and has produced rich resources of support and help for the weak and hurting in particular.

3. STRENGTHS. The charismatic stress on faith in a living Lord, learning of God from God through Scripture, openness to the indwelling Spirit, close fellowship in prayer and praise, discernment and service of personal need, and expecting God actively to answer prayer and change things for the better, are tokens of true spiritual renewal from which all Christians should learn, despite associated oddities to which mistaken theology gave rise.

4. GLOSSOLALIA. Charismatic glossolalia, a chosen way of nonverbal self-expression before God (chosen, be it said, in the belief that God wills the choice), has its place in the inescapable pluriformity of Christian experience, in which the varied makeup of both cultures and individuals is reflected by a wide range of devotional styles. It seems clear that as a devotional exercise glossolalia enriches some, but that for others it is a valueless irreverence. Some who have practiced it have later testified to the spiritual unreality for them of what they were doing, while others who have begun it have recorded a vast deepening of their communion with God as a result, and there is no reason to doubt either testimony. Glossolalic prayer may help to free up and warm up some cerebral people, just as structured verbal prayer may help to steady up and shape up some emotional people. Those who know that glossolalia is not God's path for them and those

for whom it is a proven enrichment should not try to impose their own way on others, or judge others inferior for being different, or stagger if someone in their camp transfers to the other, believing that God has led him or her to do so. Those who pray with tongues and those who pray without tongues do it to the Lord; they stand or fall to their own Master, not to their fellow servants. In the same sense that there is in Christ neither Jew nor Greek, bond nor free, male nor female, so in Christ there is neither glossolalist nor nonglossolalist. Even if (as I suspect, though cannot prove) today's glossolalists do not speak such tongues as were spoken at Corinth, none should forbid them their practice; while they for their part should not suppose that every would-be top-class Christian needs to adopt it.

5. SIN. Two questions needing to be pressed are whether, along with a sense of worship and of love, the charismatic movement also fosters a realistic sense of sin and whether its euphoric ethos does not tend to encourage naive pride rather than humility among its supporters.

6. THE SPIRIT. Though theologically uneven (and what spiritually significant movement has not been?) the charismatic renewal should commend itself to Christian people as a God-sent corrective of formalism, institutionalism, and intellectualism. It has creatively expressed the gospel by its music and worship style, its praise-permeated spontaneity and bold ventures in community. Charismatic renewal has forced all Christendom, including those who will not take this from Evangelicals as such, to ask: What then does it mean to be a Christian and to believe in the Holy Spirit? Who is Spirit filled? Are they? Am I? With radical theology inviting the church into the barren wastes of neo-Unitarianism, it is (dare I say) just like God—the God who uses the weak to confound the mighty—to have raised up, not a new Calvin or John Owen or Abraham Kuyper, but a scratch movement, cheerfully improvising, which proclaims the divine personhood and power of Jesus Christ and the Holy Spirit not by great

theological eloquence, originality, or accuracy, but by the power of renewed lives creating a new, simplified, unconventional, and uncomfortably challenging life-style. *O sancta simplicitas!* Yet the charismatic life stream still needs an adequately biblical theology and remains vulnerable while it lacks one.

7. TOTALITY. The central charismatic quest is not for any particular experience as such, but for what we may call thoroughgoing and uninhibited *totality* in realizing God's presence and responding to his grace. In worship, this totality means full involvement of each worshiper and the fullest openness to God. In ministry, it means not only nor even chiefly the use of sign gifts, but the discerning and harnessing of all capacities to serve. In Christian expression and communication, it means a great deal of singing, both from books and "in the Spirit"; clapping, arm raising, hand stretching; muttering together in group prayer, delivering of prophecies from God to the fellowship, passing the lead from glossolalics to interpreters, loose improvisatory preaching and corporate dialogue with the preacher by interjection and response; hugging, dancing, and so on. In fellowship, it means giving oneself and one's substance generously, even recklessly, to help others. The charismatic quest for totality is surely right, and even if this way of pursuing it is not one which all believers can happily buy into, it comes as a salutary challenge to the muddleheaded ideals of restraint and respectability that have bogged down so many within our older churches in a sort of conscientious halfheartedness. This challenge must be received as from God.

Specifically, then, those who stand aloof, while doubtless not obliged to adopt the charismatic ethos or forbidden to think that some of what they see in the movement is childish and zany, must face these questions, How are you, in your church and fellowship, proposing to realize comparable totality before the Lord? What are you going to do, for instance, about the brisk, stylized sixty-minute canter—clergy and choir performing to a passive congregation—that is the worship diet of so many churchgoers on so many Lord's Days? This is not total worship; how then are you going to turn it into such?

Again, how will you respond to the often-heard complaint that the talents of gifted folk in the congregation lie unused and needs in personal and neighborhood ministry are going unmet because the pastor insists on being a one-man band, will not think of his flock as a ministering team, and seems to run scared lest it should appear that some parishioners can do some things better than he can?

What about the equally common complaint that people in the pews are unwilling to intrude into the spiritual ministry that they pay their pastors to fulfill? Lay passivity is not total ministry; indeed it negates the every-member ministry idea in a way that is spiritually ruinous. How then will you proceed in order to realize the full ministry potential of pastors and people together?

Then, too, what are you going to do about the singing in whispers, the chilly formalities, the locked-up lives, and lack of mutual commitment that have won for so many congregations the derisive description "God's *frozen* people"?

If the charismatic handling of all these problems fails to grab you, what is your alternative? Any who venture to criticize charismatic practices without facing these questions merit D. L. Moody's retort, a century ago, to a doctrinaire critic of his evangelistic methods: "Frankly, sir, I prefer the way I do it to the way you don't do it." The charismatic movement is a God-sent gadfly to goad the whole church into seeking more of totality before the Lord than most Christians today seem to know. Face the challenge!

8. IMMATURITY.   The charismatic movement is theologically immature, and its public speech and style seem on occasion half-baked as a result. Its exponents of renewal have not in every case learned to be consistently God centered, Trinitarian, and forward looking, and on occasion appear to be man centered and experience centered in their interests, tritheistic in their theology, and mindlessly mesmerized by the present moment, as children are.

˟ The movement's intellectual and devotional preoccupation with the Holy Spirit tends to separate him from the Son whom he was sent to glorify and the Father to whom the Son brings us. The result too often is a concentrated quest for intense experiences, emotional highs, supernatural communications, novel insights, exotic techniques of pastoral therapy, and general pietistic pizzazz, not closely linked with the objectivities of faith and hope in Christ and the disciplines of keeping the Father's law. The charismatics' passion for physical and mental euphoria (health in the sense of feeling good and functioning well) reflects strong faith in the supernatural but feeble grasp of the moral realities of redemption, of the significance for our discipleship of self-denial, accepted weakness and apparent failure, and of the spiritual values that belong to hard thought, frustrated endeavor, pain accepted, loss adjusted to, and steady faithfulness in life's more humdrum routines.

What emerges, therefore, is intensity with instability, insight not always linked with intelligence, an oversimplified one-sidedness in spirituality, and an enthusiasm that is too often escapist. Thomas Smail, theologian of the British renewal, sees all this as the result of not sufficiently focusing on the Father,[38] and that is certainly part of the story; but I think it is part two rather than part one and that the root of the trouble is failure to focus sufficiently on the Jesus of the New Testament—Jesus, the incarnate Son of God, who is man for God, our model of discipleship, as well as being God for man, our sin-bearing Saviour—I mean by that, not that charismatics do not trust, love, and worship Jesus—to say such a thing would be absurd—but that they do not sufficiently grasp the link between what he was in his state of humiliation in this world and what his people, individually and corporately, are now called to be since Pentecost, as they were before (*see* Luke 14:25–33; John 15:18–16:4; Acts 14:22; Romans 8:17–23, 35–39; 2 Corinthians 4:7–18; 12:7–10; Hebrews 12:1–11). If I am right, this would be, ironically enough, a Spirit-frustrating, Spirit-grieving and Spirit-quenching feature right at the heart of this Spirit-exalting movement, and it would throw much light on the renewal's disconcerting tendency, underlined by Smail, to run out of steam and get stuck.

But in any case, whichever is the right diagnosis, it can hardly be doubted that the immaturities of the charismatic vision of Christian life can only be cured through a theological deepening that will result in an acuter self-awareness and self-criticism. It is to be hoped that such a deepening will soon come.

9. REVIVAL. The charismatic movement, though a genuine renewing of much that belongs to healthy biblical Christianity, does not exhibit all the features that belong to God's work of revival. While vigorously grasping the joys of firm faith, it knows too little of the awesome searchlight of God's holiness and the consequent godly sorrow of radical repentance. Also, in settling for the joys of faith and the celebrating of gifts the movement has, as it seems, been satisfied too easily and too soon. There is need to go, not back, but on from the point it has currently reached to seek the richer reality of God's reviving visitation, toward which this movement, please God, will prove to have been a step on the way. In my final chapter I shall explore this further.

Come, Holy Spirit

Now let me try to pull some threads together.

Two convictions have been reflected in all that I have written so far. It is time for them to break surface, so that you may look at them directly. Here they are.

First: Understanding the Holy Spirit Is a Crucial Task for Christian Theology at All Times. For where the Spirit's ministry is studied, it will also be sought after, and where it is sought after, spiritual vitality will result. This has happened historically through Augustine and his patristic and medieval disciples (who had in mind the Holy Spirit when they spoke of God's "grace"), and through Calvin (whom history hails as *the* theologian of the Holy Spirit, just as Athanasius is *the* theologian of incarnation and Luther of justification), and through the Puritans (theologians of regeneration and sanctification to a man), and through the first Wesleyans and the last-century holiness teachers, and through this century's Pentecostals and charismatics. Whose opinions have been right on the disputed questions within this heritage does not matter here; my point rather is that those who have thought about and sought after the power of the Spirit in their own lives have regularly found what they were seeking, for in such cases our generous God does not suspend his blessing upon our getting details of theology all correct. Conversely, where the Spirit's ministry arouses no interest and other preoccupations rule our minds, the quest for life in the Spirit is likely to be neglected, too. Then the church will lapse, as in many quarters it has lapsed already, into either the formal routines of Christian Pharisaism or the spiritual counterpart of sleeping sickness, or maybe a blend of both.

The Christian scene today in the Western world highlights the importance of attending to the doctrine of the Holy Spirit. The lack of divine energy and exuberance in most congregations, even some of the most notionally orthodox, is painful to see. The current quest for church renewal, whatever true renewal might be (and one problem today is that so many have no idea), demands that we get clearer in our minds about the divine Renewer. The zany notion of contemporary Christian mission that the World Council of Churches seems to sponsor (see all faiths as valid and all men as actually saved; stop being church-planting evangelists and start being sociopolitical revolutionaries) makes us ask, Is that what the Spirit was sent to help us do? The bland acceptance by professional churchmen of doctrinal relativism as an ultimate necessity and doctrinal pluralism as an unavoidable fact prompts the question, Is that the best we can expect when the Spirit teaches? The charismatic challenge forces on us the query, Have we ever yet grasped the supernatural reality of Holy Spirit life? It is as if God is constantly flashing before us on huge billboards the message REMEMBER THE HOLY SPIRIT! and our eyes are so lowered and trained on one another as we gossip about our current interests that we have not yet noticed what he is doing. Once I canvassed with a candidate for election to Britain's Parliament; he did the talking while I passed out leaflets headed in big black type WORKERS WAKE UP! I should like to shout from all housetops today CHRISTIANS WAKE UP! CHURCHES WAKE UP! THEOLOGIANS WAKE UP! We study and discuss God, Christ, body life, mission, Christian social involvement, and many other things; we pay lip service to the Holy Spirit throughout (everyone does these days), but we are not yet taking him seriously in any of it. In this we need to change.

SECOND: HONORING THE HOLY SPIRIT IS A CRUCIAL TASK IN
CHRISTIAN DISCIPLESHIP TODAY. "Honor the Holy Spirit!"
was Evan Roberts' constant cry from pulpit after pulpit in the
Welsh revival of 1904. Honoring the Holy Spirit has, I believe, been the secret of every revival movement in Christendom from the start, whether or not the actual words have
been used. Believers honor the Holy Spirit when they give
him his way in their lives and when his ministry of exalting
Christ and convincing of sin, sinking them ever lower and
raising Christ ever higher in their estimate, goes on unhin-
dered and unquenched. The records of all fruitful times in
the church's past confirm this. How, then, starting from situations in which the Holy Spirit has long been quenched, are
we to honor him in these days?

This question, which is really at the heart of most of the
church's current intramural discussions, takes us into an area
of confusion and uncertainty. Charismatics and the Cursillo
movement answer it one way: Release the Spirit within you
by opening yourself to his direct influence. Exponents of relational renewal have another answer: Dare to be real and
become vulnerable to other believers. Christians in the tradition of Jonathan Edwards have a third: Pray and prepare for
the Spirit's outpouring. Professional ecumenicals in the
main-line churches offer a fourth: Cultivate a reforming social activism. Granted, these answers do not entirely exclude
each other, yet their points both of concern and of unconcern
are far from coinciding. So the question continues to press on
us all: How should we honor the Holy Spirit today? How
may we keep in step with him in his work among us? After
which of our many different drummers should we who seek
more of the Spirit march? All movements mentioned and
others, too, claim the Spirit's leadership; how can we tell how
far any of them has a right to make that claim?

The Authority of Scripture

† TESTING BY SCRIPTURE.   The methodological formula for answering these questions is that we must test the rival views

by the teaching of the canonical Scriptures. That involves asking whether they are built on biblical truth, rightly applied. It involves also asking whether they miss anything Scripture stresses and whether they need any change of direction or emphasis in order to match biblical priorities. For the teaching of Scripture is God's own message to us, and the mental discipline of systematically submitting our thoughts, views, and purposes to the judgment of Scripture as it interprets itself to us in regard to our relationship with God, is more than one Christian tradition among many; it is a discipline intrinsic to Christianity itself.

Jesus, the Founder, ". . . the pioneer and perfecter of our faith . . ." as the writer to the Hebrews calls him (12:2), demonstrably took his Bible—that is, our Old Testament—to be his Father's eternally valid word of promise, direction, and control and no less demonstrably tagged his own teaching and that which the Apostles were to give in his name as divine and authoritative. So the principle of living under Scripture (meaning now the two Testaments put together) may fairly be said to come to us straight from the mind of Christ. It is as if he himself handed each one of us our Bible and told us that only as we follow it do we follow him.

THE SPIRIT AND REVELATION.   The principle of biblical authority embodies and expresses several basic truths about the Holy Spirit. For the Spirit was and is the agent of all communication from God. Both the giving and the receiving of revelation are his work. The reason why it can be said that "the spirit of man is the lamp of the Lord . . ." (Proverbs 20:27) is not that we pick up divine truth naturally, without special divine help, as some have supposed; the reason is that the Holy Spirit brings revealed truth home to our otherwise impervious hearts. In other words, the spirit of man is a lamp that is out till the Holy Spirit lights it. Earlier we looked at Jesus' account of the Teacher-Spirit's coming ministry as set forth in John 14–16. Now we should note that Paul and John elsewhere both confirm that only through the Spirit do our sin-darkened minds gain sure knowledge of divine things (*see*

1 Corinthians 2:9–16; 12:3; 2 Corinthians 3:12–4:6; Ephesians 1:17, where "a spirit" in RSV, should be "the Spirit," as NIV; 3:5, 16–19; 1 John 2:20, 27; 4:1–6; 5:7, *see also* 20) and that Luke speaks of the risen Jesus, both before and after his Ascension, not only "opening" the Scriptures to men's hearts (Luke 24:32, *see also* 24) but also "opening" eyes, minds, and hearts to understand and receive the divine message that the Scriptures and the gospel declare (Luke 24:45; Acts 16:14; 25:18). It is through the Spirit that Jesus thus communicates understanding, and apart from the Spirit there is no understanding. The whole New Testament assumes this.

So the truth, analytically put, comes out as follows. The lordship of the Spirit was exercised in the whole process of producing the Bible and setting it before us, and that same lordship is exercised as the Spirit moves us to receive, revere, and study the Scriptures and to discern their divine message to us. Five processes went into producing the Bible as we have it: first the disclosure of wisdom and truth to its writers; then the inspiring, canonizing, preserving, and translating of their text. The Spirit was active in all five. Three processes now go into the effecting of communication through the Bible, namely authentication, illumination, and interpretation. These, too, are areas of the Spirit's action. *Authentication* is of Scripture as such. It is that work of the Spirit that Calvin called his inner witness and described, not as a special sort of feeling nor a secret disclosure of new information, but as the creating of a state of mind in which one cannot doubt that whatever the Bible says is from God. *Illumination* is of our dark and perverted minds. It is that aspect of the authenticating process whereby we are made able to recognize divine realities for what they are. *Interpretation* is of the text. It is the Spirit's activity, effected through our own labor in exegesis, analysis, synthesis, and application, of showing us what the text means for us as God's present word of address to our hearts. The wide range of the Spirit's ministry in connection with Scripture is not always appreciated, but we abuse our minds and miss the truth if we overlook it.

Two comments should be added here, for the sake of

clarity. First, it is sometimes thought that the Spirit's lordship
in the transmission and translation of Scripture implies that
somewhere there must exist an infallible manuscript tradition and a faultless English rendering of the infallible text.
This however is not so. What the evidence shows is that the
text has always been well enough preserved and translated
for the Spirit to be able to use it to give true knowledge of
God in Christ. But such adequacy falls far short of faultlessness. We should therefore trust whatever versions of the
Bible we have, and not mistrust them, while yet being willing
to learn what is always true, namely, that in many details
they could all be better than they are. Second, it is sometimes
thought that when the Spirit interprets Scripture, guiding us
into its "spiritual" meaning, the process may involve finding
allegories and applications that could not be read out of the
text by any normal means. But that is not so either. The
"spiritual" sense of Scripture is nothing other than the literal
sense—that is, the sense the writer's words actually
express—integrated with the rest of biblical teaching and applied to our individual lives.

There is, then, a correlation between the Holy Spirit and
what the twentieth Anglican Article of Religion calls "God's
Word written." Each teaches by means of the other. Apart
from the Spirit, there is no true learning of divine things from
Scripture, and supposedly "spiritual" thoughts not founded
on the Word are godless flights of fancy. (We should note
that in the New Testament the word *spiritual* regularly relates
to the new life in Christ that the Spirit gives and *never* means
"intellectual, high-minded, or fastidious" as distinct from
"physical, material, or coarse," as it does in modern secular
speech.) So those who would live under the authority of the
Spirit must bow before the Word as the Spirit's textbook,
while those who would live under the authority of Scripture
must seek the Spirit as its interpreter. Negligence and one-
sidedness either way could be ruinous, and since a proper
balance in this as in other matters comes naturally to none of
us, we do well to be on our guard.

But does not the Spirit lead Christians beyond the limits

of the specific situations with which Scripture deals? It depends what you mean by that. If you mean, Does he lead us to apply biblical principles to modern circumstances with which, in the nature of the case, Scripture does not deal, the answer is yes. But if you mean, Does he lead us to treat as historically and culturally relative principles that Scripture sets forth as revealed absolutes and so to treat them as not binding us, the answer is no. Those modern movements that appeal to isolated texts or extrapolated biblical principles in a way that the rest of biblical teaching disallows and those that appeal to alleged revelations of future fact or present duty which are neither clear implications nor clear applications of what is actually said in the text have no right to claim the Spirit's leading. Nor may any caucus or consensus in the church claim to be Spirit-led simply because for the moment it commands a majority vote.

The Call to Christ Centeredness

We must, then, critically weigh all formulas for honoring the Holy Spirit today by allowing Scripture to judge them in the way I have described, and with that we must bring New Testament norms of faith and life to bear on us as we are, so that we may see both what we lack and how our lack might be supplied. A full study of all the renewal formulas of our time cannot be attempted here, but I would urge as I close this book that at least two pressing needs have become very obvious from what has been said so far.

First, the New Testament's Christ-centered view of the ministry of the Holy Spirit needs to be recovered. I argued this point earlier; here I briefly review it. We saw that, whereas today the Holy Spirit, outpoured at Pentecost, tends to be thought of man centeredly as the source of whatever perceptions, experiences, and abilities raise folk above, and so free them from, their prior limitations, the New Testament writers think of the Pentecostal Spirit Christ centeredly and explain all his work of supernaturalizing our lives in terms of his making our Lord Jesus Christ present to us and in us and to others through him. Without questioning the continuance of the Spirit's pre-Christian activity as Creator and Sustainer, animating beasts and human beings and bestowing good gifts of all kinds from God upon everyone in what some call "common providence" and others "common grace" (you may choose your phrase; both mean the same), the New Testament writers focus on the saving distinctives of the Spirit's new covenant ministry, which are these:

> The definitive revelation of Christ and the truth about him to and through themselves
> The illuminating of human hearts to receive and respond to this revelation
> The new birth, whereby we sinners are quickened to trust Christ as our sin bearer and baptized—that is, initiated and introduced—into Christ's body, in which we become living limbs (see John 3:3–15; 1 Corinthians 12:12, 13)
> ₭The Spirit's witnessing to the fact that we are Christ's forever by giving us foretastes of heaven's joy
> His sanctifying transformation of us into Jesuslikeness of character
> And his fitting the saints for service and actually putting them into it by showering upon them spiritual gifts

In the Spirit's new covenant ministry, according to the New Testament, the glorified Christ is shown, known, loved, served, modeled, and expressed throughout.

From this it follows that no convictions and experiences save those that center on Christ as God incarnate and man's only Saviour ought ever to be ascribed to the Spirit of Christ as their source. It is right to see the work of Christ's Spirit in any changes of conviction or significant experiences that in retrospect appear as steps in a person's pilgrimage to Christian faith, but this can only be seen after faith has emerged. We cannot know in advance whether or not any particular person who rethinks or revalues life is being led toward faith. The Spirit as Creator sustains both the life that is being revalued and the revaluing process, but that does not mean one who becomes, say, a serious Moslem or Hindu or Buddhist or humanist is being led by the Spirit in Saint Paul's sense of that phrase or that the Spirit of Christ is the patron of non-Christian religion as well as of Christian faith.

Surely it is plain that these Christ-centered emphases need to be stated more clearly and stressed more strongly than is often done today.

What difference would their recovery make? A great deal. It would bring fellowship with Christ right to the center of our worship and devotion. It would make that fellowship the key factor in any definitions we offered of our Christian identity. It would give new substance to the time-honored description of a Christian as one who "loves the Lord," and the description would then fit us in a way that just at present it hardly does. Recovery at this point would set us seeking a deeper experiential realization of the love of Christ, according to Paul's prayer in Ephesians 3:14–19, so bringing us back into line with saints of former days. Also it would stop us mistaking Christian Pharisaism, legalistically preoccupied with moral standards and stopping there, for the holiness of those who walk with their Saviour and grow like him. It would stop us from ascribing to the Spirit any of the current forms of supernaturalist superstition that while offering themselves as religion, lead minds and hearts away from Christ rather than toward him. It would stop us from glibly claiming that the Spirit prompts programs, in or outside the church, in which the unique glory of Christ the Redeemer is obscured instead of being exalted and celebrated. And it would help us realize that the sin that in this era of the gospel should be seen as most scandalous of all is unbelief concerning our crucified and now vindicated Saviour (*see* John 16:8–11). It would give us a jealousy for Christ's honor that would change our whole way of thinking about both the church and the world. Would these be changes for the better? I think so, and I hope you agree.

Beyond the Charismatic Renewal

This leads to the second step it seems to me that we are being called to take. *The ultimacy sometimes assumed by exponents of charismatic renewal needs to be queried.*

Anyone who did not thank God for all the new life, in all Christian traditions, of which the charismatic movement has been the human channel would stand condemned. Anyone who saw the movement as concerned only with an alleged resurgence of the sign gifts would be failing to see it whole, and anyone who did not look beyond its zany side and see its cheerful simplicity of faith and infectious warmth of love as a divine corrective of the inhibited intellectualism, barren formalism, and theological skepticism that operate as a kind of creeping paralysis in much of the world church would stand revealed as spiritually shortsighted. But every movement, like every member of the human race, tends to show the defects of its qualities, and if the now conventional pattern of charismatic renewal were idolized as the *ne plus ultra* of spiritual quickening ("thus far shalt thou go, and no farther"), much that has been gained during the past quarter century could easily be dissipated and lost. We need to move, not away from, or past, but through and then beyond the charismatic renewal. For Scripture shows that there is more to the renewing of the church than the common charismatic emphases cover.

Scripture points to a recurring process whereby, following upon coldness, carelessness, and unfaithfulness among God's people, God himself acts in sovereignty to restore what was ready to perish by means of the following set of events:

GOD COMES DOWN.   (*See* Isaiah 64:1). He makes known his inescapable presence as the Holy One, mighty and majestic, confronting his own people both to humble and to exalt, and reaching out into the wider world in mercy and in judgment. Other biblical ways of saying this are that God "awakes," "arises," "visits," and "draws near" (*see* Psalms 44:23–26; 69:18; 80:14 KJV). God's coming forces folk to realize, like Isaiah in the temple, the intimacy of the supernatural and the closeness, majesty, and knowingness (that is, the heart-searching omniscience) of the living Lord (*see* Isaiah 6:1-8; Revelation 1:9-18).

GOD'S WORD COMES HOME.   The Bible, its message, and its Christ reestablish the formative and corrective control over faith and life that are theirs by right. The divine authority and power of the Bible are felt afresh, and believers find that this collection of Hebrew and Christian literary remains becomes once more the means whereby God speaks to them, clears and changes their minds, and searches and feeds their souls.

GOD'S PURITY COMES THROUGH.   As God uses his Word to quicken consciences, the perverseness, ugliness, uncleanness, and guilt of sin are seen and felt with new clarity, and the depth of each person's own sinfulness is realized as never before. Believers are deeply humbled; unbelievers are made to feel that living as they do with sin and without God is intolerable, and the forgiveness of sins becomes the most precious truth in the creed.

GOD'S PEOPLE COME ALIVE.   Repentance and restitution, faith, hope, and love, joy and peace, praise and prayer, conscious communion with Christ, confident certainty of salvation, uninhibited boldness of testimony, readiness to share, and a spontaneous reaching out to all in need become their characteristic marks. There is a new forthrightness of utterance, expressing a new clarity of vision with respect to good and evil; and a new energy for reformation—personal, ecclesiastical, and social—goes along with it.

While all this is happening, *outsiders come in*, drawn by the moral and spiritual magnetism of what goes on in the church.

Whence comes this analysis? First, from accounts of this restoring work of God in Scripture—the early chapters of Acts, plus the narratives of spiritual awakening under Asa,

Hezekiah, Josiah, and Ezra (2 Chronicles 15, 29–31, 34, 35; Ezra 9–10; Nehemiah 8–10). Second, from the theology of restoration set forth by the prophets, most notably Isaiah, Ezekiel, and Zechariah, and by the prayers for restoration in such psalms as 44, 67, 80 and 85. Third, from the annals of similar stirrings in later days under such leaders as Bernard, Francis of Assisi, Savonarola, Jonathan Edwards, George Whitefield, John Wesley, Charles Finney, Robert Murray McCheyne; the Puritan awakening in seventeenth-century England; England's Evangelical Revival and America's Great Awakening in the mid-eighteenth century; spiritual quickenings round the globe in the 1850s and again in the 1900s; and late movements like the East African revival, which began in the 1930s and still goes on. The family likeness of these movements, both to each other and to biblical prototypes, is remarkable. What we are looking at here is a distinctive and recurring work of God whereby again and again he rouses languishing churches and through the consequent evangelistic overflow extends the kingdom of Christ.

What name shall we give to this momentous divine work? The time-honored term since the seventeenth century has been *revival*. But because of its associations with certain types of preaching mission, of emotional piety, and of public hysteria, this word presents difficulties to some, and one can understand charismatics and others with other programs preferring to talk of *renewal* instead. We should not make an issue of this or any other verbal preference. As Thomas Hobbes observed long ago, words are the counters of wise men ("they do reckon by them"), but they are the coinage of fools, in the sense that unless certain words are used—the right buttons pressed, as we say—fools cannot recognize that the thing to which they apply the words has been spoken of at all, however many equivalent words may have been employed in place of their beloved shibboleths. We should take to heart Hobbes' warning and remember that two people can use different words and mean the same thing, just as they can use the same word and mean different things. What we need to ask, however, is whether the charismatic ideal and experience of renewal is fully equivalent to the evangelical ideal and experience of revival. And the answer, I think, is: not quite.

The charismatic movement, as we have seen, seeks the renewal of the whole church by at least the following means:

1. Rediscovery of the living God and his Christ and the supernatural dimensions of Christian living, through Spirit baptism or the Spirit's "release"
2. Returning to the Bible as the inspired Word of God, to nourish one's soul upon it
3. Habits of private and public devotion designed to bring the whole person, body and soul, into total, expectant dependence on the Holy Spirit (glossolalia comes in here)
4. A leisurely, participatory style of public praise and prayer
5. A use of spiritual gifts for ministry in the body of Christ by every member of Christ
6. Exploration of the possibilities of ministry through a communal life-style
7. An active commitment by this and other means to reach out to the needy in evangelism and service
8. A high level of expectancy that the hand of God will again and again be shown in striking providences ("miracles"), prophetic messages to this or that person, visions, supernatural healings, and similar manifestations

Does this ideal of renewal at any point go beyond the historic evangelical notion of revival? Yes: A vein of what I have called super-supernaturalism runs through it, becoming visible in the stress on tongues, prophecies, healing, and the expectation of miracles. In evangelical thinking about revival this has no warrant, and in evangelical experience of revival it has constantly been diagnosed as a mark of disturbing immaturity rather than of high spirituality.

Does the charismatic ideal of renewal at any point fall

short of what Evangelicals mean by revival? Yes: The notes of humility and awe in the presence of the holy God and of the need to realize the sinfulness of sin, the evil of egoism and the radical nature of repentance are rarely struck. As a result, the child-to-Daddy, buddy-to-Jesus informality that charismatics often embrace and cultivate as a corrective of the cold and distant formalism of prerenewal religion easily becomes more childish than childlike and actually stunts growth.

Now that is a serious shortcoming, for a deepened sense of who and what God is and a quickened realization of one's own unworthiness and of the marvel of God's grace to so rotten a sinner as oneself is the taproot of all real revival. So it is further into this sense of things that all who appreciate the charismatic movement and have benefited from its enormously fruitful delineations of openness to the Spirit and responsiveness to Christ should now be seeking to move. For the Spirit's work of magnifying the Mediator in Christian eyes today will not be fully done till he has brought us all to a more galvanizing awareness of the holiness of God and the greatness of our need of the mercy that Christ has brought than any of us has yet known.

Revival conditions are not with us at present; this is a day of small things, and we remain pygmy saints. One can be thankful for the contemporary willingness of Bible-believing, Christ-loving Christians to receive from each other across denominational boundaries and despite theological differences within the evangelical spectrum; it was not always so. Each of us has cause for gratitude for what we personally have received from sources with which, in terms of theology, we could not altogether identify. Yet none of us is entitled to be satisfied and complacent with what we now have; all of us must seek, rather, to be led on to a profounder quickening yet, and it is in this quest that charismatic and noncharismatic, old Augustinian, old Wesleyan, and old Keswick believers should be finding unity in the Spirit today.

Questions to Live With

Those who would honor the Holy Spirit and keep in step with him as he leads must learn to live with at least the following questions and respond constantly to their pressure at every turn of the road.

THE FIRST QUESTION CONCERNS REALITY IN CHURCH LIFE. Its thrust can be pinpointed by reference to 1 Corinthians 12-14; for whatever evils these chapters may confront us with, they do in fact show us a church in which the Holy Spirit was working in power. Reading them makes one painfully aware of the degree of impoverishment and inertia that prevails in churches today. If our reaction as readers is merely to preen ourselves and feel glad because our churches are free from Corinthian disorders, we are fools indeed. The Corinthian disorders were due to an uncontrolled overflow of Holy Spirit life. Many churches today are orderly simply because they are asleep, and with some one fears that it is the sleep of death. It is no great thing to have order in a cemetery! The real and deplorable carnality and immaturity of the Corinthian Christians, which Paul censures so strongly elsewhere in the letter, must not blind us to the fact that they were enjoying the ministry of the Holy Spirit in a way in which we today are not.

Let us go a little further into this. At the start of the letter, Paul had written (1:4-7): "I give thanks to God always for you because of the grace of God which was given you in Christ Jesus, that in every way you were enriched in him with all speech and all knowledge—even as the testimony to Christ was confirmed among you—so that you are not lacking in any spiritual gift. . . ." This was not empty politeness. Paul had not got his tongue in his cheek; he meant what he said. The Corinthians really had been "enriched" by Christ in the manner described. Consequently, when they met for the fellowship of worship, they brought with them gifts and contributions in abundance. Whereas congregations today too often gather in a spirit of aimless and unexpectant apathy, scarcely aware that they come to church to receive, let alone to give, the Corinthians met with eagerness and excitement, anxious to share with their fellow believers the "manifestation of the Spirit" (12:7) that was theirs. ". . . When you come together," wrote Paul (14:26), "each one has a hymn, a lesson ["some instruction," NEB], a revelation, a tongue, or an interpretation." Public worship at Corinth was thus the reverse of a drab routine; every service was an event, for every worshiper came ready and anxious to contribute something that God had given him. In the words quoted, Paul is not (*pace* our Brethren friends) prescribing an order for worship, making a rule that Christian worship always and everywhere should take potluck form where every guest brings something for the common pool; he is just describing the actual state of affairs in one particular church and giving directions, not for creating it, but for handling it once it had arisen. The state of affairs itself, however, was the spontaneous creation of the Holy Spirit.

Furthermore, when the Corinthians met for worship, the presence and power of God in their midst was an experienced reality. There was a sense of God among them that struck awe into men's souls, as at Jerusalem in the early days (*see* Acts 5:11–13), and gave every word that was spoken in God's name heart-searching force. Hence Paul—who, remember, knew the church, having watched over the first eighteen months of its life, and could therefore speak of it at firsthand—could write to them almost casually something that would sound staggering, indeed fatuous, if said to a congregation today. "If, therefore, the whole church assembles," Paul declared, "and . . . all prophesy [that is, announce the message of God in intelligible speech, whether by direct inspiration or biblical exposition we need not here determine], and an unbeliever or outsider enter, he is convicted by all, he is called to account by all, the secrets of his heart are disclosed; and so, falling on his face, he will worship God and declare that God is really among you" (14:23–25). Can you imagine that being seriously said to any church you know today? Yet Paul could say it to the Corinthians in a matter-of-fact manner, without the least sense of unreality, as if it were unquestionably true.

How was this possible? It could only have been possible if in fact the statement was one whose truth both Paul and the Corinthians had repeatedly proved in experience. This alone can explain why Paul expected the Corinthians to accept it, as he clearly does. Evidently it had happened more than once at Corinth, and no doubt elsewhere in Paul's experience, that a casual visitor, coming by accident into a church service, had heard all that was spoken as a message from God to his heart and had gone out a changed man. Nor should we be surprised at this, for the same thing has happened many times since Paul's day under revival conditions, when the sense of God's presence among his people has been strong.

Granted, the Corinthian disorders were grievous, yet the Corinthian church was being carried along by a great surge of divine life. Disorder, as such, is demonic and not to be desired, but it remains a question whether Holy Ghost life, with all its exuberance and risk of disorder, is not preferable to spiritual deadness, neat and tidy though that deadness may be. It is true that there is no problem of disease or malfunctioning where death reigns, but is lifelessness therefore the ideal?

Three centuries ago, in his *Discourse of Spiritual Gifts,* John Owen reviewed the Puritan revival (for revival it truly was) and frankly acknowledged the extravagance and misuse of spiritual endowments that had disfigured it. "By some, I confess," he wrote, "they [that is, "the eminent abilities of a number of private Christians"] have been abused; some have presumed on them; . . . some have been puffed up with them; some have used them disorderly in churches, and to their hurt; some have boasted . . . all which miscarriages also befell the primitive churches." But then he went on to say: "And I had rather have the order, rule, spirit, and practice of those churches which were planted by the apostles, with all their troubles and disadvantages, than the carnal peace of others in their open degeneracy from all these things."[1] Frankly, and before God I declare it, so had I, and I hope my readers feel the same. The question presses, and always will: What kind and degree of spiritual reality do we seek in our church routine? And how much, or rather how little, of the life and power of God are we prepared to settle for?

THE SECOND QUESTION CONCERNS RADICALISM IN THE REALM OF CHURCH ORDER AND ORGANIZATION. Radicalism is the attitude that goes ruthlessly to the root of problems (the word comes from *radix*, Latin for "root") and refuses to accept solutions that only scratch the surface. What nowadays is called radicalism in theology is to my mind a great evil, and I would not want any of my readers to be enmeshed in it; but none of us dare evade God's constant summons to radicalism in our congregational life. Let me explain.

The New Testament writers expect that every Christian community will show forth the power of the Holy Spirit, for to enjoy a rich outpouring of the Holy Spirit is a privilege entailed upon the New Testament church as such. For churches to lack the Spirit's powerful working in their corporate life is by biblical standards unnatural, just as heresy is; and this unnatural state of affairs can only be accounted for in terms of human failure. The New Testament has a phrase for the failure in question: We may, it says, *quench* the Spirit by resisting or undervaluing his work and by declining to yield to his influence (*see* Acts 7:51; Hebrews 10:29). The picture is of putting out a fire by pouring water on it. It is noteworthy that in 1 Thessalonians 5:19 the words "do not quench the Spirit" are flanked, on the one hand, by exhortations to follow the good, and to rejoice, pray, and give thanks at all times, and on the other hand, by warnings against disregard for "prophesying" (meaning, God's messages, however and by whomsoever declared), against failure to discriminate, and against evil involvements. It is natural to suppose that these things were linked in Paul's mind and that he meant his readers to understand that heedlessness of these exhortations and warnings was likely to quench the Spirit both in personal and in corporate life. It should be noted, too, that while one may effectively put out a fire by dousing it, one cannot make it burn again simply by stopping pouring water; it has to be lighted afresh. Similarly, when the Spirit has been quenched, it is beyond our power to undo the damage we have done; we can only cry to God in penitence, asking that he will revive his work.

Now it is hard to deny that we inherit today a situation in which the Spirit of God has been quenched. Unnatural as it may be, the Spirit's power is absent from the majority of our churches. What has caused that? In some quarters, certainly, it is the direct result of devaluing the Bible and the gospel and wandering out of the green pastures of God's Word into the barren flats of human speculation. In other places, however, where the "old paths" of evangelical belief have not been abandoned, the quenching of the Spirit is due to attitudes and inhibitions on the personal and practical level, which have simply stifled his work. Perhaps the words *conventionality* and *traditionalism* best express what I have in mind. There is a subtle tenacity abroad that remains wedded to the way things were done a hundred years ago. It thinks that it renders God service by being *faithful* (that is the word used) to these outmoded fashions; it never faces the possibility that they might need amending today if ever we are to communicate effectively with each other and with those outside our circles. Letting our inherited buildings dictate what we do and do not do when we meet in them is part of this traditionalist syndrome—and is often a very potent part, as surely we can all see. Churches tend to run in grooves of conventionality, and such grooves quickly turn into graves.

Here is where the challenge to institutional radicalism comes in: a challenge to which charismatic groups have been noticeably more alert than some others. Only styles and structures that serve the Spirit should stand. Everything bogging us down in lifeless routines or restraining the fruitful use of spiritual gifts or encouraging people in the pews to become passengers should be changed, no matter how sacrosanct we previously took it to be. The Holy Spirit is not a sentimentalist as too many of us are; he is a change agent, and he comes to change human structures as well as human hearts. Change for its own sake is mere fidgeting, but change that gets rid of obstacles to God's fullest blessing is both a necessity and a mercy. In Acts 2–5 we read of a church with, it seems, no buildings of its own, with loose and sometimes improvised leadership, but with each member apparently pulling his or her weight in the work and witness that went on, and the impact on Jerusalem was great. Around us in the modern West we see big church buildings—some of them housing four-figure congregations, and others certainly intended to house congregations of that size—often furnished with an impressive hierarchy of ministers and other officials; but the congregations, such as they are, are mostly passengers, and city life proceeds as if the churches were not there. When full allowance has been made for sociological differences between first-century Jerusalem and twentieth-century Liverpool, Vancouver, or New York, the question still presses: How much change are we willing to accept, in order to reach the point where the Spirit is no longer quenched? Are we radical enough in our view of traditional patterns as potential Spirit grievers and Spirit quenchers? Are we sufficiently ready to alter them if it should appear that this really is their effect? This question will not go away; we have to live with it, and much depends, for the health both of our own souls and of our churches, on how we face up to it.

THE THIRD QUESTION HAS TO DO WITH REACHING OUT IN LOVE TO OTHERS.   How should we love our neighbor? One of the nightmares of our time is that massive chunks of the church seem to be committed to the idea that evangelism is passé; that church planting is no longer a main task; that God himself is now at work directly in the world, not through the church, but in the first instance bypassing it, as he fights injustice in the secular sphere in all its current forms; and that the church's business is no more than to perceive this and join in where the action is. This idea of the church's mission assumes universalism; the thought behind it is that since our neighbor is spiritually safe anyway, helping him to faith is not a priority, and other forms of service and support to him may appropriately come first. (Universalism always undermines the urgency of evangelism in this way.) But what if universalism is false, as until this century most Christians thought? Then the modern view would have to be totally rethought.

In fact, if the teaching of Scripture is God's truth and if we take that teaching as a whole, not picking and choosing within it, but fitting together all its strands and facets, then universalism is unquestionably false, and evangelism is what it was previously thought to be—the primary form of neighbor love. As such, it is sustained in practice by the promise that the Spirit himself will convince the world of sin, righteousness, and judgment (John 16:8), and Christians who engage in it are sustained by the knowledge that the Spirit regularly empowers disciples for witness to their Master (Acts 1:8; 4:31, 33; 6:5, 8–10; 9:17–22). But then the questions press: What is the most effective and telling way to share the message of Christ? How may we get it across? And it can safely be said that only the believer and the community that are constantly exercised over this question, so that they may spread the gospel as widely and fruitfully as they can, will ever know the full power of the Spirit. Others will effectively quench him by their unconcern about the evangelistic task into which he would lead them and end up knowing little or nothing of his day-to-day ministry in their lives.

THE FOURTH QUESTION WITH WHICH WE MUST EVER LIVE CONCERNS REVIVAL. Is revival a meaningful hope in our time? Is it our personal hope? What expectations from God do we settle for? As we saw, the reviving that the church needs today has not come yet, and to equate the charismatic phenomenon with the fullness of revival would show some ignorance of what revival is. I gave earlier a description of what revival involves, but did not formulate a theology of it. It is worth spending a moment doing that now, so that we may know for sure what we are talking about. Here are the main points.

Revival is God revitalizing his church. Revival is a work of restoring life. Spiritual life is fellowship with God. The Holy Spirit is the architect and agent of that fellowship, as we have seen, and he revives the church by bringing believers into a new quality of fellowship with the Father and the Son—perhaps I should say, with the Father through the Son, although the former phrase is apostolic (1 John 1:3). Revival is a social, corporate thing, touching and transforming communities, large and small. Bible prayers for revival implore God to quicken not *me* but *us*. Bible prophecies of revival depict God visiting and enlivening not one or two individual Israelites, but Israel, the whole people. Records of revival, in biblical and later Christian history, tell of entire communities being affected. Revival comes to Christians individually, no doubt, but it is not an isolated, individualistic affair; God revives his church, and then the new life overflows from the church for the conversion of outsiders and the renovation of society.

Revival is God turning his anger away from his church. For God's people to be impotent against their enemies is a sign that God is judging them for their sins. In the Old Testament the cry for revival springs from the sense of judgment (*see* Psalms 79:4-9; 80:12-14; 85:4-7; Habakkuk 3:2), and the coming of revival is God comforting his people after judgment. In the New Testament Christ counsels the Laodiceans to seek revival from his hand as an alternative to the judgment he would otherwise inflict on them (Revelation 3:14-22).

Revival is God stirring the hearts of his people, visiting them (Psalms 80:14; Jeremiah 29:10-14), coming to dwell with them (Zechariah 2:10-12), returning to them (Zechariah 1:3, 16), pouring out his Spirit on them (Joel 2:28; Acts 2:17-21), to quicken their consciences, show them their sins, and exalt his mercy—in the New Testament epoch, to exalt his Son, bringer of mercy—before their eyes. Times of revival bring a deep sense of being always in God's sight; spiritual things become overwhelmingly real, and God's truth becomes overwhelmingly powerful, both to wound and to heal; conviction of sin becomes intolerable; repentance goes deep; faith springs up strong and assured; spiritual understanding grows quick and keen; and converts mature in a very short time. Christians become fearless in witness and tireless in their Saviour's service. They recognize their new experience as a real foretaste of the life of heaven, where Christ will disclose himself to them so fully that they will never be able to rest day or night from singing his praises and doing his will. Joy overflows (Psalms 85:6; 2 Chronicles 30:26; Nehemiah 8:12, 17; Acts 2:46, 47; 8:8), and loving generosity abounds (Acts 4:32).

Revival is God displaying the sovereignty of his grace. Revival is entirely a work of grace, for it comes to churches and Christians that merit only judgment; and God brings it about in such a way as to show that his grace was decisive in it. Men may organize conventions and campaigns and seek God's blessing on them, but the only organizer of revival is God the Holy Spirit. Again and again revival has come suddenly, breaking out often in obscure places, through the ministry of obscure men. To be sure, it comes in answer to prayer, and where no one has prayed it is likely that no one will be revived either; yet the manner in which prayer is answered will be such as to highlight God's sovereignty as revival's only source and to show that all the praise and glory of it must be given to him alone.

If God is sovereign in revival and we cannot extort it from him by any endeavor or technique, what should those who long for revival do? Twiddle their thumbs? Or something more?

There are three things to do. First, preach and teach God's truth; second, prepare Christ's way; third, pray for the Spirit's outpouring. Preach and teach, because it is through truth—Bible truth, gospel truth, truth taken into the mind and heart—that God blesses. Prepare, in the sense of removing boulders from the road—obstacles such as habitual sins, neglect of prayer and fellowship, worldly-mindedness, indulgence of pride, jealousy, bitterness, and hatred as motives for action. Repentance on the part of Christians is regularly a harbinger of revival from one standpoint and the real start of it from another. Pray, because God has told us that we need not expect to receive unless we ask, and in the words of Jonathan Edwards, the classic theologian of revival: "When God has something very great to accomplish for his church, it is his will that there should precede it, the extraordinary prayers of his people; as is manifest by Ezekiel 36:37. . . . And it is revealed that, when God is about to accomplish great things for his church, he will begin by remarkably pouring out the spirit of grace and supplication (Zechariah 12:10)."[2]

Those who would keep in step with the Spirit must learn to seek revival where it is needed (and that is almost everywhere in the Western world), just as they must learn to commit themselves to spreading the gospel, changing the church's ways where these are Spirit quenching, and making every-member ministry happen in the church's ongoing life. For these are central concerns of the Spirit himself, whereby he pursues his mission of glorifying our Lord Jesus Christ.

Spiritual Realism

The last question the Spirit of God makes us live with is that of *realism*. This is not the same as the question of *reality*, which came first in my list. The question of reality has to do with the goals we set in church and personal life, and the issue there is how much or how little of the life of God we are prepared to settle for. The question of realism has to do with our willingness or lack of willingness to face unpalatable truths about ourselves and to start making necessary changes.

Most of us are not realists when it comes to self-assessment, however brutally matter-of-fact we may become when assessing others. In our attitude toward ourselves we are either starry-eyed romantics, kidding ourselves that all is well, or at least well enough, or at any rate will magically come right some day without our needing to take any action; or else, like Adam blaming Eve and Eve blaming the serpent, we are assiduous blamers of others for whatever goes wrong in our marriages, families, churches, careers, and so on. In neither case do we accept responsibility for present shortcomings; in both cases the root of our attitude is pride, which tells us that whoever else needs to change, we don't. Romantic complacency and resourcefulness in acting the injured innocent are among the most Spirit-quenching traits imaginable, since both become excuses for doing nothing in situations where realism requires that we do something and do it as a matter of urgency. Both traits stifle conviction of sin in the unconverted and keep Christians in a thoroughly bad state of spiritual health. But the inducing of realism, both in thought and in action, is part of the Spirit's regular ministry.

We may learn this from that section of "what the Spirit says to the churches" that was specifically addressed to the Laodicean church in the Book of the Revelation 3:14-22. An exposition of Revelation 2, 3 was once published with the title *What Christ Thinks of the Church*, and no better title could be devised; that is exactly what the letters to the seven churches of Asia Minor show us. What the Spirit says is always what Christ thinks (he speaks what he hears [John 16:13]), and in this case Jesus presents himself as the speaker, so that there can be no possible doubt that what is said to the Laodiceans is the Saviour's own message. What is that message? It is a call to spiritual realism, in three parts.

First, *Jesus exposes unrealism.* "I know your works"—and your works tell me that in fact you are—lukewarm, tepid, nondescript, apathetic; in short, nauseating and like lukewarm water, fit only to be spat out in disgust. Thus I know you, says Jesus—but you do not know yourselves! "For you say, I am rich, I have prospered, and I need nothing; not knowing that you are wretched, pitiable, poor, blind and naked." The Spirit ought to be blowing like the wind and flowing like a stream of water through your lives (John 3:8; 7:38), and under his influence you should be growing in grace and showing the Spirit's fruit in ways one can see (2 Peter 3:18; Ephesians 4:15; Galatians 5:22-24). But, says Jesus, no such thing is happening; instead, you are spiritually stagnant—and that is a scandal!

Let us be clear that if, through complacency or the habit of externalizing blame, we should become similarly stagnant, and then fail to recognize our stagnation and fancy that we are doing well, Jesus' attitude to us will be the same as his attitude was to the Laodiceans. He does not change.

Next, *Jesus recalls to realism.* "Therefore I counsel you to buy from me" (at no cost save your own self-acquaintance and self-humbling, as in Isaiah 55:1, 2) the authentic wealth of a pure, ardent, sincere, wholly devoted heart, plus "salve to anoint your eyes, that you may see"—in other words, that you may learn to be spiritual realists henceforth, discerning how to live and walk with Christ so as to please him. In other words (stating it now in terms of what the Spirit says in his own person), the Laodiceans must learn to change both their attitude of taking Jesus and his love for granted and their complacent habit of bland self-approval. Learn to be realistic, says Jesus to them; as ivy kills the tree to which it clings, so the unrealism that clings so closely is ruining you, for it keeps you from dealing with me as you need to do.

Let us be clear that this will be Jesus' word to us, too, if we lapse as the Laodiceans did.

Finally, *Jesus extols realism.* He does this by showing the supreme benefit to which it leads. "Behold, I stand at the door and knock; if any one hears my voice and opens the door" (that is, by realistic admission of need and approach to Jesus to "buy" what he offers) "I will come in to him and eat with him, and he with me." When we approach Jesus thus realistically, knowing our need to change and seeking grace to do it, honestly recognizing what has offended him in our lives and asking for power to turn from it, we shall find him: That is his promise to us, as to the Laodiceans. It is a promise of close, conscious, sustained fellowship, a promise of knowing that one is loved and cared for, a promise of power to conquer the opposition of sin and Satan, a promise of heaven on earth before one reaches heaven. But it is a promise only spiritual realists ever inherit.

As knowing the Holy Spirit means precisely knowing Christ, so honoring the Holy Spirit means precisely honoring Christ—honoring him by realism in facing spiritual issues, in willingness to have Christ expose to oneself one's faults and in readiness to change one's ways according to his word. Are you a spiritual realist? Am I? If the Spirit has his way in our lives, he will be forcing this question on us constantly and leading us to measure ourselves by Scripture in order that we may be sure that we do not fall short of this kind of realism at any point at all. "Search me, O God, and know my heart! Try me and know my thoughts! And see if there be any wicked way in me, and lead me in the way everlasting" (Psalms 139:23 24).

To adapt a familiar question: if you were accused of honoring the Holy Spirit, would there be enough evidence to convict you? We see now what sort of evidence would be relevant. As was said at the start of this book, there are many mistaken ideas abroad today about what constitutes the life of the Spirit. As we have seen throughout our argument, the essence of life in the Spirit is acknowledgment of Jesus and fellowship with Jesus, whom the Father has given us to save us from the folly, guilt, and power of sin. The evidence that shows us to be honoring the Spirit is that we are endeavoring each day to live this life, to which Revelation 3:20 invites us. This is what counts, and nothing counts apart from it.

Come, Holy Spirit

Is it proper to pray to the Spirit? There is no example of doing this anywhere in Scripture, but since the Spirit is God, it cannot be wrong to invoke and address him if there is good reason to do so. The New Testament shows that though prayer to the Father is the ordinary norm (for that is the way of prayer that Jesus himself practiced and taught), prayer to Jesus is proper also (as when Paul prayed three times specifically to Jesus the healer [2 Corinthians 12:8–10]), and prayer to the Spirit will equally be proper when what we seek from him is closer communion with Jesus and fuller Jesuslikeness in our lives. Now that we see what the Spirit, if invoked, is to be asked for, and why, we can make our own hymns like this, from Joseph Hart, which as a plea for spiritual realism, responsiveness, repentance, righteousness, and reviving of

spirit in and through Christ is as near perfect as we are ever
likely to get:

> Come, Holy Spirit, come!
>   Let thy bright beams arise;
> Dispel the sorrow from our minds,
>   The darkness from our eyes.
>
> Convince us of our sin,
>   Then lead to Jesus' blood,
> And to our wondering view reveal
>   The secret love of God.
>
> Revive our drooping faith,
>   Our doubts and fears remove,
> And kindle in our breasts the flame
>   Of never-dying love.
>
> Show us that loving Man
>   That rules the courts of bliss,
> The Lord of Hosts, the Mighty God,
>   Th' Eternal Prince of Peace.
>
> 'Tis thine to cleanse the heart,
>   To sanctify the soul,
> To pour fresh life in every part,
>   And new-create the whole.
>
> Dwell, therefore, in our hearts,
>   Our minds from bondage free;
> Then shall we know, and praise, and love,
>   The Father, Son, and Thee.

AMEN.

APPENDIX
The "Wretched Man"
in Romans 7

I want to discuss the identity of the "I" in Rom.
7:14–25—the passage which leads to the cry: "Wretched man
that I am! Who will deliver me from this body of death?"
This is a problem which has divided expositors since Augustine's day, and on which differences of view still remain
wide.

The problem arises as follows. In Rom. 7:7, Paul poses the
question: "Is the law sin?" Having in the previous chapter
linked together the states of being "under law" and "under
sin" (6:14; 7:5), and having spoken of the rule of sin as being
exercised and made effective through the law (5:20; 7:5, cf. 1
Cor. 15:56), he now fears lest the conclusion be drawn that
the law itself is evil. So he raises the question of verse 7, answers it at once with an emphatic negative—μὴ γένοιτο, "by
no means!" or as KJV has, "God forbid"—and then proceeds
to justify his negation by giving a positive analysis of what
the relation between the holy law of God and sin really is.
This takes up the rest of the chapter. In Paul's analysis, the
main points seem to be three:

1. The effect of the law is to give men knowledge of
sin—not merely of the abstract notion of sin, but of sin as a
concrete, dynamic reality within themselves, a spirit of re-

bellion against God, and of disobedience to His commandments (vss. 7, 13, cf. 3:20).

2. The way in which the law gives this knowledge is by declaring God's prohibitions and commands; for these first goad sin into active rebellion and then make men aware of the specific transgressions and shortcomings of motive and deed into which sin has led them (vss. 8, 19, 23).

3. The law gives no ability to anyone to perform the good which it prescribes, nor can it deliver from the power of sin (vss. 9–11, 22–24).

In making these points, Paul speaks throughout in the first person singular, and his teaching takes the form of personal reminiscence and self-analysis. What he says falls into two sections, each of which (as is common with Paul) starts with a summary statement of the thesis which the following verses seek to explain.

The first section (vss. 7–13) is all in the past tense, and the natural way to understand it is as autobiography. Its thesis is stated in vs. 7: "I had not known sin, except through the law"—i.e., it was the law that made sin known to me. The section goes on to tell how the law's prohibition of coveting stirred up in Paul uncontrollable covetousness, so that the actual effect of its marking out the way to life was to fix Paul's feet firmly on the road to death.

The second section (vss. 14–25) is written entirely in the present tense. Grammatically, therefore, the natural way to read it would be as a transcript of Paul's self-knowledge at the time of writing; but its contents seem to some to make this reading of it quite incredible. It presents the experience of a man who sees himself constantly failing to do the good which the law commands, and which he himself wants to do, and who through reflecting on this fact has come to see the bitter truth which is announced at the outset as the thesis of the whole section—"I am carnal, sold under sin" (v. 14). It is this perception that prompts the cry: "Wretched man that I am! Who will deliver me. . . ?"

What creates our problem is the *prima facie* contradiction between the state of the "wretched man" and that of Paul of

Rom. 8, the Paul who declares that "the law of the Spirit of life in Christ Jesus has set me free from the law of sin and death" (v. 2), and who counts himself among the "us" who "walk not according to the flesh, but according to the Spirit" (v. 4), who "have the first fruits of the Spirit" (v. 23), and whose infirmities the Spirit helps (v. 26). The following questions arise: 1. Is the "wretched man" really Paul, or is he some ideal figure? 2. If he is Paul, is he Paul the Christian, or Paul the still unconverted Jew? We will consider these questions in order.

First: Is the "wretched man" really Paul at all?

That Paul in this paragraph is describing an experience which was, or once had been, his own is the view of nearly all commentators and can hardly, I think, be disputed. The suggestion that this passage "does not represent a personal experience at all, but is no more than a second-hand account of the experience of others, or even an imaginative picture of a condition of mind into which men might fall were it not for the grace of God" is, says Kirk, "difficult to believe"[1]. It is indeed. The idea that Paul, despite his shift from the plural "we", denoting all Christians, to the first person singular (v. 14, cf. vss. 5–7), is yet describing an experience which, so far as he is concerned, is purely hypothetical and imaginary— the idea, that is, that the emphatic "I" (ἐγώ, vss. 14, 17, 24; αὐτὸς ἐγώ, v. 25) means "not I at all, but you, or somebody else", and that the spontaneous outcry, "Wretched man that I am!", was one that he had never himself uttered—seems altogether too artificial and theatrical to be treated as a serious option. It is true that, as is often pointed out, Paul means the whole experience recorded in vss. 7–25 to be understood, not as a private peculiarity of his own, but as a typical and representative experience, for he presents it as affording a universally valid disclosure of the relation between the law and sin in human life. His very certainty, however, that this experience is characteristically human makes it apparent that it was an experience from which he himself was not exempt.

The "wretched man", then, is Paul in person. But is he the Paul of the past, or the Paul of the present? Is he Paul the

Pharisee, representing unconverted religious mankind, mankind in Adam, knowing the law in some form, but without
the gospel, and faith, and the Spirit; or is he Paul the Christian, speaking as a representative man in Christ? It is clear
that, on the one hand, vss. 7–13 of Rom. 7 depict Paul before
conversion, and, on the other hand, that the whole of Rom. 8
is a transcript of the theological consciousness of Paul as a
Christian; but to which of these states do the verses between
belong? Here, as we said before, expositors divide.

Some hold that the Paul of vss. 14–25 is the same unconverted Paul as we meet in vss. 7–13, so that this paragraph, of
self-analysis is simply a comment on the events which vss.
7–13 record. On this view, the passage is thrown into the
present tense merely for the sake of vividness, although to
Paul at the time of writing this experience itself was a thing of
the past. So Bultmann, for instance, describes the paragraph
as "a passage in which Paul depicts the situation of a man
under the Torah as it had become clear to a backward look
from the standpoint of Christian faith"[2]. If this is right, then
the wretchedness of the "wretched man" is due to the failure
of his religious self-effort. He has sought righteousness by
works, and not found it. He feels his impotence, and knows
himself to be heading for final ruin. Hence his cry for deliverance. It is the unconverted man's cry of self-despair, and the
gospel grace of 8:1–4 is, on this view, God's answer to it. Accordingly, the verb to be understood in the elliptical first half
of v. 25 ("I thank God through Jesus Christ our Lord") will be
a verb proclaiming past or present deliverance—something
corresponding to ἠλευθέρωσέ με in 8, 2. This view of the passage is probably the one most commonly held today. But
there are overwhelming objections to it.

1. The change from the aorist to the present tense at
verse 14 remains unaccounted for. On this view, the change
is exceedingly unnatural, occurring as it does in the middle of
a passage which, *ex hypothesi*, is dealing with a single unit of
experience, and one, moreover, which is now past and gone.
There is nothing comparable in Paul, and the use of the historic present in the gospels to give vividness to narrative does

not provide a parallel, for here the narrative part is in the aorist, and what is in the present is not narrative, but generalised explanatory comment. But if, as seems to be the case, there is no recognised linguistic idiom which will account for the change of tense, then it follows that the only natural way for Paul's readers to interpret the present tenses of vss. 14 ff. is as having a present reference, and as going on to describe something distinct from the past experience which the previous verses have recalled; and we must suppose that Paul knew this when he wrote them. Are we, then, to accuse Paul of wantonly obscuring his own meaning, and laying himself open to needless misunderstanding, by a change of tense for which there was no reason at all? The view under consideration involves in effect just such an accusation. This, surely, makes it suspect.

2. If v. 25a be held to proclaim present deliverance from the bondage to sin described in vss. 15–25, then the inference of v. 25b ("so then I myself with the mind serve the law of God, but with the flesh the law of sin," as RSV and NAS have it) is *prima facie* a *non sequitur*, and a shattering anticlimax into the bargain. Two expedients have been employed to deal with this problem; neither, however, is very convincing. The first is to construe the emphatic αὐτὸς ἐγώ ("I myself") as meaning, not "I, even I", which would be the natural rendering, but "I by myself; I alone, without Christ; I thrown on my own resources" (RSV). Among others Meyer, Denney[3], Dr. C. L. Mitton[4], and Arndt-Gingrich (s.v. αὐτός, l. f.), take this view. But it is really very doubtful whether αὐτός can bear such a weight of meaning. Arndt-Gingrich gives no parallel (the two passages cited as comparable, Mk. 6:31 and Rom. 9:3, are not parallel in meaning at all). Grammatically, the explanation is forced. Moreover, if this had really been Paul's meaning, it is hard to believe that, after v. 25a, he would not have put the verb in the aorist or imperfect ("I served . . .", "I used to serve . . ."); he could hardly have been unaware that to return to the present tense would be bewilderingly harsh. It is not clear, therefore, that this explanation can stand. The second expedient is to assume, without the

least manuscript evidence, that verse 25b is misplaced, and should follow verse 23 (so Moffatt, Kirk, and C. H. Dodd). But this is a *tour de force* which must cast doubt upon the theory which makes it necessary.

3. On this view, Paul speaks of a man in Adam as having a natural affinity with the law of God—approving it (v. 16), delighting in it (v. 22), willing to fulfil it (vss. 15, 18–21), and serving it with his *νοῦς* and in his "inmost self"—literally, "inward man" (v. 22, cf. v. 25). But, elsewhere Paul consistently denies the existence of any such affinity, affirming that the mind and heart of man in Adam is blind, corrupt, lawless, and at enmity with God (cf. Eph. 2:3; 4:17ff.). Indeed, we find a very clear assertion to this effect in the first paragraph of chapter 8 which ASV renders thus: "they that are after the flesh mind the things of the flesh . . . the mind of the flesh is enmity against God; for it is not subject to the law of God, neither indeed can it be" (vss. 5, 7). Unless we are to suppose that Paul had reversed his anthropology within the space of less than ten verses, we are surely forced by this to conclude that in Rom. 7:14–25 Paul is not, after all, describing a man in Adam, but a man in Christ.

4. The freedom from sin's power which Christ bestows in this world is less than the deliverance for which the "wretched man" cries out. For what he desires is deliverance "out of (*ἐκ*) this body of death", i.e. this mortal body, which is at present sin's place of residence (v. 23). But that deliverance will not come until "the mortal puts on immortality" (1 Cor. 15:54): a consummation for which, according to Rom. 8:23, those who have the Spirit wait, groaning. And it is surely this groaning, in exact terms, which Rom. 7:24 voices. What the "wretched man" is longing for is what 8:23 calls "the redemption of our bodies". But if this is so, then what he gives thanks for in v. 25a must be the promise that through Christ this blessing will ultimately be his. And if 25a is a thanksgiving, not for a present deliverance from the condition described in vss. 15–23, but for a hope of future deliverance from it, then the juxtaposition of v. 25b ceases to present a problem. On this exegesis, v. 25b is neither a *non se-*

quitur nor an anticlimax: it is simply a summing-up of the situation thus far described, a state of affairs which will last while mortal life lasts. The man in Christ serves the law of God with his mind, in the sense that he wants and wills to keep it perfectly, but with the flesh he serves the law of sin, as appears from the fact that he never is able to keep the law as perfectly and consistently as he wishes to do. The emphatic αὐτὸς ἐγώ, "I, even I", expresses Paul's sense of how painfully paradoxical it is that a Christian man like himself, who desires so heartily to keep God's law and do only good, should find himself under the constant necessity of breaking the law and doing what in effect is evil. But such is the state of the Christian till his body is redeemed.

What has been said in developing these criticisms has already indicated what seems to me to be the more satisfactory view of the passage. The main points in this view are as follows. The paragraph is in the present tense because it describes a present state. It reproduces Paul's present theological self-knowledge as a Christian: not all of it, but just that part of it which is germane to the subject in hand—namely, the function of the law in giving knowledge of sin. (The other side of Paul's self-knowledge, that given him by the gospel, is set out in chapter 8.) The thesis of the paragraph, "I am carnal, sold under sin", is stated categorically and without qualification, not because this is the whole truth about Paul the Christian, but because it is the only part of the truth about himself that the law can tell him. What the law does for the Christian is to give him knowledge of the sin that still remains in him. When he reviews his life by the light of the law, he always finds that he has done less than the good that he wanted to do; thus he "finds" and "sees" that sin is still in him, and that he is still to a degree being taken captive by it (vss. 21–23). The wretchedness of the "wretched man" thus springs from the discovery of his continuing sinfulness, and the knowledge that he cannot hope to be rid of indwelling sin, his troublesome inmate, while he remains in the body. He is painfully conscious that for the present his reach exceeds his grasp, and therefore he longs for the eschatological deliverance through which the tension between will and achievement, purpose and performance, plan and action, will be abolished. This interpretation seems to fit the context and details of the passage, and in particular to make sense of vss. 24–25, in a way that the commoner interpretation quite fails to do.

Notes

Preface

1. Jonathan Goforth, *By My Spirit* (Grand Rapids: Zondervan, 1942), pp. 17, 18.

Chapter 1

1. Steven Barabas, *So Great Salvation* (London: Marshall, Morgan & Scott, 1952), p. v. This book offers a full analysis of Keswick teaching. See also J. C. Pollock, *The Keswick Story: The Authorized History of the Keswick Convention* (London: Hodder & Stoughton, 1964).
2. "'Keswick' and the Reformed Doctrine of Sanctification," *Evangelical Quarterly*, 27 No. 3 (July 1955): 153–167. See the comments of the then editor, the pacific F. F. Bruce, *In Retrospect: Remembrance of Things Past* (Grand Rapids: Eerdmans, 1980), pp. 187, 188.
3. John Owen, *Works*, ed. W. Goold (London: Banner of Truth, 1967), 4:437. Arguably the New Testament category of spiritual gifts include dispositional qualities that Owen's intellectualist analysis does not cover, but that does not affect the truth of what he says about the gifts of utterance of which he is speaking.
4. John V. Taylor, *The Go-Between God* (New York: Oxford University Press, 1979), p. 212.
5. Ibid., p. 102.

6. Ibid., pp. 58–62.
7. Ibid., p. 241.
8. Emil Brunner, *Revelation and Reason* (Philadelphia: Westminster, 1946), p. 265.
9. Taylor, pp. 191–197.
10. Anglican Article 20.
11. Samuel Terrien, *The Elusive Presence: Toward a New Biblical Theology* (San Francisco: Harper & Row, 1978), p. 457.

Chapter 2

1. For fuller surveys of the New Testament material, see Michael Green, *I Believe in the Holy Spirit* (Grand Rapids: Eerdmans, 1975); David Ewert, *The Holy Spirit in the New Testament* (Scottdale, Penn.: Herald Press, 1983); James D. G. Dunn, *Jesus and the Spirit* (Philadelphia: Westminster Press, 1979).
2. Since "The Phoenix and the Turtle" is such a stunning expression of the lovers' sense of intertwinedness, I venture to subjoin the key stanzas. *Turtle* is of course the turtledove.

> So they lov'd, as love in twain
> Had the essence but in one;
> Two distincts, division none:
> Number there in love was slain.
>
> Hearts remote, yet not asunder;
> Distance, and no space was seen
> 'Twixt the turtle and his queen:
> But in them it were a wonder.
>
> Reason, in itself confounded,
> Saw division grow together:
> To themselves yet either neither,
> Simple were so well compounded
>
> That it cried, "How true a twain
> Seemeth this concordant one!
> Love hath reason, reason none,
> If what parts can so remain."

3. Richard Wagner, *Tristan und Isolde,* trans. R. B. Moberly, Everyman Opera Series HMV HQM 1001–1005. The fact that Wagner

was caught up with murky ideas about lovers only finding true union in death does not affect the truth of his portrayal of how they feel in life.

4. Start with the volumes by Christian authors in the series The Classics of Western Spirituality (Ramsey, N.J.: Paulist Press, 1978–); and two items in the series Classics of Faith and Devotion, Bernard of Clairvaux, *The Love of God*, ed. James M. Houston (Portland, Ore.: Multnomah Press, 1983), and Teresa of Avila, *A Life of Prayer*, ed. James M. Houston (Portland, Ore.: Multnomah Press, 1983).

5. See John Owen's treatise "Communion With God," *Works*, ed. W. Goold (London: Banner of Truth, 1966), 2:1–274; Jonathan Edwards, "A Treatise Concerning Religious Affections," *Works*, ed. E. Hickman (London: Banner of Truth, 1974), 1:234–343; John Fletcher, *Christ Manifested: The Manifestations of the Son of God*, ed. David R. Smith (Braughing: Rushworth, 1968); etc.

6. A full English text of Pascal's record, which was found after his death, sewed into the lining of his coat, is in Emile Cailliet, *The Clue to Pascal* (London: SCM Press, 1944), pp. 47, 48, and Denzil Patrick, *Pascal and Kierkegaard* (London: Lutterworth Press, 1947) 1:76, 77. The original is in L. Brunschvig, P. Boutroux, and F. Gazier, eds., *Oeuvres de Blaise Pascal* (Paris: Hachette, 1904–1914), 12:3–7.

Chapter 3

1. John Owen, *Works*, ed. W. Goold (London: Banner of Truth, 1966), 3:386.
2. Peter Williamson, *How to Become the Person You Were Meant to Be* (Ann Arbor, Mich.): Servant, 1981), pp. 42, 43.

Chapter 4

1. B. B. Warfield, *Studies in Perfectionism* (New York: Oxford University Press, 1931), 1:113–301. Classic accounts of holiness from a Reformed Augustinian, "miserable sinner" standpoint include J. C. Ryle, *Holiness* (Old Tappan, N. J.: Fleming H. Revell, n. d.) and the incomparable presentation that emerges from the following treatises by John Owen: "Indwelling Sin in Believers," *Works*, ed. W. Goold (London: Banner of Truth,

1966) 6:154–322; "Mortification of Sin in Believers," Works, 6:2–86; "Temptation," Works, 6:88–151; "Spiritual Mindedness," Works, 7:263–497; "The Holy Spirit," Books 4, 5, Works, 3:366–651.

2. John Owen, Works, 6:79.

3. J. Telford, ed., The Letters of John Wesley (London: Epworth Press, 1931), 5:43.

4. Albert Outler, ed., John Wesley (New York: Oxford University Press, 1964), p. 257.

5. The main biblical passages on which Wesley relied are listed by W. E. Sangster, The Path to Perfection (London: Hodder & Stoughton, 1943), pp. 37–52, as follows: Ezekiel 36:25, 26, 29; Matthew 5:8, 48; 6:10; Romans 2:29, 12:1; 2 Corinthians 3:17, 18; 7:1; Galatians 2:20; Ephesians 3:14–19; 5:27; Philippians 3:15; 1 Thessalonians 5:23; Titus 2:11–14; Hebrews 6:1; 7:25; 10:14; John 8:34–36; 17:20–23; 1 John 1:5, 7–9; 2:6; 3:3, 8–10; James 1:4. To these should be added Deuteronomy 30:6.

6. Among significant critical presentations of Wesley's doctrine those by Harald Lindström, Wesley and Sanctification (London: Epworth Press, 1946); Sangster, The Path to Perfection; R. Newton Flew, The Idea of Perfection in Christian Theology (London: Oxford University Press, 1934), pp. 313–341; Outler, John Wesley, pp. 30–33, 251–305 are especially noteworthy.

7. Sangster, Path to Perfection, p. 147.

8. Outler, John Wesley, p. 286.

9. Sangster, Path to Perfection, p. 282.

10. Outler, John Wesley, p. 292.

11. E. H. Sugden, ed., The Standard Sermons of John Wesley, 4th ed. (London: Epworth Press, 1956), 2:459, footnote.

12. Sangster, Path to Perfection, p. 135.

13. Outler, John Wesley, p. 290.

14. Sangster, Path to Perfection, p. 289.

15. Flew, Idea of Perfection, p. 330.

16. See John Wesley, Notes on the New Testament.

17. Outler, John Wesley, p. 287.

18. For a warm, friendly overview of half a century of Keswick teaching, see Steven Barabas, So Great Salvation (London: Marshall, Morgan & Scott, 1952); for a cool, critical analysis of it in some of its first American exponents, see Warfield, Studies in Perfectionism, 2:463–611.

19. Walter Marshall published *The Gospel Mystery of Sanctification* in 1692. It has often been reprinted.

20. The main source of quietist influence seems to have been Madame Guyon, whose biography, written by T. C. Upham (1854), was popular reading in holiness-oriented circles in the second half of the nineteenth century. Bishop H. C. G. Moule, probably Keswick's best theologian, described the believer's part in the life of holiness as "a blessed and wakeful Quietism" (*Veni Creator*, [London: Hodder & Stoughton, 1890], p. 197).

21. From my Preface to the centenary edition of Ryle's *Holiness* (Welwyn: Evangelical Press, 1979), pp. vii, viii.

22. It has sometimes been maintained that the emphatic conjunction of two personal pronouns (*autos egō*) in verse 25 calls for the rendering "I of myself" (so RSV), "I, left to myself, when I rely on my own unaided effort" (Donald Guthrie et al., eds., *The New Bible Commentary*, rev. ed. [Grand Rapids: Eerdmans, 1970], p. 1029). But the implied contrast with "I, when divinely helped" is not there in the text, and "I, one and the same person" is the natural nuance to find in *autos egō*. The Jerusalem Bible expresses it well: ". . . it is I who with my reason serve the Law of God, and no less I who serve in my unspiritual self the law of sin."

23. A useful study of learned opinion on the interpretation of Romans 7:14–25 is Brice L. Martin, "Some Reflections on the Identity of ἐγώ in Romans 7:14–25," *Scottish Journal of Theology*, 1981, 1:39–47. I venture to reproduce as an appendix an essay in which I argue my own view more fully.

Chapter 5

1. M. Harper, *None Can Guess* (Plainfield, N.J.: Logos, 1971), pp. 149, 153. Harper provides an interesting, up-to-date profile of the movement as he sees it from inside, in *Three Sisters* (Wheaton, Ill.: Tyndale House, 1979).

2. R. Quebedeaux, *The New Charismatics* (New York: Doubleday, 1976), p. 111.

3. L. Newbigin, *The Household of God* (London: SCM, 1954), p. 110.

4. Much of the following material appeared in *Churchman*, 1980, in an article entitled "Theological Reflections on the Charismatic

Movement," pp. 7–25, 103–25, with more extensive academic documentation than is given here.

5. Eleven times in 1 Corinthians 14 (verses 2, 4, 5, 6, 9, 13, 18, 19, 23, 26, 27), and in 12:28, 13:8, NEB renders glōssa(i) as tongues *of ecstasy* or *ecstatic speech*. Edward D. O'Connor's observation is on target: "The New Testament *nowhere* describes prayer in tongues as 'ecstatic utterance.' That term has been coined by modern scholars in their efforts to conjecture what the gift must have been like. The experience of the Pentecostal movement suggests that their guesswork has been ill-advised." (*The Pentecostal Movement in the Catholic Church* [Notre Dame, Ind.: Ave Maria Press, 1971], p. 126).

6. D. Bennett, "The Gifts of the Holy Spirit," *The Charismatic Movement*, ed. Michael P. Hamilton (Grand Rapids: Eerdmans, 1975), p. 32. Bennett is warding off the idea that Christian glossolalia is schizophrenic, hypnotic, or demonic in origin.

7. Richard Baer, quoted by Josephine Massyngberde Ford, "The Charismatic Gifts in Worship," in *The Charismatic Movement*, p. 115.

8. R. Quebedeaux, *The Young Evangelicals* (New York: Harper & Row, 1974), p. 43; *see also The New Charismatics*, pp. 153, 154.

9. Charles E. Hummel, *Fire in the Fireplace: Contemporary Charismatic Renewal* (Downers Grove, Ill.: Inter-Varsity, 1977), p. 47; *see also* the description of charismatic prayer groups among Roman Catholics in United States in O'Connor, *The Pentecostal Movement*, pp. 111–121.

10. O'Connor, *The Pentecostal Movement*, pp. 225–227.

11. "Thus, there are people who want their entire lives to be guided by heavenly messages and revelations, and hence neglect the planning and deliberation that are within their power. Some people want all sicknesses to be healed miraculously, and refuse to see a doctor or take medicine. On similar grounds, others would like to see theological study and sermon preparation replaced by a kerygma [pulpit utterance] of purely charismatic inspiration, and the institutional offices in the Church ... replaced by a purely charismatic leadership." (O'Connor, *The Pentecostal Movement*, p. 227). All this expresses very clearly and typically the super-supernaturalist cast of mind.

12. "Deliverance from sickness is provided in the atonement, and

is the privilege of all believers" (Declaration of Faith of the Assemblies of God, 12); "Divine healing is provided for all in the atonement" (Declaration of Faith of the Church of God [Cleveland], 11). Cited from Walter J. Hollenweger, *The Pentecostals,* trans. R. A. Wilson (Minneapolis: Augsburg, 1977), pp. 515, 517. That total healing for the body, with total sinless perfection, are "in the atonement," in the sense that entire personal renewal in Christ's image flows from the cross (*see* Romans 8:23; Philippians 3:20, 21), is true, but it is a potentially disastrous mistake to expect on earth what will only be given in heaven.

13. *See also,* for instance, Francis MacNutt, *Healing* (Notre Dame, Ind.: Ave Maria Press, 1974), pp. 13, 14: "I would no longer have to tell people whose sicknesses were disintegrating their personalities that their illness was a God-sent cross, but I would hold up the hope that God wanted them well, even when medical science could not help." Assessing claims to supernatural bodily healing through prayer is hard, for the evidence is regularly incomplete and disputed. Sample skeptical evaluations highlighting this difficulty are B. B. Warfield, *Counterfeit Miracles* (London: Banner of Truth, 1976), and W. Nolen, *Healing: A Doctor in Search of a Miracle* (New York: Random House, 1974), a study of the healing ministry of Kathryn Kuhlman, who in 1962 had ventured to publish a book called *I Believe in Miracles.* The argument in the text does not depend on, nor does it justify, assessments as negative as these, though it is hard to see on what grounds one could safely be more positive.

14. Epaphroditus, Philippians 2:27; Timothy, 1 Timothy 5:23; Trophimus, 2 Timothy 4:20; Paul himself, the agent of widespread supernatural healings of others (*see* Acts 19:11, 12, 28:8, 9), according to the natural exposition of 2 Corinthians 12:7–10, where "thorn" points to physical pain and "flesh" to created, flesh-and-blood humanity.

15. *See* on this the superb book by the quadriplegic Joni Eareckson and Steve Estes, *A Step Further,* rev. ed. (Grand Rapids: Zondervan, 1980).

16. *See also* John Richards, *But Deliver Us From Evil* (London: Darton, Longman & Todd, 1976).

17. T. Goodwin, *Works,* ed. J. C. Miller (Edinburgh: James Nichol 1861), I:227–52.

18. *See* pp. 142, 143 above.
19. In his *Memoirs* (New York: Fleming H. Revell, 1876), pp. 17, 18, Charles Finney tells how he wept and "bellowed out the unutterable gushings" of his soul when he received a baptism of the Spirit in 1821. Asa Mahan describes his experience extensively in Part 2 of *Out of Darkness Into Light:* (London: T. Woolmer, 1882). In 1871 D. L. Moody "dropped to the floor and lay bathing his soul in the divine" while his room "seemed ablaze with God" (J. C. Pollock, *Moody: A Biographical Portrait,* [New York: Macmillan, 1963], p. 90.). A. B. Simpson expounded the baptism as "power to receive the life of Christ" in *The Holy Spirit, or Power From on High* (Harrisburg: Christian Pubs. 1896). R. A. Torrey's exposition is in *The Person and Work of the Holy Spirit* (London: Nisbet, 1910), pp. 213–37. F. D. Bruner summarizes his views, *A Theology of the Holy Spirit* (Grand Rapids: Eerdmans, 1970) pp. 335–37.
20. *See also* Evan H. Hopkins, *The Law of Liberty in the Spiritual Life* (London: 1884). On F. B. Meyer, *see* Bruner, ibid., pp. 340, 341.
21. E. C. Rickards, *Bishop Moorhouse of Melbourne and Manchester* (London: John Murray, 1920), pp. 15, 16. The account continues: "At the time I did not think of it as Christ, but as God the Father: but now I see that he manifested himself through Christ." In a description of the same experience written in a letter when he was eighty-three Moorhouse said: "To prevent myself from crying aloud in my joy, I was obliged to wrap myself in my bedclothes. And for days this divine rapture lasted . . . it made me love everyone intensely . . . it was heaven . . . I had been in heaven" (pp. 245, 246).
22. Cited from Josephine Massyngberde Ford, "The Charismatic Gifts in Worship," *The Charismatic Movement,* pp. 115, 116.

Chapter 6

1. A. A. Hoekema, *Holy Spirit Baptism* (Grand Rapids: Eerdmans, 1972), p. 10.
2. *See also* the Statement of Fundamental Truths of the Assemblies of God (U.S.A.), 7: "All believers are entitled to, and should ardently expect, and earnestly seek, the Baptism in the Holy Ghost and fire, according to the command of our Lord Jesus

Christ. This was the normal experience of all in the early Christian Church. . . ."

3. For this idea, see F. D. Bruner, *A Theology of the Holy Spirit* (Grand Rapids, Eerdmans, 1970), 185–188; James D. G. Dunn, *Baptism in the Holy Spirit* (Naperville, Ill.: Allenson, 1970); G. W. H. Lampe, *The Seal of the Spirit* (London: Longmans, Green, 1951).

4. Dunn, *Baptism*; Bruner, *Theology*;; John R. W. Stott, *Baptism and Fulness*, rev. ed. (Downers Grove, Ill.: Inter-Varsity, 1976); Hoekema, *Holy Spirit Baptism*.

5. *See also* R. A. Torrey, *The Person and Work of the Holy Spirit* (London: Nisbet, 1910), pp. 177, 178: The baptism is potential for all, actual only for some. Bruner notes Torrey's role as "a kind of John the Baptist figure for later international Pentecostalism" (*Theology*, p. 45).

6. *See* Dunn, *Baptism*, pp. 127 ff.

7. *See* Hoekema, *Holy Spirit Baptism*, pp. 21 f.

8. Bruner, *Theology*, pp. 196 f, rightly quoted Acts 2:39; 3:16, 26; 5:31; 11:18; 13:48; 15:8, 9; 16:14; 18:27 to show that in Acts faith and repentance are no less God's gift than is the Spirit.

9. Ibid. p. 161.

10. In *The Charismatic Movement*, ed. Michael P. Hamilton (Grand Rapids: Eerdmans, 1975), p. 53.

11. Bruner, *Theology*, p. 60, note 12.

12. Or it may not. *Akarpos* ("unfruitful") in verse 14 may mean either "helping nobody" (GOODSPEED, as in Ephesians 5:11; Titus 3:14; 2 Peter 1:8; Jude 12) or "blank." The former meaning is consistent with the speaker understanding the tongue he utters, which Charles Hodge, *An Exposition of the First Epistle to the Corinthians* (London: Banner of Truth, 1958), p. 288, held to be implicit in the passage. But today's charismatics confessedly do not understand their tongues.

13. Ibid., pp. 248–52, 276–302. Robert G. Gromacki, *The Modern Tongues Movement* (Philadelphia: Presbyterian and Reformed, 1967), p. 113, takes this view.

14. Abraham Kuyper, *The Work of the Holy Spirit* (Grand Rapids: Eerdmans, 1956), pp. 133–138.

15. A. A. Hoekema, *What About Tongue-Speaking?* (Grand Rapids: Eerdmans, 1966), p. 83; *see also* p. 128: "The baffling question remains: how can Pentecostals . . . be sure that what goes on in

tongue-speaking circles today is the same thing that went on in New Testament days?"

16. *See* Nils Johansson, "1 Cor. XIII and 1 Cor. XIV," *New Testament Studies* 10, no. 3 (April 1964): 389.

17. *See* Gromacki, *Modern Tongues Movement*, pp. 125–129.

18. *See* Hodge, *An Exposition*, p. 281, on verse 4: "The speaker with tongues did not edify the church, because he was not understood; he did edify himself, because he understood himself . . . the understanding was not in abeyance." On verse 18 he says: "That Paul should give thanks to God that he was more abundantly endowed with the gift of tongues, if that gift consisted in the ability to speak in languages which he himself did not understand, and the use of which, on that assumption, could according to his principle benefit neither himself nor others, is not to be believed." Hodge's axiom that edification presupposes understanding is hard, biblically, to get round; accepting it, however, would seem to entail the conclusion that glossolalia as practiced today cannot edify, which is a most unfashionable view to hold.

19. Interestingly, Nils Bloch-Hoell in his authoritative survey, *The Pentecostal Movement* (London: Allen & Unwin, 1964), p. 146, noted that "glossolalia is definitely decreasing within the Pentecostal Movement." Whether this was what the charismatic Derek Prince had in mind when he said in 1964: "They have programmed the Holy Spirit out of most Pentecostal churches, do you know that?" (*Baptism in the Holy Spirit*, [London: Fountain Trust, 1965], p. 27) can only be surmised. Virginia H. Hine, in an enquiry into tongues speaking that embraced the United States, Mexico, Colombia, and Haiti, found that second-generation Pentecostals generally used tongues less than did their fathers, and that "the most frequent glossolalics were those who had been least socialized to accept the practice"—in other words, those for whom it had most charm of novelty and boldness in breaking with their past ("Pentecostal Glossolalia: Towards a Functional Interpretation," *Journal for the Scientific Study of Religion* 8 (1969): 221, 222). I am told by British charismatic leaders that glossolalia has been less stressed in their circles during the past decade than it was before, but I cannot test that generalization.

20. *See*, among recent books, William J. Samarin, *Tongues of Men*

and *Angels* (New York: Macmillan, 1972), an authoritative, broad-based sociolinguistic study); John P. Kildahl, *The Psychology of Speaking in Tongues* (New York: Harper & Row, 1972), a careful and fair-minded report on a ten-year investigation, plus his chapter, "Psychological Observations," *The Charismatic Movement,* ed. Michael P. Hamilton; Morton T. Kelsey, *Tongues Speaking* (New York: Doubleday, 1964), a welcoming assessment bringing Jungian personality theory to bear. *See also* Virginia H. Hine, "Pentecostal Glossolalia." More negative assessments, reflecting older models, are those of Julius Laffal, *Pathological and Normal Language* (New York: Atherton Press, 1965): glossolalia voices, while yet concealing, a "conflicted wish"; and Wayne Oates in Frank E. Stagg, Glenn Hinson, and Wayne E. Oates, *Glossolalia* (Nashville: Abingdon, 1967): glossolalia is a regressive symptom of a deprived personality. Among older authorities, George B. Cutten, *Speaking With Tongues* (Northford, Conn.: Elliots, 1927), sees glossolalia as a syndrome found among nonverbalizers of low mental ability and social privilege; and Emile Lombard, *De la Glossolalie chez les Premiers Chrétiens et des Phénomènes Similaires* (Lausanne: Bridel, 1910), depicts it as a kind of entranced automatic speech. A well-digested pastoral treatment is C. W. Parnell, *Understanding Tongues-Speaking* (Johannesburg: South African Press, 1972). See also Hoekema's two books already cited.

21. "Quite clearly, available evidence requires that any explanation of glossolalia as pathological must be discarded. Even among those who accept this position, however, there often remains a sort of non-specific suspicion of emotional immaturity, of sub-clinical anxiety, or of some sort of personal inadequacy. This is particularly true of churchmen in whose denominations the ranks of Spirit-filled Christians are swelling." (Hine, "Pentecostal Glossolalia," p. 217).

22. "There is no mystery about glossolalia. Tape-recorded samples are easy to obtain and to analyze. They always turn out to be the same thing: *strings of syllables, made up of sounds taken from among all those that the speaker knows, put together more or less haphazardly but which nevertheless emerge as word-like and sentence-like units because of realistic, language-like rhythm and melody* ... Nothing 'comes over the speaker's vocal chords.' Speech ... starts in the brain ... when someone speaks in tongues, he is only using in-

structions to the vocal organs that have lain dormant since childhood. 'Finding' them and then being willing to follow them are the difficult things. So the only *causes* that need to be found are those that explain why a person should *want* to use these rules again and how he becomes *willing* to do so" (Samarin, *Tongues of Men*, pp. 227, 228). Samarin parallels glossolalia with the "nonsense vocalizations" of Armstrong, Ella Fitzgerald, and others; he might have added to his list Adelaide Hall in Duke Ellington's 1927 "Creole Love Call" and Billy Banks in "Yellow Dog Blues" (1932), which in my youth was a front runner for the title of the hottest track ever. It is unfortunate that Samarin miscalls scat singing bebop (pp. 145, 146); bebop was a name for "progressive" instrumental jazz, and was coined in 1946.

23. Dennis Bennett in *The Charismatic Movement*, p. 26.
24. See Kildahl, *The Psychology of Speaking in Tongues*, pp. 83, 84.
25. See Kildahl in *The Charismatic Movement*, pp. 141, 142.
26. John V. Taylor, *The Go-Between God* (New York: Oxford University Press, 1979), p. 218.
27. Kildahl, *Psychology*, p. 63.
28. Kildahl in *The Charismatic Movement*, p. 136. He continues: "I have gained the impression that interpreters who translate tongue-speech literally are often poorly integrated psychologically. Their view of their gift of interpretation borders on the grandiose. This impression has not been tested clinically, and I offer it to the reader simply to see whether it coincides with the general impression left by this type of interpretation of tongues."
29. Samarin, *Tongues of Men*, p. 166. See his whole discussion, pp. 162–172.
30. Hoekema, *What About Tongue-Speaking?*, pp. 135, 136.
31. For a positive survey of healing in Christian history, *see also* Morton T. Kelsey, *Healing and Christianity*, (New York: Harper & Row, 1973), and Evelyn Frost, *Christian Healing: A Consideration of the Place of Spiritual Healing in the Church of Today in the Light of the Doctrine and Practice of the Ante-Nicene Church* (London: Mowbrays, 1940). For negative assessments, *see* Warfield, *Counterfeit Miracles*, and Wade H. Boggs, Jr., *Faith Healing and the Christian Faith* (Richmond, Vir.: John Knox Press, 1956). For a charismatic healer's perspective, *see* Francis MacNutt, *Healing*

(Notre Dame, Ind.: Ave Maria Press, 1974) and *The Power to
Heal* (Notre Dame, Ind.: Ave Maria Press, 1977). For wisdom on
the whole subject, *see* an older book written to counter the unbalanced views of A. J. Gordon and A. B. Simpson, Henry W.
Frost, *Miraculous Healing* (Old Tappan, N.J.: Fleming H. Revell,
1951); also John MacArthur, *The Charismatics: A Doctrinal Perspective* (Grand Rapids, Zondervan, 1978), pp. 130–155, and
D. M. Lloyd-Jones, *The Supernatural in Medicine* (London: Christian Medical Fellowship, 1971).

32. David J. Atkinson, *Prophecy* (Bramcote: Grove Books, 1977), p.
22.

33. For further discussion of Christian prophecy *see*, along with
Atkinson, *Prophecy*, David Hill, *New Testament Prophecy* (Atlanta:
John Knox Press, 1980); H. A. Guy, *New Testament Prophecy*
(London: Epworth Press, 1947); James D. G. Dunn, *Jesus and the
Spirit* (London: SCM, 1975); and Wayne Grudem, *The Gift of
Prophecy in 1 Corinthians* (Lanham, Md.: University Press of
America, 1982).

34. Regrettably, many charismatics have spoken and written as if
these postconversion deepenings of fellowship with the Father
and the Son through the Spirit have only ever happened with
any frequency in the Wesleyan-holiness tradition and then in
their own Pentecostal-charismatic circles. To those who know
the history of Christian devotion, patristic, medieval, and modern, Protestant and Catholic, this must seem an arrogant pro-
vincialism matching in the realm of spirituality the so-called
Anabaptist ecclesiology, which in effect tells us to ignore the
centuries between the apostles and ourselves and see God as
starting again with us. Such an attitude suggests not only ignorance of the Christian past but also forgetfulness of the Lord's
promise that the Spirit should abide with the church always (*see*
John 14:16).

35. Charles E. Hummel, *Fire in the Fireplace: Contemporary Charismatic
Renewal* (Downers Grove, Ill.: Inter-Varsity, 1978), chapter 17,
does this typically and judiciously, but in a way that makes
rather obvious the difference between the miraculous healing
of the New Testament and today's ministry of spiritual healing
by congregational prayer, when "nothing is promised . . . but
much is expected" (p. 218).

36. John Owen wrote: "Of this joy there is no account to be given, but that the Spirit worketh it when and how he will; he secretly infuseth and distils it into the soul, filling it with gladness, exultations, and sometimes with unspeakable raptures of mind" (*Works*, ed. W. Goold, London: Banner of Truth,[1967], 2:253).

37. Charismatic theologians such as Thomas Smail, to whom the "second blessing" view of Spirit baptism is unacceptable, theologize the event as one aspect of a unitary initiation into Christ of which water baptism is the outward sign. But Christian initiation is essentially the establishing of a relationship with God and God's people in and through Christ, and the essence of Spirit baptism, as we saw, is the vivid realization (God given, as I hold) that you *have been* initiated into Christ; that is, you are his and he is yours. Surely it is not very plausible to call this *a part or aspect* of God's initiating work, especially when it comes to a Christian many years after his conversion, as on Smail's own showing it did to him. The more straightforward thing to say is that it *presupposes* initiation, being in fact the Spirit's witness to it. See Thomas A. Smail, *Reflected Glory* (Grand Rapids: Eerdmans, 1976), chapter 10.

38. *See* Thomas A. Smail, *The Forgotten Father* (Grand Rapids: Eerdmans, 1981), especially pp. 9–20.

Chapter 7

1. John Owen, *Works*, ed. W. Goold (London: Banner of Truth, 1967), 4:518.

2. Edwards, *Works*, ed. E. Hickman (London: Banner of Truth, 1974), 1:426.

Appendix

1. Romans *Clarendon Bible*, (Oxford: Clarendon Press, 1937), p. 206.

2. *Theology of the New Testament 1*, (London: SCM Press, 1952), p. 247. In 1932, Bultmann wrote: "It seems to me that these questions (about the identity of the 'I' in Rom. vii) have been sufficiently discussed and that there can be no doubt as to the answer: the situation characterised here is the general situation of man under the law, and, to be sure, as it appears to the eye of

one who has been freed from the law by Christ" (*Existence and Faith: Shorter Writings of Rudolf Bultmann*, trans. Schubert M. Ogden, [London: Hodder & Stoughton, 1961] p. 147).

3. In *The Expositor's Greek Testament.*

4. C. L. Mitton, "Romans VII Reconsidered: III," *Expository Times* 65 (1954): 133.

Scripture Index

Topical Index